Very

CLASSY

BE A
LADY
NOT A
TRAMP

Very CLASSY

· DEREK BLASBERG ·

DESIGN BY

RODRIGO CORRAL DESIGN

· RAZORBILL ·

Very Classy

RAZORBILL

Published by the Penguin Group
Penguin Young Readers Group
345 Hudson Street, New York, New York 10014, U.S.A.
Penguin Group (USA) Inc., 375 Hudson Street, New York, New York 10014, U.S.A.
Penguin Group (Canada), 90 Eglinton Avenue East, Suite 700, Toronto, Ontario, Canada M4P 2Y3
(a division of Pearson Penguin Canada Inc.)
Penguin Books Ltd, 80 Strand, London WC2R 0RL, England
Penguin Ireland, 25 St Stephen's Green, Dublin 2, Ireland (a division of Penguin Books Ltd)
Penguin Group (Australia), 250 Camberwell Road, Camberwell, Victoria 3124, Australia (a division of
Pearson Australia Group Pty Ltd)
Penguin Books India Pvt Ltd, 11 Community Centre, Panchsheel Park, New Delhi - 110 017, India
Penguin Group (NZ), 67 Apollo Drive, Rosedale, North Shore 0632, New Zealand
(a division of Pearson New Zealand Ltd.)

Penguin Books (South Africa) (Pty) Ltd, 24 Sturdee Avenue, Rosebank, Johannesburg 2196, South Africa

Penguin Books Ltd, Registered Offices: 80 Strand, London WC2R 0RL, England

10 9 8 7 6 5 4 3 2 1

ISBN 978-1-59514-438-6

Designed by Ben Wiseman/Rodrigo Corral Design

Library of Congress Cataloging-in-Publication Data is available

Printed in the United States of America

CLASSY

"He is to parties what Rob Pattinson is to Vampires. But you don't get bitten, you get smitten!"

—Glenda Bailey, editor-in-chief, *Harper's Bazaar*

"What's a gal to do in this age of tacky pseudo-celebrity? Enter New York fashionisto Derek Blasberg, whose new book may just be the saving grace."

—*TeenVogue*

"[Blasberg] dispenses advice on everything from table manners to tattoos in cheeky essays—a thoroughly modern guide to living like a lady."

—*Vanity Fair*

"...the Truman Capote of his generation, or the Carrie Bradshaw."

—*New York Times*

"Derek Blasberg's social calendar reads like *WWD*'s "Eye" column, a Bravo reality series and an episode of 'Gossip Girl' rolled into one."

—*Los Angeles Times*

"Blasberg's compiled everything he's learned from Hollywood, fashion, and high society into *Classy*, a guide to becoming a true lady."

—*Elle*

"The book could equally be subtitled 'How To Get Ahead Without Being A Bitch.'"

—*Grazia*

"Derek Blasberg gives hilarious, blunt direction about how young women can be ladies and not tramps."

—*The Today Show*

"*Classy* is a fizzy mix of decorum, style and dating advice with crib notes on arts and culture, and advice and opinions on heavier topics such as drugs, drinking and driving and pole dancing."

—*Toronto Star*

"He's like a male Elsa Maxwell. He is a social catalyst who can cut across all different levels, mixing society ladies with strippers."

—Simon Doonan, creative director, Barney's New York

"Making the transition from girl into woman is a minefield, and there's a set of problems my generation will need to navigate that hasn't been addressed. Derek's book is a fun, witty way of discussing them. He really knows what he's talking about!"

—Emma Watson, actress

For Mom and Dad, who bought me Tiffany's Table
Manners for Teenagers *when I was a little boy,
and then supported me and encouraged me to chase
my dreams so that one day I would have the opportunities
to put the lessons in that book to good use.*

Table of Contents

Foreword

NOW THAT *Classy* is a bona fide success (a *New York Times* bestseller, no less), I can make the following confession: Before it was published, I was extremely trepidatious and hesitant about writing a collection of humorous essays covering etiquette and social behavior. When the book was still a rough idea in my head, there were moments when I thought penning a book on ladylike behavior would be futile. I was scared it wouldn't sell, and people would think I was completely clueless. In a culture where it seems tramps and reality stars can rule the world, why would anyone buy a book on manners and class?

However, after it sold on all four corners of the globe and was translated into various languages, I could breathe a sigh of relief. Turns out people who want to get *Classy* exist in the world after all. Even better? Writing and promoting *Classy* at parties and signings around the world was a truly rewarding experience: Speaking directly to the reader—and sharing a few jokes along the way—was a fabulous exercise in social interaction.

I loved meeting you, future *Classy* ladies, and loved hearing your anecdotes (both personal triumphs and horror stories) while stumping everywhere from L.A. to London, from Cannes to Canada. It was comforting to discover there are still a few young women in the world getting bored with today's get-famous-quick culture, even if, like me, they are amused by it. But allow me this full disclosure: I can watch guilty-pleasure reality programming for hours. (I liked how Marc Jacobs described it: "a vacation for your brain.") But I've always said the trick is knowing what behavior is entertainment-based, and what behavior is inspirational.

The chord *Classy* struck with its readers was something I hadn't entirely anticipated. Young girls came to my book signings to say hi and ask for hugs, and they stopped me in the street and on the subway to introduce themselves. The deluge of letters (often written on nice stationary, which I loved) I got from young women, and the occasional *Classy*

young man, was truly touching and reinforced what an important message this book preaches: Although we live in a day and age when rich housewives and overly tanned alcoholic club rats can reach immediate reality show superstardom, a book promoting sophisticated style and respectable behavior can be successful in this social climate. (And what a relief!)

I met girls who read the chapter on vices and realized that even though they had lived their life until that point as a tramp, it was possible to clean up their act. (Oscar Wilde's line "Every saint has a past and every sinner has a future" apparently had a profound effect.) In Toronto, a girl came up to me at a book signing and showed me her own lady-to-tramp before and after pictures. When I did NBC's *Today Show* in New York City, a young girl waited outside and wanted a hug. (I felt like Justin Bieber.) People sent me messages on Twitter thanking me for telling them how rude it was to be glued to their phones at the dinner table (which makes me now wonder if they were in fact Tweeting me from the dinner table, but never mind that).

I have many of these girls to thank for this new expanded edition of *Classy*. (The two new chapters in the book—"A Lady Decorates" and "A Lady Stays Healthy"—were conceived directly from questions and e-mails I received in the months after *Classy* came out.) And there's also a new feature in the book where I've taken many of the issues I've received

and answered them in Q&As. While the first edition of *Classy* could teach a girl to be a sophisticated woman, there's always room to get *Classy*-er. So, here we go: Let's get *Very Classy*, ladies!

Love,
Derek

Some of the classy ladies who joined me on my book tour: Previous spread, left page: me with Nicole Richie, Margherita Missoni, and Kate Bosworth. Previous spread, right page, from top: me with Chloe Sevigny; Milla Jovovich. Opposite page, from top: me and Eugenie Niarchos; Kirsten Dunst; Leighton Meester. This page, from top: Lou Doillon; Alexa Chung; Daphne Guinness.

Introduction

I KNOW, I KNOW: It seems a little suspicious. What could someone like me, a scruffy-faced, Midwest-born twenty-something, know about being a lady? What does a boy from suburban Missouri who drove a Pontiac to his public high school know about black-tie galas and VIP Rooms? What does this guy, who grew up buying clothes at strip malls, know about diamonds and the haute couture?

Well, let me tell you: a lot. To be honest, I probably know more about being a lady than any grown man should. (I'm not sure if this will assuage your reservations about this book or give you new ones, but I digress.)

Through observation and experience, by working in the fashion and entertainment industries and forging friendships with chic young women, and thanks to my own brand of pluck and moxy, I've learned how to spot a responsible young lady. I know the difference between a *smart casual* and *cocktail* dress code. I have a good idea of what's sexy and what's slutty; I'm all too familiar with the proper way to lay buffet; and I've realized that nothing good can come from a young woman's amateur attempt at pole dancing (for one thing, it's just not hygienic).

I grew up in America's Heartland, with a solid family and an old-fashioned sense of values. But as a teenager I moved to New York City, mixing that Midwest moral code with an instant dose of metropolitan sophistication—and temptation. My wholesome girlfriends from home were replaced with a full spectrum of women—from the graceful sort who wore ball gowns to charitable benefits and said "please" and "thank you," to the types of social climbers who would have sold their grandmother's prosthetic leg to get their picture in a fashion magazine. In just my few decades on this earth I've done everything from mow lawns in cutoff jeans for pocket money, to work at *Vogue* magazine and sit front row at fashion shows. I've attended tiny parties in retail spaces, and been a chairman for black-tie balls in world-renowned museums.

Looking back, I can categorize the young women I've met through my trials and travails into two groups: ladies and tramps. The ladies were pleasant, well-groomed girls who knew to keep their phones off the dinner table and wear underwear when sporting a short skirt. The tramps were a much more sordid sort: types who wore clothes two sizes too small, ate with their hands, and always smelled of cigarettes. And designer imposter perfume. And tequila. And worse.

My shocking realization? There are far too many tramps in the world!

Hence this book: Too often have I found myself surrounded by bad-mannered young women, or out with friends who are dressed outrageously inappropriately. Too often have I witnessed nasty girls get propped on society's pedestal and become famous for all the wrong reasons. These tramps are getting away with—and showing!—far too much. (No offense if you are a tramp. You've come to the right place.)

I wasn't just seeing these train wrecks in person, either. I'd look in magazines—and not just the nasty tabloid magazines I have the good sense to deny reading—and find girls who had broken up marriages, who had starred in sex tapes, who had flashed their girlie bits to paparazzi.

This made me think of the challenges facing a young woman

today: Where are the role models? No wonder there are so many girls out there who are disillusioned by the modern notion of what it means to be a lady, and no wonder so many of you fine young women think it's perfectly normal to stand in your mom's shower and e-mail pics of yourself in a wet white T-shirt to the cute boy in your algebra class.

Here's the thing: There are young women—women both in the public sphere and women who shy away from red carpets—who aren't going out every night fully

equipped with beer, bongs, and bad decisions. Although it might not always seem to be the case, I'm here to tell you it's not always the loudest, least covered, blondest, biggest-chested girl at the party having the most fun. Quite the con-trary. Speaking as a person who has been to his fair share of parties—from house parties in L.A. to nightclubs in New York to palaces in Europe and beyond—I can say with authority that it's the smart, sweet, thoughtful girls who are actually the most attractive.

So I'm taking a stand, and encouraging young women to be better behaved—and to realize that life can be so much more than the happy-hour special at your local strip club.

In fact, that's the whole point of this book: to celebrate the ladies of the fu-ture. This book is for girls who know to keep their tops on and their legs closed when someone asks for a picture. Girls who understand the drunkest person at the party isn't the coolest. Girls who can identify their bread plate at an elegant dinner. Girls who know that friends don't let friends blog drunk. Girls like the girls on these pages, who strive for their goals but understand their limits.

You might not have been born a lady. But there's no rea-son you can't learn to be one. As Coco Chanel once said: "A girl should be two things, classy and fabulous."

Behold, the classy women in my life and the unofficial muses of this book: Previous spread, right page, from top: me with Lauren Santo Domingo and Chloe Sevigny; Mary-Kate and Ashley Olsen. Opposite page, from top: me with Kate Bosworth; Christy Turlington; Agyness Deyn. This page, from top: me with Tinsley Mortimer; Liya Kebede and Rachel Roy; Emma Watson.

A Lady
Gets Dressed

▬▬▬▬▬

"Fashion is not something that exists in dresses only.
Fashion is in the sky, in the street. Fashion has to do with ideas,
the way we live, what is happening."

Coco Chanel

THE WAY YOU LOOK, as materialistic and silly as it may sound, is paramount. Apart from the fact that appearance is the basis for most first impressions, it is one of the things that best differentiates ladies from tramps.

Mind you, life isn't a beauty contest. It's not like you have to be six feet tall, blue-eyed, blonde, and emaciated to be a beautiful lady, and if you're not a supermodel, you're automatically grouped into the tramp category. I'm talking about the way that anyone—no, *everyone*—can dress to look respectable. Not "respectable" in the old-fashioned granny sense, like a lady should never show her clavicle or more than a hint of ankle. If you want to rock a mini at the Vatican or a sheer knit at granny's house, that's your prerogative. But ladies—real ladies—dress to respect themselves. Specifically, ladies dress up their assets and cover their asses. (Tramps, on the other hand, confuse their asses with their assets.)

True, it can be difficult to differentiate between sexy gear and skankville. (Believe me, those tramps are a sneaky lot.) For example, when short skirts are in style, how short is too short? If all the cool girls aren't wearing underwear, why should you? (The answer to that one is pretty simple: 'cause it's not hygienic to press that part of your body to public seats or the inside of sweaty trousers. But I'm getting ahead of myself.)

In this section, I'll help you navigate the sometimes savage and always complex world of style—and help steer you away from pleather asslesschaps and rhinestone-studded tube tops. Whoa, that visual just sent a shiver down my spine.

Fashion and Style: The Critical Difference

Allow me to clarify a common confusion about a lady's wardrobe: the difference between fashion and style. Fashion is a constantly changing sensibility promoted by fashion designers and translated to stores and to customers every six months. Style, on the other hand, refers to the way that you, your friend, your mom, your boyfriend, your future ex-husband take individual trends and fashion pieces and incorporate them into a personalized wardrobe.

Let's use jeans as an example. Even before the rebellious days of James Dean and Co., denim was an all-important element of the modern wardrobe. But everyone wears jeans a different way, a way that corresponds to his or her personal style. A total type A who needs to match her Starbucks cup to her shoes every morning will want crisp jeans that are perfectly fit (fig. 1); an artistic boho type might prefer a flared look (fig. 2). A retro girl who hangs out with film nerds and talks about Fellini might like her jeans to end above the ankle; a goth girl will want everything in black (fig. 3); and the captain of the JV field hockey team might prefer a boyish, baggier look. (A skank will want acid wash jeans with holes in the ass so her leopard-thong underwear hangs out; but, needless to say, we won't be providing a visual for that look.)

One girl might pair a man's button-down with a ball skirt and wear it to a black-tie gala; another girl might take that same shirt and wear it over a tank top to go grocery shopping. This is a testament to the ver-

A Lady does not change too many times in a day, and she never changes between fashion shows or appointments.

A Lady knows not to answer her phone at a fashion show. Ever.

satility of personal style. It's all about interpretation.

An analogy: Fashion provides for a common vocabulary, but style is how you learn to say something new and unique with those words.

Here's the thing: Personal style is just that—personal. It's important to cultivate a look of your own. It's easy to confuse being fashionable with looking trendy (looking, in other words, like everybody else). But fashion magazines and friends' wardrobes are templates for a person's style, not a dictum. No one wants to see you looking like you've been photocopied out of a page of *Vogue* magazine—that's boring and unoriginal. And people definitely don't want to see you looking like you've been photocopied out of a teeny-bop magazine or off of a flyer taped above a urinal in a men's room.

This is what the legendary designer Yves Saint Laurent (the man, according to the French press, who saved all of France when he took over for Christian Dior in 1957 and then went on to revolutionize the entire fashion industry) said before his death in 2008: "Fashions fade; style is eternal."

FIG. 1: Preppy   **FIG. 2**: Hippie   **FIG. 3**: Goth

Here, the exact same pair of jeans is incorporated into three completely different looks. That pair of jeans might be *in fashion*, but the extras (preppy pearls, stoner posture, black leather) give each girl a style of her own.

Lady vs. Tramp: In Fashion

Is your mini too short? Your shirt too low-cut? And other important questions answered

Let's get one thing straight right now: An exposed thong is not sexy. Neither is an exposed nipple. Or exposed pubic hair. Hell, barring a few exceptions (we'll give it to you, Madonna and Sarah Jessica Parker), even an exposed bra strap can take a girl from sexy territory into slutty-land. (For the record, a lady never shows her bra strap. Madonna may be fierce, but she is not a lady.)

Keep in mind that overexposed body parts aren't the only thing that differentiate sexy and slutty: Makeup, body language, and general attitude can also give off the wrong idea. Super-red lips and loads of eye makeup are more lady of the night than ladylike; lifting up your skirt for pictures, or constantly making an orgasm face when gentlemen make eye contact, is plain unnecessary.

Not that anyone can be blamed for the error—in modern times, the distinction between sexy and slutty is often tricky territory. After all, the desire to be sensual is no doubt the reason that preeten girls are showing up to recess in miniskirts and tube tops.

Wanting to feel sexy? Okay, I get that. Dressing up and acting like a teenage truck stop prostitute, however, is a different issue. Sure, a young girl may confuse classy and trashy, but certain things so clearly fall on the skanky side of the line.

For example, when teen starlets began going out wearing short skirts without underwear and climbing out of their Mercedes convertibles like a bunch of basketball players at halftime, driving the blogs into a frenzy with their uncensored photos, surely they did it to feel sexy.

> "The only real elegance is in the mind; if you've got that, the rest really comes from it."
>
> DIANA VREELAND

> "Elegance is a question of personality, more than one's clothing."
>
> JEAN-PAUL GAULTIER

But it backfired: Instead of applauding their adolescent sensuality, the entire world thought they were sluts with poor hygiene. (Except in your case, Britney Spears; you were going through a real rough patch. But you've gotten over it, now. Bless. Love you.)

Same thing with skirt length.

While the fashion industry may dictate different lengths for different seasons—sometimes above the knee, sometimes down to the ankle—there will never be a time when a woman's reproductive organ should be exposed to the elements. I don't think I'm going out on a limb here when I say that *Vogue* will never have a story claiming that this season's hottest accessory is an exposed crotch. "Your Baby Maker: Spring's Big Reveal" just won't sell copies.

It might seem old and archaic. It might seem like something your mother might tell you or something that you'd read in a '50s prom brochure, but there's nothing wrong with generating some mystery and keeping covered. Flashing skin and showing bum aren't the only things you can do to draw attention to yourself: Wear bright colors, or wear a bra with enough support to create cleavage. (But if you're wearing a revealing top, make sure your bottom half is covered.) There's a fine line between looking sexy and slutty, and you want to err on the side that doesn't also include dominatrices and strippers.

You might be thinking: Why? Why, in these modern times, would I need to be at all prim or ladylike? (Chances are, however, if you're reading this book right now—as opposed to, say, having an entire fraternity suck tequila out of your belly button—

you already know the answer to this.) But let's attend to the query: Sluts hardly ever win. Sure, occasionally the girl who constantly flaunts her goodies parlays such exposure into success (Hi, Paris Hilton!), but overall it's not a good idea. I have met models and actresses who have lost endorsement deals because they insist on showing up at clubs with their butt cracks out, or because they catch the eye of the wrong type of man while rocking an outfit that screams: "My daddy didn't love me, so I'll make up for that now by showing every man in the room my nipple piercing."

If the hottest girl in the world loses a million-dollar cosmetics contract because she wears a crop top to a nightclub, don't you think that maybe, just maybe, you could lose the affection of Johnny Quarterback if he knows you're willing to show the entire team your footballs?

A smoky eye, tousled hair, tight tops, short skirts with tights—there are a million ways to look sexy without looking like you've been rode hard and put away wet. Perhaps you have a great pair of legs—wear a slightly more conservative top and go ahead and bare those gams. Maybe you have a beautiful, slender neck, or perfect pale arms, or a beautiful collarbone. I've always thought the back is one of the sexiest parts of a woman's body. In fact, to this day, when a Cate Blanchett (at her first Golden Globes) or a Gwyneth Paltrow (see: the pink Ralph Lauren dress she wore when she won the Oscar for *Shakespeare in Love*) works

THAT'S =YES= CLASSY!

A Lady **wears underwear.**

A Lady **knows not to pick anything but a dress at a store; she doesn't pick her nose or her panties in public.**

an open-backed dress, she finds herself in both best-dressed lists and men's fantasies. The point is, the sexy parts of the body aren't necessarily the parts of the body that are used during the act of having sex.

Remember: Cultivating some mystery is still one of the greatest weapons of mass seduction there is. The other one is confidence. I don't want to get too Oprah on you here, but it's true that how you carry yourself is often more important than what you wear. You might have the sexiest outfit on, but if you hold yourself like a timid granny at a rock concert, you won't look nearly as hot as the confident girl in the turtleneck.

Looking Chic

A quick survey of what famous women are wearing can give a girl a complex about what is considered fashionable nowadays. If that tween sensation is in a mini-mini-skirt and hooker boots, is that what all the girls are wearing? If she's in a sheer bodysuit, should I be? (The answer is no to both questions, FYI.) Here is a visual that helps clarify the difference between sexy and slutty.

POSE
The look is coquettish: invitation only, not open house.

MAKEUP
Here, we're focused on a single feature—a smoky eye. Only hookers, clowns, and stage actresses pile makeup on the eyes, lips, *and* cheeks.

SKIN
Although the shoulders are exposed, the rest of the body is considerably covered, leaving something (anything) to the imagination.

LADY

THAT'S YES CLASSY!

SKIRT LENGTH
Because the top of this outfit is so bare, the hem of the Chanel skirt is considerably low, almost below the knee. The modern girl knows balance: A short skirt means a covered top, and vice versa.

FIT
The skirt is tight, but not too tight. You can appreciate her silhouette without getting a full-on lesson about the female anatomy.

DOSE OF COLOR
Subdued doesn't necessarily mean boring, and these Louboutin stilettos are tall, shiny, and sexy—without being gauche.

POSE
I've seen this pose before. In a strip club.

MAKEUP
A heavily darkened eye, a very red lip, lots of foundation—one has to wonder what she's hiding under there (rashes? brushes? what?).

CROP TOP
Unless you're a cheerleader or prepubescent little girl, there is no reason to run around town in a half tee. Surely you can afford a whole shirt.

SKIN
If 75 percent of your body is exposed—and you're not at a beach—there is a problem.

TRAMP

UNDERGARMENTS
An exposed bra strap? Really? There are other ways to remind a guy that you have breasts.

LACE-UP TROUSERS
Leather trousers can be dangerous enough (though I've seen some effective pairs in my day), but traditionally—unless you're in a *Moulin Rouge* remake or a Versailles costume party—anything that laces up is a no go. Especially if skin can poke through said lacing.

CHEAP CLOTHES
Even if they are expensive, nice clothes on a skank will look cheap. Like these Manolo heels with lace-up trousers and a baby tee. They look like stripper shoes.

TRAMP
NO
STAMP

Do You Dress Like a Tramp?

People who dress as though they are good for only one thing (hint: It involves black satin bed sheets and a hangover) are still that: people. And sometimes they don't even know they're sending out a big Slut Symbol. In case you're one of those people, here is a quiz to help you find out if you are inadvertently dressing like a ten-dollar hooker.

1. It's Christmas morning and your grandmother has given you a very conservative turtleneck sweater. You:

- (A) Love it completely. It is the best Christmas gift you could have gotten.
- (B) Think it will be great for a cold winter's day, but know you won't be wearing it to the clubs.
- (C) Almost throw it away, until you realize that if you cut the neck out and the sleeves off, you can easily convert it to a knit tube top.

2. Your favorite pair of jeans has just ripped up to your upper thigh, so you:

- (A) Throw them away.
- (B) Patch them, or turn them into shorts.
- (C) Love the bare-ass look so much, you rip all of your other jeans to match.

3. You've just had a growth spurt. Your favorite white T-shirt now barely covers your stomach and is very tight across the chest. Your response?

- (A) Buy a new T-shirt.
- (B) Keep the T-shirt for the beach and slumber parties.
- (C) Relief! *Finally*—something that looks great at a wet T-shirt contest *and* church.

4. You have a gift certificate to a department store. The first section of the store you go to is:

- (A) The sleepwear section.
- (B) The jewelry section.
- (C) The lingerie section, specifically for crotchless panties.

5. A family member has died, and you have to attend the funeral service. You decide to wear:

- (A) A black hooded sweatshirt, a black floor-length skirt, and flat black shoes.
- (B) A dark dress with dark tights.
- (C) A tight tank top tucked into a PVC skirt with high heels. What? They're all black.

6. Your sister is getting married, and at the wedding you wear:

(A) A long dress with long sleeves and no jewelry whatsoever.

(B) A cute dress in a bright color that makes you feel pretty.

(C) A sexy white dress, slit up to your thighs. Why should your tramp of a sister get all the attention today?

7. Your favorite fashion icon is:

(A) Mary Magdalene

(B) Audrey Hepburn

(C) Those pole dancers–turned–reality-TV-show stars who make out with fallen '80s musicians on camera.

8. Your favorite fabrics are:

(A) Wool and polyester

(B) Cashmere and silk

(C) Anything see-through. Or leopard print, to match your leopard-print satin bedsheets.

9. Your favorite color is:

(A) Beige.

(B) Blue. It brings out your eyes.

(C) Is *transparent* a color? What about *patent leather?*

10. You're going to the beach with friends. You pack:

(A) A one-piece swimsuit with an extra-long sarong and oversize black men's T-shirt to wear over the whole look. Tan lines be damned.

(B) A cute tankini that shows a bit of skin but has a generous amount of coverage, plus a cute sundress.

(C) A thong string bikini and a white T-shirt—for the wet T-shirt contest, obviously.

QUIZ KEY

Count up all your answers and see which of the three letters you had the most of. If you are:

Mostly A's. Are you Amish? Yes, there are more important things in life than fashion, but that's no reason to dress like an 18th-century housemaid. There's nothing wrong with being conservative, but remember that clothing can be *fun:* a form of personal expression and a way to show the world how you feel.

Mostly B's. Finally, a classy bird. You experiment with your fashion choices, but you also know that pleather is not appropriate beachwear.

Mostly C's. Even if you don't sell your womanly charms for money, you *look* like you do. There's a difference between looking sexy and looking cheap. Remember: People will find you even more attractive if the goodies aren't always on display. Who wants to eat a half-melted cookie that's been left out in the sun and manhandled by a dozen other people?

RECESSIONISTA

Looking Chic on the Cheap

O ne of the biggest misconceptions associated with the fashion industry is that a girl has to spend a lot of money to look good. It's not true: I've often seen rich women look awful when they load on their designer duds, piling on label after label and hair treatment after hair treatment. They end up looking like overstuffed designer teddy bears with mops on their heads.

Just because you can't afford clothes off the Paris runway doesn't mean that you will automatically look like a homeless woman in Queens. A girl on a budget needs to remember several key things: A) Classic silhouettes never go out of style; B) It's important to invest in certain staple pieces; and C) As with glass and newspapers, you should always reuse and recycle.

A half century ago, Coco Chanel designed a little black dress that could go with anything. Since then, every single magazine has done a story on the LBD every single season. And famous designers aren't the only ones making garments that flatter the body. Sure, Marc Jacobs can send a chic black number down the runway every season, but your local mall will have a few of its own versions at prices nearly everyone can afford. Classic things—things that fit well and are understated and elegant—don't have to be expensive.

Shop the sales. Wait until the end of the season to stock up your wardrobe (but be care-

ful you're not buying something that is already out of style—remember to think "classic"). Go to discount stores. The trick is to know what looks good on you, and what you'll wear in the future. And by future I don't just mean at spring homecoming. I mean (gasp) in college and (double gasp) even after college.

> "It's not money that makes you well-dressed, it's understanding."
>
> CHRISTIAN DIOR

The best lesson to remember when it comes to shopping: If something fits correctly and you look good in it, it will look expensive. The opposite is true as well. You might have an unlimited budget, but if you don't buy things that fit well, you'll look bad. And you'll probably look poor. (This is probably the most insulting thing you can say to a rich person, by the way.)

Don't worry about wearing your clothes too frequently. (Within reason; don't wear the same blouse every day for a week or the same dress at every single cocktail party. Mix it up by pairing the blouse with a skirt at one event, and then with jeans and a blazer at the next.) But know that there's nothing wrong with having articles of clothing that you like and wear often.

The chicest girls I know look put together no matter what they're wearing, whether their dresses are from the haute couture in Paris or the mall in Lexington, Kentucky. To be completely honest, the most stylish girls know how to mix their wardrobes with pieces from both worlds. This is the whole idea behind High/Low, the stylistic integration of both inexpensive and expensive pieces. Just remember: The best black dress is one that looks like it cost a bunch even if it didn't, and the stylish girl looks good, happy, and confident in whatever she's wearing, no matter where she bought it.

TIPS FOR ONLINE SHOPPING

Purchasing items online should be an easy, convenient experience, and a great way to score deals when you're buying on a budget. You can do it from the comfort of your home and think about a purchase for as long as you like without some shop assistant giving you the stink eye.

However, it can also provoke major anxiety. How do you know you're getting the best deal? How can you be sure the seller is legit and that the item in question actually looks like its picture—and will arrive at your house intact? What if those leather pants are too small? Too big? (For those of you who have MOSA—Major Online Shopping Anxiety—it's best just to go to a store.)

For the rest, here are some tips to keep in mind before you start draining your PayPal account:

❯ Use common sense. It's easy to get caught up in the passion of a purchase—especially if you're participating in an online auction and it's getting down to the wire—and lose your head. Listen, if something is too good to be true, it probably is. If Louboutin shoes are on sale for $10, they're either fake or they're missing a heel. Don't fall for it.

❯ When buying something online, make sure the web address is secure. This means it will have an s in its domain, and will read "https:," as opposed to "http:."

❯ Keep a record of any correspondence you exchange with the seller. If you are in possession of an e-mail that says the bag you're buying is authentic, with the original lining intact and a detachable shoulder strap included, it will be easier to get compensated when a battered, moth-eaten designer imposter clutch shows up in the mail.

❯ Whenever possible, use a credit card. The good folks behind American Express, MasterCard, and other major credit cards have claims departments, which can help you stop payments or contest bogus charges. This is not true of money orders or services like PayPal. Never send cash.

❯ Don't respond to unsolicited e-mails, and make sure the e-mails you receive are from legitimate sellers. Once you enter the worldwide mall of Internet shopping, you will often be solicited by people peddling sub-par merchandise. Just like you would be on the street, be wary of people who come up to you hawking goods you didn't want in the first place.

❯ Do your homework. See if the seller has been positively reviewed by other buyers. Ask yourself if the site feels legitimate. Larger, corporate sites will help buyers (and sellers, for that matter) who are wronged—but some dinky website thrown together by dodgy Nigerian rebels should be avoided, particularly if the sellers request your direct banking information.

This isn't meant to discourage you from purchasing things online. I've found some major goods online—like a vintage Christian Dior beaded cummerbund that makes me smile every time I see it—but I've been disappointed too. Online shopping is a gamble, so don't blow all your chips on some guy named $am who sells "iPhones" out of his basement for $5.

Vintage: It's New to Me

Sometimes your favorite new thing is really, really old

Thanks to the pioneering efforts of an entire spectrum of stylish women—from Penélope Cruz and Renée Zellweger at the Oscars to Kate Moss and Mary-Kate Olsen at music festivals—vintage clothing is not a new trend. In fact, we have these ladies to thank for the boutiques around the world that now charge more for an old dress than a new one. But just because a 1950s original Christian Dior couture dress can go for thousands doesn't mean there aren't plenty of amazing (and cheap) vintage finds for those of us who don't have million-dollar shopping budgets.

One great thing about vintage is its accessibility. But while used clothes are cheap and vintage stores are everywhere, a lot of the stuff on offer is sub-par. Unlike in the mall, where you'll be able to find a cute shirt in a variety of sizes, the discarded fashion relics from generations past might only come in a man's size 42. Most likely there will only be one of the item you want. If something doesn't fit correctly, you have to move on or find a good tailor.

Also, shopping vintage makes for hours and hours of sifting through racks and racks—or, if the place is particularly budget, piles and piles—to find something cute. And who knows, you might not find anything at all after your exhaustive rummaging. It's like a treasure hunt. But don't be discouraged: The thrill of locating a lost fashion artifact is worth it.

When I was growing up in Missouri, I found resale shops were great places to shop when I wanted to look good for less. My parents thought my obsession

A lady is always on the lookout for a good deal when it comes to stocking her closet.

with vintage was frivolous (my dad had some moral issues with shopping at thrift stores: He was convinced they were stocked with the apparel of dead people). But I was on a budget. Thrift shops were full of undiscovered gems; they were places I could go to find '70s suits, '50s shirts, and fabulous cardigans and bow ties.

Whenever I go home to my parents' house I still—without fail—work in a trip to a local resale shop. I'll find a few suits, which I'll turn over to a cute old

Italian woman who runs a tailor shop from a bedroom in her house. She takes the pants in (if they were originally bell bottoms), or lets the waist out (if they were designed '50s-style, to be worn above my belly button). A suit might cost $10. My lovely tailor will fit it to my body for an even $15—and then I'll show up on the Manhattan party circuit and tell everyone I'm wearing a Prada suit that retails at $4,000. (Suckers!)

The Midwest isn't the only place for good vintage shops. I've found really terrific shops all over, though be warned: In rural parts of the world, and even this fine country, it is considered weird to actively covet and seek out the fashions of deceased people. A simple Internet search can provide a good selection of fancy stores and the discount bargain bins. (Even big cities like New York have Salvation Armies, and recent reports say that whenever the economy hits a snag, sales at the stores go up.)

Another appealing aspect of vintage clothing is that, for the most part, it's completely and utterly unique. The chances of someone else showing up to a party wearing the same 1960s caftan you found at a yard sale on a back-country road (another great place to find vintage) are, needless to say, extremely slim.

Caveat: A great risk of dressing exclusively in vintage is looking like you're living in a time warp, or permanently in costume. The trick is updating the stuff, mixing a vintage silhouette with contemporary elements. Even if you're into '60s sensibilities, don't turn full-on hippie with colored glasses, a maxi dress over bell-bottoms, and a headband. Even if you love '50s movies, you don't need to show up to the prom in a pintucked chiffon dress, a pillbox hat, and white gloves. There's a fine line between vintage and costume. You want to look cute, not like you're in a community theater production of *Hair* or *Bye, Bye Birdie*.

And most important when it comes to vintage: Be sure to get whatever you buy cleaned or dry-cleaned before you wear it. Not only do you want to get the stains and any possible lingering smells out of the fabric, I've had a few friends report very unfortunate stories of contracting rashes and certain other skin conditions after wearing the unwashed garments of others. Vintage is worth everything to me— except a case of the crabs.

Everything in this look is vintage. The 1970s Chanel jacket might be found at a designer vintage boutique, whereas the denim shorts, T-shirt, and strappy sandals could be picked up on the cheap at your average thrift shop, like the Goodwill or Salvation Army. Remember: Half the fun of shopping vintage is the hunt.

COLORS AND COMPLEXION

It's one of the first fashion lessons many of us learned: matching! (Or at least, understanding that certain colors "go" with certain colors and clash with other shades.) The exact same principle applies to skin and hair tones, and which colors do them justice. This little chart will help ensure that you're wearing things that make the most of your coloring. Heed this chart wisely: All it takes is one super-blonde wearing something bright red to prove that the wrong color combo can have disastrous consequences. (In this case, consequences that involve being mistaken for a hooker.)

**BLONDE HAIR,
FAIR COMPLEXION**

**BRUNETTE,
OLIVE SKIN**

**BLACK HAIR,
DARK SKIN**

**RED HAIR,
FAIR COMPLEXION**

WHAT TO LOOK FOR IN A FASHION INVESTMENT

○ **FIT** The way a garment fits is the single most important feature of a purchase. Pay special attention to sleeve length and the way the garment drapes off the shoulders. If there are darts, make sure they fall under the breasts. And use tailors! No one is a perfect size 2, or a perfect size 14. Minor alterations can make a garment look custom-made.

○ **MATERIAL** Not everyone can afford cashmere. Nonetheless, material is important. A good test? Brush the material to your face. If you don't recoil in horror or break into a rash, this is suitable material. Remember to check the care instructions before you buy something. Are you really going to want to hand wash that synthetic rhinestone-encrusted shirt every time you wear it? (Also, in general, stay away from rhinestones.)

○ **PRACTICALITY** Ask yourself where this piece fits into your wardrobe. Will this jacket/skirt/shirt serve its purpose? For example, once I picked up a raincoat that wasn't waterproof. That was stupid.

○ **PATTERN & COLOR** These can be tricky. Not only do specific colors go in and out—which is why I'm always buying blacks, grays and blues—patterns can flatter your figure, or completely trash-talk it. For example, horizontal stripes and busy patterns can make a person look heavier. Likewise, if you're tall, a pinstripe—which attenuates the frame—can make you look lanky. Color is hard: Bright colors draw attention to and exaggerate certain features, while neutral colors can wash out a person's skin color. A good rule of thumb? Pick subdued patterns—you can never go wrong with a light floral or a subtle pinstripe—and when it comes to color, listen to loved ones. (Surely a parent or loved one has told you by now that you look good in red or blue or green.) Michael Kors once told me that, if possible, you should always have white next to your face—it makes all skin types look glorious.

○ **LONGEVITY** It's difficult to think about what you'll wear a few decades from now—ew, you'll be, like, old then—but it's never too soon to think about the quality of your purchases. Will a leather bag last longer than a nylon one? Fashion can be fun and frivolous, but when it comes to staple pieces, pay attention to a garment's construction and quality—or you might have to buy it again in a few weeks.

○ **PRICE** I've put this last on the list for a reason—and not because I don't remember the days of my very budgeted childhood. Believe me, I can still recall paying for cardigans at thrift stores in quarters. But chic isn't always cheap. When something feels, fits, and looks good, buy it. Remember: If you buy one pair of jeans that costs a lot of money, it's okay if you buy only one pair—it's better, and in the long run cheaper, than buying four pairs of cheaper jeans you don't like as much. While many bemoan that some of fashion's greatest prizes are priced out of range—it pisses me off too—for some things it's okay to splurge. Just don't make it a habit, ladies. Credit-card debt is never chic.

A Couple of Classics

While it's true that every young woman needs a pair of jeans that make her look ten pounds thinner and a little black dress that can be worn anywhere (dressed up for a formal occasion, dressed down for a casual event), be on the lookout for these additional wardrobe staples.

"All it takes are a few simple outfits. And there's one secret—the simpler, the better."

CARY GRANT

Cardigans and Cashmere

When I was a little boy I tried counting the many ways I could wear my first cashmere sweater: over the shoulders, around the waist, over one shoulder and then looped under the other arm and tied around the chest—the options were endless. Just make sure the cashmere is good quality. Cardigans are great investments: A chic cardigan can be thrown over jeans for a casual afternoon about town, but also dressed up when belted over a tight pencil skirt.

Jackets

A smart jacket is one that can be paired with anything, from jeans to ball gowns. A smartly tailored tweed jacket like this one from Chanel (left) can dress up a pair of slacks or be draped over the shoulders and worn with a dress on a chilly night. Same thing with a good trench coat (above): It's the perfect chic cover-up when you're dealing with the cold, the rainy, or the last-minute dash out the door.

Perfect Shoes

Countless articles have been devoted to the search for the perfect pump, and women have long been obsessed with their footwear. (One whole *Sex in the City* episode was devoted to a pair of shoes so enticing they were stolen at a party.) Every girl needs a smart, well-built pair of heels and a good, classic flat. Most girls I know would prefer costume jewelry to the real thing if it means they will have extra money to spend on chic, comfortable, classic shoes.

"I don't know who invented high heels, but all women owe him a lot."

MARILYN MONROE

Logomaniacs!

Be careful when rocking out with your labels out

Make a fist. Nothing you wear should feature a logo bigger than the size of your fist right now. Actually, half that. Nothing should be bigger than half of your fist right now. Okay, fine: Nothing should be bigger than half the size of your fist when you were five years old.

Logomania can be vulgar. A little bit of fashion history: In the past decade, with the fashion world on a hazy financial high reflective of the more-more-more mentality of the investment bankers (before they all went bust), a chic woman's wardrobe went a little bling. Fendi logos were everywhere, and so were

> "Above all, remember that the most important thing you can take anywhere is not a Gucci bag or French-cut jeans; it's an open mind."
>
> **GAIL RUBIN BERENY**

Prada's metal triangles and Gucci's double G's. It didn't last long, and soon labels went back inside the garments. (Note: There are a few exceptions to the rule, like the Louis Vuitton monogram, which remains classic and probably always will.) But for some reason, most tramps still think that giant, overbearing designer logos are a passport to cooldom. But I'm telling you right now: They're not. They reek of desperation.

Look at it this way: Logos are the equivalent of blinged-out hubcaps. Sure, you can spend a bunch of money buying four hubcaps that look like disco

In small doses, a classic monogram or a fashion house's print can be the perfect decorative motif on an accessory. But be careful that you're not so loaded down with logos you become a walking advertisement for a design house.

balls, but if you're slapping them on the four flat tires of a beat-up Buick, it's going to look ridiculous. I'm not suggesting that you are a Buick, not by any means. But common sense should dictate that it's a much better idea to invest in the whole transportation package, buying a sensible car with classy rims. You might not be able to afford a Rolls-Royce yet, but that doesn't mean you can't focus on the basics, like well-made wardrobe staples, a personal sense of style, and, most importantly, confidence.

Similarly speaking, I should mention here that just because something has a name brand or a logo does not mean it's cool.

A lady does not wish to be defined by her purchases.

I've known people (typically, the types who have just inherited some money or found a rich boyfriend) who will walk into a Chanel store and buy the tackiest,

loudest, most gauche bag they can find, then carry it around like a prize pig at a state fair. Take this to heart: A fancy logo doesn't automatically make an article of clothing fashionable. (And FYI: People shouldn't like you because you can spend a lot of money on a handbag.)

Always remember this: People who can afford really expensive clothes very rarely make it a priority to let others know they spent a lot of money on their wardrobe. Being stylish means buying fashionable things and making them your own, not showing up in head-to-toe Dior just to prove that you managed to up your credit limit.

Never Trust a Faker

Designer knock-offs can be tempting, but like anything disingenuous, they can often lead to heartbreak

When the question of designer-imposter luxury goods comes up, my response is simple: absolutely not. More often than not the fakes are easy to spot—and believe me, the people who can actually afford the real ones can easily spot the people who can't. And furthermore, knockoffs do serious damage to the fashion world we so dearly adore and cherish.

If a designer at a high-fashion house spends six months designing this season's It Bag, dedicating all his resources and time and company money to its design, and using all the best materials and workmanship, it's going to be expensive. And then if some factory in Brooklyn runs off a thousand very similar bags and sells them on Canal Street, not only does that insult the integrity and vision of the designer, it also makes the bag less desirable. And when the desire is gone, sales go bye-bye. Sure, Marc Jacobs once said that it's flattering when his designs get copied, but he's rich already and can afford to be flattered. That's why,

ahem, knockoffs are illegal. (For proof of the importance of legit fashions and the illegality of their imposters, look no further than the court case of Jacobs' very annoyed employer Louis Vuitton vs. eBay, in which the French-luxury-goods house sued the pants off the online auction website for not doing a good job of policing the knockoff Vuittons sold on the site.)

Here's the bigger issue: If you truly think that your life will be better if you own a Murakami Louis Vuitton handbag, real or fake, there is something wrong with your way of thinking. Not to say a cute bag isn't a thrilling purchase or that sales aren't miracles from retail heaven. I have friends who go absolutely orgasmic at the after-Christmas sales and sample sales (and by "friends" I mean me).

But an expensive logo will not make you more stylish—and if you really think it will, you should take that designer-imposter money and get a shrink, not a handbag.

"Costly thy habit as thy purse can buy, But not expressed in fancy; rich, not gaudy; For the apparel oft proclaims the man."

SHAKESPEARE, *HAMLET*

A lady understands that just because people think she can afford expensive things does not mean they think she deserves them.

A lady, if she desires a designer item, will work hard and pay for the authentic version.

On my first trip to New York City, when I saw folding tables full of discount merchandise on Canal Street and men selling designer handbags off of bedsheets and out of the backs of moving trucks, I was confused. Why, I wondered, are these Chanel bags so much cheaper than the ones in the stores? And why would anyone go all the way to Madison Avenue when there are perfectly chic ones right here in the back of this man's Buick for a fraction of the cost? Only later, upon closer inspection, did I realize the bags were fakes: Fucci instead of Gucci, Prado instead of Prada. It was an honest mistake, though. To the untrained eye, a double E might look awfully similar to Fendi's signature double F. So here's a little diagram to help remind you which are the real logos and which are the impostors. But remember: When in doubt, just buy a bag in basic black.

THE ACTUAL LOGOS

Chanel

Fendi

Gucci

Dior — Christian Dior

Louis Vuitton

PRADA — Prada

Borrowing & Lending Etiquette

Even with clothes, sharing is caring

In the fashion world, there are two major types of borrowing. The first is pretty simple: When a friend of yours has an article of clothing that you like, you ask if you can borrow it. If she's not selfish or anal, chances are she'll lend it to you. Which is nice of her. So it's up to you to return it in a similar (or better) condition: Wash it, or offer to have it dry-cleaned—even if it wasn't dry-cleaned when you borrowed it. (What? It's still cheaper than buying a new dress.) You must also return it in a timely fashion, typically within a week of borrowing it. (P.S. This also means that you have to be equally unselfish and give her something out of your wardrobe if she asks for it, even if you're selfish and anal.)

Borrowing from friends and loved ones boils down to common sense. For example, don't ask to borrow a friend's favorite skirt to wear to a party that she hasn't been invited to. Nothing hurts more than knowing you are not on the guest list at the party everyone else, including your skirt, will be attending.

The importance of common sense, of course, is not limited to the borrower. Lenders should have the brilliance to know not to lend anything so valuable—sentimentally or monetarily—that they could never bear to see it stained, stolen, or lost. It's okay to say no in these situations; a true friend will understand if you explain that you are saving the item for a special occasion or that it's in too delicate a condition to part with. Are you lending your mom's wedding dress to a friend who is a known smoker and drunkard? 'Cause that's probably a bad idea.

A Lady is not gluttonous with her wardrobe.

A Lady, if she borrows, returns items promptly and in the same condition she received them.

The second type of borrowing, specific to big cities and fashion capitals, is when a noteworthy person borrows a dress from a fashion house. Typically, this happens when the dresses are fresh off the runway and aren't available to the public yet. Designers are more than willing to lend the garments to famous people, as it is essentially free press.

Even if you've never made it beyond the local cornfields, and the fanciest party you've ever been to is Big Tommy's Moonshine Hoedown, you never know what the future will hold for you, so it's important to know the guidelines for this type of exchange. Of course, you must return the dress in a timely fashion and be careful not to ruin it, but it's also considered tacky to wear something that someone else has already been photographed in. (Sometimes people deliberately break this rule in order to garner free press. I can think of one particular instance when an overly ambitious socialite intentionally wore a dress someone legitimately famous had worn previously, hoping to wind up in the tabloids on the Who Wore It Better lists.)

Borrowing clothes is perfectly acceptable, but make sure it doesn't become an addiction. Nan Kempner was a famously skinny and photogenic socialite in New York City who made it a point to pay for clothes (granted, often at a discounted rate). When Kempner died, she donated her entire "closet"—a renovated spare bedroom in her Upper East Side apartment—to the Metropolitan Museum of Art's Costume Institute. Sometimes I've seriously thought that if some of today's "fashion icons" died and specified their closets be donated to a fashion museum

Fake eyelashes, hair extensions, velour jumpsuits and broken sunglasses: the calling card of pathological borrowers. Don't let this happen to you.

as Kempner did, all the museum would get is a bunch of false eyelashes and Juicy Couture jumpsuits. Scary thought.

Appreciate your own closet, ladies. Sure, when you're in a pinch it's okay to borrow a dress from your BFF, but don't abuse

"Happy, happy fashion—there is not much more to it than that."

MARC JACOBS

the privilege. If you're wearing all your friends' dresses, what kind of style do you have? If you don't have any fabulous clothes in your closet, then what the hell is in there? And don't say sex toys, trampy tramp.

Decoding the Dress Code

Broadly speaking, it's always better to be overdressed than underdressed. (Ivana Trump said this in an interview when I was a little boy; I remember reading those words then and thinking, "You're *so* right, Ivana"). Sure, you might feel silly if you're in a dress when everyone is in jeans—but you will feel ridiculous if you're in jeans when everyone else is in a dress. I was once asked to escort a young actress to what she thought was just another cocktail party in Los Angeles. I wore jeans and a suit jacket; she was wearing black pants and a blouse. When we arrived and noticed all the other girls in long dresses and the men in suits, she was completely mortified—and made me leave before we even got to the door. We went to Domino's Pizza instead (so it wasn't all bad). But not every dress-code horror story ends happily in melted cheese and pepperoni, so beware.

Below are a few common dress codes. I've also listed some less traditional—but just as common—types of parties you might attend, and some general guidelines to ensure you don't show up at a backyard barbecue dressed in a leather bustier and Lucite wedge heels. Not that you should own either item.

One rule of thumb: If a hostess or party organizer has gone to the trouble of specifying a certain type of dress on the invitation, she expects you to adhere to it. It is incredibly impolite to disregard a dress code.

Casual

At a family Christmas party, casual might mean that you should break out your "fancy" sweatpants. On a more traditional invitation, however, casual doesn't mean looking like you just spent the afternoon lounging around the house watching *Roseanne* reruns. You should still be wearing unwrinkled clothes, a bra, and shoes that have soles. Casual means putting on your nice jeans; it means a pretty sweater or blouse; it means a leather shoe and not an Ugg boot. The point of putting "casual" on an invitation is to encourage people to look relaxed, not lazy.

Smart Casual

This is typically a business-type term. For all you aspiring moguls out there with internships, know that, again, you should appear to be casual, though you shouldn't actually be casual. Avoid jeans unless they're perfectly tailored and without holes. A skirt is a good choice here, or a nice cocktail dress with a cardigan over it to dress it down.

BBQ

I love a BBQ. The unhealthy food, the warm weather, the smell of charcoal. But dressing for one isn't the easiest thing. It's important to look nice, but a BBQ is not the place to test-drive your new cocktail dress or blouse. My biggest tip: Do not wear white. A girlfriend of mine once wore her new pair of white pants to a family BBQ and promptly sat on a half-eaten chicken wing. It looked like she was having a "female emergency." Gross. Also, avoid super-flowy garments. Nobody wants a long chiffon scarf dangling over an open flame.

Cocktail

Just because it's called "cocktail" does not mean you should dress to get drunk. This isn't a keg party. Slacks are okay, but not jeans. Something more formal—like, ahem, the aptly named cocktail dress—is certainly more appropriate. If you have a job, going from the office to a cocktail party can be as simple as putting on a nice pair of heels and a few statement pieces of jewelry, like a large broach or a few bracelets.

A Lady never wears an evening gown during the day; if a formal function is during the day, she wears a cocktail dress.

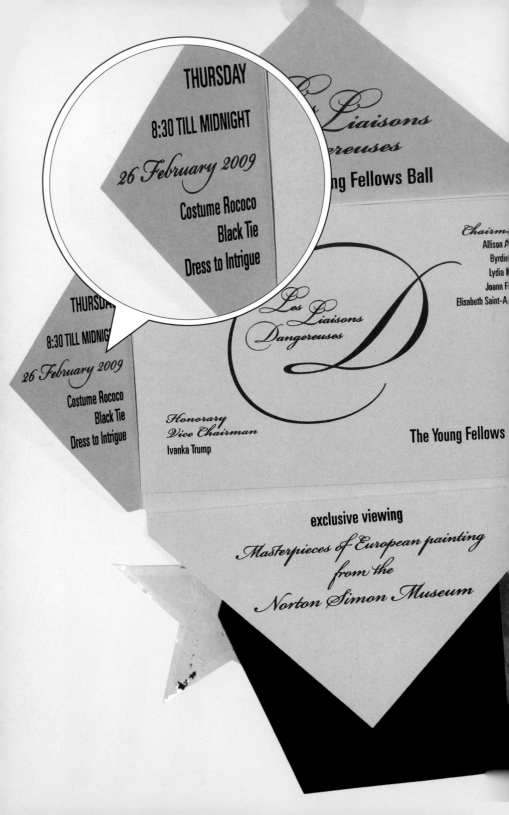

THURSDAY

8:30 TILL MIDNIGHT

26 February 2009

Costume Rococo
Black Tie
Dress to Intrigue

Les Liaisons Dangereuses

...ng Fellows Ball

Chairm...
Allison A...
Byrdie...
Lydia...
Joann...
Elisabeth Saint-A...

D

*Honorary
Vice Chairman*
Ivanka Trump

The Young Fellows

exclusive viewing

*Masterpieces of European painting
from the
Norton Simon Museum*

THURSDA...

8:30 TILL MIDNIG...

26 February 2009

Costume Rococo
Black Tie
Dress to Intrigue

The first thing I look at when I get an invitation is the dress code. Before I look at the date, or the time, or even the location of the party, I look for a theme: Is it a birthday? Will I be breaking out the ol' tuxedo for this shindig? Or will I have to do something more creative? (This reminds me: A good hostess always includes a dress code on her invite, especially if there's a theme; for more on hostessing and themes, see Chapter 3.) Dress codes are just as important as the date and time of the event, so make sure you take note of and then adhere to them—especially because (as is often the case in New York) some hostesses are very specific about what they would like their guests to wear. Heaven forbid you show up in a minimalist look at a party like one of these, which clearly ask for 30s costume or something to intrigue.

The Frick Collection

One East Seventieth Street
New York City

YOU ARE INVITED TO

An Evening of Glamour and Games
Where Stars Are Born and Legends Made

Domino Tournament

Dress Code 1930s New York, The Golden Age of Jazz

BENEFIT COMMITTEE

Cocktails 6:30 pm
Domino Tournament 8:00 pm sharp

Dress Code 1930s New York, The Golden Age of Jazz

BENEFIT COMMITTEE

AMANDA ANKA GLENDA BAILEY JASON BATEMAN ADRIEN BRODY OLIVIA CHANTECAILLE
PENÉLOPE CRUZ GIANNINA FACIO DEBORAH HARRY SALMA HAYEK ROSIE PEREZ JASON POMERANC
JOEL MADDEN MIA MAESTRO OLIVIER MARTINEZ DEMI MOORE JENNIFER MORRISON
ENRIQUE MURCIANO AMAURY NOLASCO NICOLE RICHIE RIDLEY SCOTT ALI WISE

This invitation is non-transferable

Theme

Although I love a theme [see "Favorite Party Themes", pp. 92-93], some people prefer to moan about getting dressed up. But prepping a costume, especially if you're getting ready with friends, can be memorable and fun. So take a minute, be creative, find an outfit, and run with it. Bear in mind that a hostess puts a lot of time and energy into these parties, so don't rain on her parade by being a spoilsport. If you can't muster up the energy to get a plastic sword and slap on an eye patch for a pirate-themed party, stay home—because there's no way you're going to muster up the energy to be good company once you're out.

Formal and Black-Tie

Pull out the stops, ladies, and the gowns and the evening clutches and the high heels. Occasions to really dress up become less and less frequent with every generation, so when the situation arises take advantage of it. Do something with your hair, lotion up your whole body so you feel sexy, and put on some mascara. A generation ago "formal" meant long dresses, but shorter dresses have become accept-

able for formal occasions. Granted, a short dress does not mean a miniskirt. [For a review on what is a decent length, please see "Lady v. Tramp: In Fashion," pp. 4-7.] Show off your legs, not your plumbing.

White-Tie

"White tie" refers to the gentleman's tuxedo, which is even fancier than the traditional black or navy tuxedo. The white-tie dress code is traditionally reserved for formal weddings and other decadent affairs, and if you find yourself invited to one—I've only been invited to a handful—this is not the time to try out a new hair color or wear something edgy. You must wear a floor-length dress. No knobby knees or visible thighs permitted. I'm always one for breaking the rules and pushing the envelope, especially when it comes to fashion, but there's something to be said for feeling elegant once in a while. So think "sophisticated" and save those fashion experiments for another event—like your cousin's bar mitzvah!

Pool Party

Ah, the tricky pool party, the terrifying time when people are going to actually see you in a swimsuit. Girls typically fall into two categories here: the overconfident girl who wears the tiniest of swimsuits to show off her body, or the insecure girl who would wear a winter coat to the beach if she could. Both girls are in trouble when it's time to disrobe. Tiny suits are useless—and even my supermodel friends have found themselves providing free peep shows to random strangers because their bikinis don't provide sufficient coverage. (Please believe it: Even supermodels have problem areas.) Larger swimsuits and a cover-up, like a beach wrap or skirt, can prevent these issues. For the girl who hates herself in a swimsuit: Don't be afraid to wear one that is considered "boring," like a one-piece. Also, invest in a nice sundress or something to wear when you're not in the pool. Confidence is key in most situations and critical at the beach. So before you dress for anyone else, make sure you feel good in what you're wearing.

What to Wear to Weddings and Funerals

One might think this concept would be self-explanatory: look festive at a wedding and look respectful at a funeral. But, without fail, every time I attend one of these functions, I find myself staring at enough poorly dressed women to warrant an entire chapter on these sartorial tragedies.

Let's start with weddings. I remember the elegant nuptials I attended in the South of France where a female friend of the groom showed up in a strapless Lycra mini dress that looked like it was from the South of New Jersey. It ended just below the bottom part of her buttocks, and yes, she was wearing Lucite platform stripper shoes. (Now that I think about it, I wonder if the groom met her at the bachelor party.)

No matter what wedding— be it a fancy uptown wedding in New York City or a more budgeted affair in someone's backyard—every single one will include at least one scantily clad skank, a girl who shows up at church dressed for a night at the clubs. After giving it some thought, I forgive this woman: The reason many make this mistake is because so many girls think weddings are a great place to meet a future boyfriend or husband. (Guys probably have similar thoughts, but it's much harder to mess up a rental tuxedo.)

Rule number one: A wedding is not a singles bar. Please avoid skintight fabrics and anything so sheer it exposes provocative tan lines. If you insist on going the formfitting route, do it in a dark color, but remember that dark colors are better for night weddings. Also, bring a shawl or wrap to cover up during the service if you're baring your shoulders.

It's no longer considered bad luck to wear black to a wedding, but a bright, uplifting color is a nice gesture—this is, after all, a happy couple about to start their life together. And—for the love of all things matrimonial—don't wear white to a wedding! While this is largely considered an old-school rule—and yes, when Prince William married Kate Middleton, the maid of honor was in a white dress—many people still think it's gauche. At the very least, go with cream or a light grey. It's still nice to let the bride be the only person in white on her special day.

Beyond attire, let's briefly touch on behavior: Even if you've had a terrible day, try to check your drama at the door. Even if you're lonely or miserable or got some bad news on your way to the reception, dig deep and put a smile on your face for someone else's special day. You will move on from your drama, but this particular day will always be remembered (and hopefully cherished) by the newlyweds.

And finally, while we're on the topic, just a few tips on gift giving at a wedding: stick to the registry, give cash, or go in with friends on a big-ticket item for the new couple. Save those creative gift-giving ideas for birthdays and anniversaries. A new couple will need a toaster in their new apartment.

Now, let's move on to funerals: The skin-tight rule also applies here. The point of a funeral service is to ponder how someone has touched your life—not how you hope someone is going to touch you later that night.

While you want to wear bright colors to celebrate a wedding, when it comes to the funeral, you want to wear something dark. Even if you don't think black or navy blue are good for your complexion, they're a sign of respect. (And if you truly don't like to wear dark colors, be happy it's only one day. When King Albert died, Queen Victoria wore only black for the rest of her life!)

Funerals can be sad places, but don't be afraid to smile and affectionately greet friends. And remember: emotional and moral support should last beyond this one day.

When it comes to funerals and weddings (and anything else that involves a place of worship or legal papers), devote your time and energy to someone other than yourself. No, I'm not saying you need to dress like a schlub to avoid distracting from the bride or to honor the passing of a loved one. But a wedding is a day when you celebrate the life of two *other* people—and for heaven's sake, please turn off your cell phone!

While some people say that it is considered outdated to feel obliged to wear black to a funeral and to completely avoid anything white at a wedding, I say it can never hurt to err on the side of tradition. So remember: In doubt, wear darks at a funeral and something pastel or bright at a wedding—and make sure everything that should be covered up is covered up.
Funeral homes and wedding chapels are not singles bars.

Your Right to Accessorize

Hats, scarves, gloves, and other all-important wardrobe condiments

Accessories aren't exactly a new invention. People have been throwing on hemp necklaces since Jesus' time, and bracelets were a big deal even back in the Middle Ages (though cuffs, not dainty tennis bracelets, were the style then). The magic of accessories is in their ability to spruce up any ol' look. Take Audrey Hepburn in the classic film *Breakfast at Tiffany's*: Without the sunglasses, cigarette holder, giant diamond necklaces, and bracelets, she would have been just another spoiled and clueless Upper East Sider, window-shopping in a black dress.

Increasingly, however, it seems that people have forgotten the importance of accessorizing. The only time a lady wears a hat is when she's coming from the gym or avoiding paparazzi, and then it's typically an ugly baseball cap, not a couture confection from Paris. People don't wear funky glasses anymore; they get Lasik. (Not that the accessories situation is any better for the boys. Men rarely wear rings unless they're in the Mafia, and when I wear a bow tie, people look at me as if I've just stepped out of a Mark Twain novel.)

Attention ladies: Have fun with accessories! They can completely change an outfit, making it dressier (a diamond necklace) or more playful (a big chunky bracelet). One of my friends prefers to layer her bracelets, which gives her a tough-girl look. Another friend of mine has some of the prettiest hats I've ever seen— and I'll tell you, no one is looking at her flat chest when she has one of them perched on her head.

Brooches are great and can very quickly dress up the lapel of a boring jacket or even a cocktail dress and cardigan. (If you're on a budget, look for costume jewelry. When it came to brooches, Coco Chanel was famously a fan of mixing the real and the fake.) I have one brooch in the shape of Noah's Ark, complete with monkeys hanging off the stern and detachable giraffe heads peek- ing out of the cabin. Now that's a showstopper, and a great conversation piece.

Shoes are accessories too— and, honey, everyone looks good in a high heel—as are necklaces and bracelets. Use them to your advantage. If all you have in your closet is a crisp white shirt, why not tie a scarf around your neck to pep it up? You can even tie that same scarf around your head to conceal a bad hair day or a (yuck) pimple along the hairline. Add a pair of enormous sunglasses and you've got the perfect Jackie O. look working for you [see "5 Ways to Wear a Scarf," opposite page].

Michael Kors once said the quickest way to look glamorous is to throw on a pair of oversize sunglasses. It works every time. When Mary-Kate and Ashley Olsen were in college, they had handfuls of big glasses at the ready to keep prying eyes out of their business.

An accessory so many have forgotten: the fashionable hat. Here's a pill box, a high fashion confection, a trillby, a Panama, and a headwrap.

"Cock your hat. Angles are attitude."

FRANK SINATRA

The best part about these little closet pepper-uppers? An accessory can take a look from day to night faster than you can say "brooch." I know a lot of fashion editors who load their luggage with more decorative fashion pieces than garments for that very reason. If a girl spends all day in a simple gray shift dress and cardigan and then wants to hit the town at night, she can just take off the cardigan, put on a giant pair of earrings, lots of black eyeliner, a cocktail ring, and an evening shawl—and just like that, she has an evening look. Or maybe she starts the day in a T-shirt, jeans, and a jacket—if she swaps the jeans for a little skirt, puts on some killer shoes and throws a fun brooch on the lapel of a shrunken jacket, she's ready to go clubbing. Plus, accessories are a great way to spruce up your wardrobe on the cheap. In general, buying a killer hat or some fun chunky necklace is going to cost you less than trying to overhaul your whole wardrobe.

Don't forget: A lady knows how to accessorize. Russian supermodel Natalia Vodianova once told me that she thought gloves were the sexiest part of a woman's wardrobe. And if anyone knows clothes and sexy, it's Natalia.

5 WAYS TO WEAR A SCARF

a. Traditional
b. Jackie O.
c. Bandana
d. Bag Lady
e. Belted

THREE SIMPLE ACCESSORIES

Belts can be tricky: Do you wear them around the waist or hips, or below the sternum for an empire silhouette? Same thing with earrings: pierces or clips? Studs or chandeliers? On this page, however, are three easy accents that can go with anything. Big sunglasses are a no-brainer, an easy way to both add mystery to your appearance and to protect your pupils from UV rays (here are a squared vintage pair from Valentino and a pair of round Chanels). Cocktail rings—whether they're fake and bought for two bucks at the supermarket or real diamonds and precious stones, like these David Yurman pieces—are bold and fun, but remember to wear them in moderation. And then there's the brooch, which can be classic, like the two flowers, or more funky, like the martini glass. Often-overlooked, brooches are surprisingly versatile: On a blouse, on a dress, on the lapel of a jacket, or even on a hat, they go with more than you think.

"I'm a big believer in fashion. Fashion is history. Fashion is a whole lot of things, because as a woman embellishes herself, she looks like the times she lives in. Some people take it seriously. What does a woman do more often in her life than get dressed? And it's fun to stay with the fads. You keep young."

NAN KEMPNER

It was a phrase that made me shudder whenever I heard my mother say it: "Organize your closet!" And she'd follow up with, in her Midwestern twang, "I don't know why you want all these nice things if you don't treat them well." Looking back—and I do this begrudgingly—she was right. (I hope she's reading this, because I don't say that very often.) It's something you don't realize until your favorite sweater has a hole, or when you spill on the favorite jeans you've left on the floor, or when your dog has made a bone out of your favorite shoes. The trick to keeping your nice things nice, of course, is to keep your closet clean. (Another thing you want to do is keep the clutter out of your life, which I talk about later in "Don't Stutter with your Clutter," pp. 112-13.) Here are my helpful tips on keeping a closet clean:

➋ Get rid of things you don't wear: When your closet is so full it's bursting, you can damage your clothes. Stop jamming more things in there, and give your favorite stuff room to breath.

➋ Box it: Pick up some clear boxes that you can label and pack with similar objects. A good closet is an organized one.

➋ Storage: You don't have to invest in a fancy storage facility, but if you have a dry basement or a clean attic, store things when they're out of season so you have more room.

➋ Plan ahead: When I was still in middle school, I'd set out my outfits the night before. Yes, it's a little anal, but it stopped me from ripping through my closet in an early morning panic, leaving my clothes and my room in chaos.

➋ Color coordination and garment organization: Adjusting your closet by color and by garment (all pants here, all tops there, all skirts over there) will save time when getting dressed. Closets get mangled when someone is searching for something in particular, so keep organized.

➋ The crème rises: Leave the stuff that you wear the most on top of the piles, so you're not digging for your favorite T-shirt. (This is also handy when you want to edit some things out of your closet—start at the bottom.)

➋ Don't leave things out that you didn't end up wearing: This is a hard habit to break. I sometimes toss an outfit that didn't work on a chair and think I'll pick it up later, which becomes a mound. Train yourself to put things back if you don't wear them.

➋ Get a hamper: No one wants to see dirty clothes lying around a room. (It's also unhygienic.) Get yourself some sort of laundry pail for things that need washing.

"I like my money right where I can see it. . . hanging in my closet."

SARAH JESSICA PARKER

HOW TO PACK A BAG

It has been said that you can judge a guy by his shoes. Well, ladies, I say you can judge a lot about a woman by the state of her purse. Is chewed-up gum stuck in the zipper? Is it lined with a permanent collection of dirt, crumpled receipts, and tobacco? Does it stink worse than a pair of gym shoes? (If the answer to any of those questions is yes, you need a new bag—and maybe to reevaluate your lifestyle.) Assuming that you have a clean bag—or a brand-new one, dirty girls—here are a few tips for packing up for a night on the town, a trip around the city, or a long day in class or at the office.

☞ EVENING CLUTCH

There is nothing worse than a girl with a giant bag at night. Giant bags are clumsy and unsightly, and can ruin an outfit. In most cases, a girl only needs her bare essentials: makeup to touch herself up, cell phone, some business cards and whatever feminine products are required for that evening. It's a good idea to use a money clip or rubber band, as bills and cards floating around can get sloppy. Also, blotting papers can be a lifesaver, especially if you're somewhere hot. The bag should be chic and elegant, and if you're wearing something in a vivid color or a more revealing style, the bag needs to be understated. Ideally, it should be light enough to hold with one hand and small enough to fold up under the arm.

A good clutch will come in handy more times than you think, so it's best to buy something beautiful that will go with everything. Several of my girlfriends keep a clutch in their day bags (see opposite page), so if they're out all day, they can get ready for a night out without going home first or (worse) lugging a big bag around the club.

WHAT NEVER TO HAVE IN A BAG

⊗ Nothing used or personally consumed, like feminine products, food you didn't like and spit into a napkin, condoms, etc.
⊗ Pictures of an ex-boyfriend or anything else stalkerish, especially if you're on a date with someone new.

⊗ Drugs or illegal substances.
⊗ Stolen merchandise.
⊗ Paternity test results.
⊗ Tabloid magazines: We all read them, but let's not own up to it in public.
⊗ Dirt, scum, or stenches.
⊗ Worn underwear.
⊗ Immodium and/or industrial-strength laxatives,

or any other very strong intestinal narcotic. If something is wrong down there, stay home until it's running smoothly.
⊗ Remember: How a girl treats her bag is how she might treat a boy. (Even dirty, kinky boys draw the line somewhere.)

☞ DAY BAG

The modern woman has a lot to do during the day, which is why she must carry a sizeable bag. Not that immense means ugly, mind you; there are many chic, smart bags with enough room—and a sufficient quantity of all-important pockets—that don't resemble a wheelbarrow. Make sure the bag is made from a tough fabric (like leather) and in a color that won't show stains. Cell phones—and a charger if, like me, you can't ever keep your phone battery full—and iPods belong in here, along with reading material (magazines for those with ADD, and maybe a book of poetry for the more artistically minded). It's good to think of these bags as your daily survival kit: some gum or mints if you're worried about your breath, dental floss so you don't have to use a fork to pick your teeth after lunch, and some hand sanitizer if you're afraid of germs. Feel free to load this puppy up with necessities—but make sure they're that: necessities. You don't need every lipstick you own just in case one day you might suddenly crave a blackberry liner. [For more on what not to have in your bag see opposite page.]

☞ LARGE TOTE

If you think that the chicest, most high-maintenance females don't own spacious purses full of stuff, you are wrong. I've met glamorous fashion editors and princesses (like, actual princesses) who know a big bag is necessary for a busy girl. I've even encountered a few cool girls carrying chic backpacks. The trick to this type of accessory is the organization: The bag should be big but well pocketed; things shouldn't be jostling around inside willy-nilly. A good tip is to compartmentalize: Use multiple cosmetics bags, one for toiletries (hair brushes, makeup, etc.) and another for electronics (a phone charger, back-up battery, iPod charger, computer charger, etc.) and yet another for writing implements (pens, Post-it notes, etc.). It's not a bad idea to have a few personal hygiene sprucer-uppers in here, including deodorant and those energizing facial wipes that don't require water. Carry something in case the weather changes, like a scarf or a cardigan. Papers should be organized, either in manila folders or in binders. Again, it's good to have a book in there—for long trips in the subway or for long waits. Why not shove a pair of flats in there too, if you think you'll be walking a lot? And finally, remember food: some carrots or a granola bar to pep you up on the go. [For more on weekend bags and packing for longer trips, see "Vital Packing Tips," pp. 146.]

Ready, Set, Groom!

F or a lady, grooming is paramount. Well-maintained hair, a neat eyebrow, clean teeth—if these boxes aren't ticked, you might as well throw on a flannel and a set of overalls and work at a construction site. A well-groomed girl looks like she cares. And if a girl is organized enough to remember to trim her nails before they get long and brown—if a girl is smart enough to know how to lather, rinse, and repeat—well, it probably means she's intelligent enough to hold a decent conversation with a person of the opposite sex.

At the risk of sounding like a L'Oreal commercial, you deserve to take care of yourself. You deserve a warm bath. You deserve to lather yourself in lotion so your skin doesn't feel like the inside of a handbag. C'mon, girls, brush your hair. Look in the mirror. Shave your legs if you're in a short skirt. For heaven's sake, even women centuries ago knew to put on perfume—and that was before department stores offered all those promotional gifts with purchase. [See "How to Put On Perfume," p. 41.]

Like personal style, brow thickness and hair length are matters of personal choice. But even if you're into thick eyebrows you should still have two of them—only Frida Kahlo got by with a unibrow, and that was because she was a crazy artist who beat up her husband and had lesbian affairs. (Speaking of excessive facial hair, let me say this once: There's no reason for excessive hair on the upper lip.

> "You can be comfortable without ever compromising glamour."
>
> **DONATELLA VERSACE**

> "Beauty is only skin deep, but ugliness goes clear to the bone."
>
> **DOROTHY PARKER**

Okay? And if you think you may have it, you probably do. Wax it, stat.) Brows can be skinny too, but if you find yourself painting on whole brows—or whole expressions—you have a problem. A thin brow is fine, but a completely painted-on brow only belongs on mimes and in retirement homes. And more often than not, tramps who hang out in the inner city and meth labs. [See "What Your Eyebrows Say About You," p. 40.]

A lady keeps her legs shaven when she's wearing a skirt. And if you're one of those hippies who thinks shaving the legs is yet another clever way males have of subjugating women through the ages, you shouldn't be wearing a short skirt anyway (miniskirts are just another tool of the patriarchy, right?). I'm sure there will be occasions when a girl doesn't have time to shave or wax, but those are great occasions for trousers or long skirts.

The impeccably groomed Daphne Guinness.

Nails should be dirt-free. Not that they need to be manicured and shiny with bright polish at all times: Cameron Diaz once came to a movie premiere barefoot with her nail polish slightly chipped, and because she was clean and otherwise put together, it worked. It looked cool and laid-back. She didn't necessarily look like the classiest lady, but she did look beautiful.

Still, be careful when you're trying to achieve effortless style. More than a few girls now attempt the beachy California look with the assistance of fake tanner. Fake tanners are dangerous. If you actually find a bronzer that doesn't make you orange, chances are when you apply the stuff, it will go all freaky-streaky, especially over your knees. Worst case scenario, it gets all over your hands, and your Day-Glo palms make you look like an Oompa Loompa. Even if you go and get a spray tan, being overly bronzed can look suspicious: If it's January and you live in Wisconsin, you're not fooling anyone.

And just in case you were wondering (or considering using a tanning bed—ew), a tan is literally a body's reaction to sun damage. Let me repeat that: It's the way the body reacts to being damaged. I'm sure you've heard all about the cancer risks associated with sun damage (yawn!), but what's even more frightening are the wrinkles associated with over-tanning. Don't overtan if you don't want to overwrinkle. Speaking of the wrinkling, don't forget to moisturize; dry skin wrinkles quickly. (And don't forget to moisturize the neck. I'm sure you've seen older

The carefully disheveled Chloë Sevigny at a party during Paris Fashion Week.

women with turkey-wattle chin, and it's not pretty.)

The hair on your head should not stink. I love a messy bun or

> "Good grooming is the one thing that is a permanently stylish element. When you are perfectly groomed, you can conquer the world . . . even in a pair of old jeans and a T-Shirt!"
>
> **ISABEL TOLEDO**

a just-off-the-beach tousle, but avoid dreadlocks and the smell of crust and dirty things in one's hair. Tasteful nonchalance is

fine when it comes to a lady's appearance (just ask the French), but remember that nonchalance is one thing—dirt is another. For example, no one should ever have dirty teeth. One needn't look polished at all times—no matter what Nicole Kidman tells us—but a lady should always look hygienic at best. Even the most desperate guy will not go for a girl who looks like she just woke up in a gutter.

(Disclaimer: Although managing one's body hair is important, it shouldn't be an obsession. While you should care about your exterior grooming, be careful you don't become an over-dyed, over-exfoliated, over-lotioned, and over-clipped twinkette. You'll end up looking like a blow-up doll.)

Wild and coarse

This screams sloppy and careless (and possibly homeless). If your brows are venturing onto parts of your face where an eyebrow shouldn't be—like above the bridge of your nose, or up toward your hairline—seek out a beautician and have them shaped. (For all the ladies looking for a boyfriend: When a guy sees a ferocious brow, one that looks like it has never come within a mile of a tweezer or a slab of wax, he will most likely be terrified. If he doesn't think you can handle your visible hair, imagine his fears about the other parts of your body.)

Arched

An arched brow is for the girl with a slight rebellious streak—which is perhaps why the arch debuted in the late '50s, when girls were slowly shaking off their quiet-and-in-the-kitchen roles. But approach the arch with caution. A little arch says, "I'm flirtatious and confident." Too much arch says, "I'm irritated and self-righteous."

Straight

A straight brow means you're no-nonsense. Straight brows are good for girls who want to come off as professional and organized (and because they convey almost no expression, they are also good for professional poker players). But remember: It's one thing to want to be taken seriously; it's another to look constantly angry.

Bushy

There's a difference between completely disregarding the care of your eyebrows and rocking a slightly bushier (but still groomed) brow. See Brooke Shields for an example of the latter. A larger brow is good for a bigger woman, and one with a certain amount of confidence. It takes a tough broad to work a big brow. (Shields is, like, six feet tall.)

Thin and/or painted on

We all know the OCG (Obsessive-Compulsive Groomer), the girl who sits in front of the mirror making a federal case out of one misplaced hair. When it comes to eyebrows, this kind of girl can lose her mind—tweezing and tweezing until she is completely bald above the eyes and looks like someone recently escaped from an insane asylum. Don't be this girl. You'll wind up having to repaint your brows with the equivalent of a Sharpie, and then you'll look like someone who escaped from an insane asylum—only to wind up in a prison gang.

Curved

A subtly curved brow can make a girl look approachable and sweet—the curved brow was big at the end of the '40s, when even pinup girls kept their clothes on. But be careful: If you go for too much of a curve, you'll look permanently surprised.

HOW TO PUT ON PERFUME

While most of us are familiar with the risks associated with perfume application—namely, smelling like a stripper or your grandmother (and I hope for your sake those aren't the same thing to you)—the actual ritual of putting on a scent is a complex one. And, no, not everything your friends and family tell you is accurate. My dad always told me that a single spritz will last all day; in high school I had friends who drowned themselves in Polo Sport. And I remember once when I was a kid reading that Marilyn Monroe used to put her perfume in her bathwater. When I was young I just sprayed the jazz everywhere.

By this stage of my life, I've sorted out the complexities of perfume application, so allow me to clear up the confusion the process often entails:

➋ Think like a vampire and search out a pulse: Traditionally speaking, the best places to apply a scent are on the wrists, the base of your throat, behind the earlobes, in the creases of your elbows, and between the breasts. In general, you are looking for pulse points. Why? Because places where the human body has a strong pulse generate a great deal of heat—and when a fragrance is warm, its scent grows more pronounced.

➋ But remember that less is more: Just because these are the common places to apply perfume doesn't mean you need to douse every place every single time. Vary your routine (and avoid applying to the wrists *and* elbows, the chest *and* throat *and* ears).

➋ Perfume first: Before you put on any clothes or any jewelry, put on your scent. Oily fragrances can easily stain clothing, and if you plan on wearing the same necklace or garment again soon and changing your perfume, you'll want to make sure it's not doused in some other fragrance.

➋ Don't clap: For some reason, people often slap their wrists together when they put on perfume. Don't. It causes the scent to degrade.

➋ Hairy situation: If you want to put fragrance in your hair, only do so if your hair is clean and not full of other products. (Not all fragrances go well together—and two nice-smelling fragrances may smell worse than a public toilet when combined.)

➋ Try new scents: Modern science has proven that odor—like music—can affect mood and other senses. Don't be afraid to incorporate new scents into your daily routine, or change perfumes every few months.

➋ The knees: I always thought it was rather undignified when a woman put perfume on the backs of her knees. (I figured it had something to do with loose women and naughty behavior.) But classy girls put perfume on their legs too. The backs of the knees are a very warm part of the body; when dotted with perfume, the scent wafts upward and creates a little sweet-smelling cloud around the wearer's body.

A Lady knows how to put on perfume without smelling like a whore. Marilyn Monroe bathed in her perfume to soak it into her skin; but then again, she slept in it too.

Girls come in all shapes and sizes, but for the most part bodies fit into one of four categories. Know your shape, and know how to dress it. But remember: Because no two girls are the exact same size, no size is perfect for any girl. Take these tips to heart, but wear what makes you feel sexy—and don't be afraid of getting a tailor to make your clothes look perfect (and custom-made).

☞ HOURGLASS

THE GOOD: You have the classic womanly shape, and possess what many men classify as the perfect breast-waist-hip proportions.

THE BAD: High-fashion clothes can often be too tight and small for you, and when you turn up the sexy it's easy to accidentally venture into slutty territory.

THE USEFUL: Be confident, and wear clothes that show off your figure: a low- (but not too low) cut blouse, a belt to accentuate your waist, a pencil skirt that will show off those lovely hips as you sashay through a crowd.

☞ EGGPLANT

THE GOOD: You have long, thin arms and a tiny waist.

THE BAD: Your thighs are your problem area, and you're probably used to wearing loose clothes to overcompensate for them.

THE USEFUL: If you want to keep fabrics off your bottom half, wear A-line and pleated skirts—but make sure you don't go baggy all over. A tight cardigan, a statement necklace, or a long jacket can help accentuate the good, while drawing attention away from your problem areas.

> "Fashion is
> architecture.
> It is a matter of
> proportions."
>
> Coco Chanel

> *A Lady* knows
> how to sew on
> buttons. And she always
> has safety pins and bobby
> pins in reserve.

☞ **BRICK**

THE GOOD: Although you weren't blessed with a womanly shape, you have an athletic and muscular body-type that doesn't attract cellulite.

THE BAD: With a figure that is essentially straight up-and-down, it's hard to define a waist and it's easy to look wide.

THE USEFUL: You need clothes that create a shape that you might not have naturally, like wrap dresses and skirts with flared hemlines. Avoid horizontal stripes and ill-fitted suits at all costs, but well-tailored pants—especially those with detailing at the waist—look great on you.

☞ **RULER**

THE GOOD: After centuries of worshipping curvaceous, Rubenesque figures, the new body type *de rigeur* is yours: long, slim, and waspish.

THE BAD: Many men prefer girls with more curves than a ruler, and your long, slender limbs probably make you a very awkward dancer.

THE USEFUL: You can wear almost anything that comes down the catwalk, but be careful not to highlight your lack of curves with tight, bright skirts or low-cut, rib-revealing tops. Trousers can be tricky for curvier girls, but thin girls will look great in almost any pair of pants.

Shake What God Gave (or Didn't Give) You

Okay, now for some ego-boosting. I'm here to tell you, in the most superficial terms, to get happy with your looks. ('Cause if you're looking for help combating anorexia or bulimia, don't read any further—that's some heavy stuff that I don't know much about, so you should talk to a therapist or someone who is trained for that kind of conversation.) What I'd like to talk about is simpler: the importance of being comfortable in your own skin. Because often the biggest obstacle to a girl's self-confidence is her struggle to accept and embrace her body.

I have friends with a little extra junk in the trunk, and I have friends cursed with the flattest chests I've ever seen. To be honest, given the whole androgynous-model thing, I have some girlfriends with negative boobs—as in, their chests are essentially concave from the neck to the belly button. (Some supermodels and prepubescent boys have this in common.) But neither the curvy nor the waifish girls have automatically been unattractive because of the shape that God or genetics gave them. On the contrary. In most cases, my girlfriends have embraced their shapes: tall or skinny, short or curvy, busty or big-butted. It's taken some longer than others—the tits are always better in the other bra—but in the end, the truly beautiful girls I've known have embraced and celebrated their bodies.

Here's the thing: You will look as sexy as you feel. You will look as confident and ravishing as you wish to be. So what if you're the tallest girl in a room? Wear a sky-high stiletto heel so your legs look even longer. My supermodel friends know that there's no shame in being the tallest girl in the room—in all probability, the tallest girl has the longest gams. (Whatever you

A Lady knows where the gym is, even if she doesn't admit to going. But if she does go, her gym clothes are clean.

do, however, don't hunch over until your spine forms a permanent hump. No guy is looking for a hunchback in high heels, even if she has the longest legs in the world.)

Do you have a long, swanlike neck? Show it off with a flattering neckline. Toned arms look great in sleeveless shirts, and if you have sweet, elegant wrists, don't load them down with jewelry—leave them exposed and wear a three-quarter sleeve.

If you have a slim waist, always cinch it with a belt. Strappy shoes look great on slim ankles, and nice legs look good in fitted pants and short skirts.

So what if you have some extra padding on your hips and tits? Give the good parts a boost, spray some perfume on that cleavage, and shake what your momma gave you. (Just remember to cover up any pale parts, if you know what I mean.) Brooke Shields is broad enough to play football, and she's been considered an icon of beauty since her teens. And so what if you're short? Either invest in some good heels, or look for a partner who is into little chicks. (There's no shortage of hot short dudes.) Just because you're short doesn't mean your self-confidence has to be tiny too. My friends Mary-Kate and Ashley Olsen are barely over five feet, but they've never once looked silly, or self-conscious, in a flat shoe.

The list goes on and on—if you have braces, don't do one of those pained, closed-mouth smiles (it will just look like you're embarrassed about your braces and constipated). If you have a gap in your teeth, flaunt it (look what it did for Madonna and Lauren Hutton). Reese Witherspoon didn't let a little thing like a prominent chin get in the way of her career, and now girlfriend has an Oscar.

The most important part of looking good is feeling good, and that starts with your head—not with the gym or a diet program.

> "Tell 'em to shake it! (Shake it!) Shake it! (Shake it!) Shake that healthy butt!"

"BABY GOT BACK," SIR MIX-A-LOT

> "All the men I've ever spoken to say they like girls to have an arse on them."

KATE WINSLET

> "Zest is the secret of all beauty. There is no beauty that is attractive without zest."

CHRISTIAN DIOR

> "Or light or dark, or short or tall, She sets a spring to share them all."

T.B. ALDRICH

PLAYLIST FOR GIRLS OF ANY SIZE

Whenever I'm getting ready I have my stereo on full blast with music that makes me feel good whether I've been paying attention to my diet and exercise regime or not. Here are some songs I think will help both skinny and curvy girls get in the groove.

"Some Girls Are Bigger than Others" — THE SMITHS
"Fat Bottom Girls" — QUEEN
"The Girls" — CALVIN HARRIS
"Got to Be Real" — CHERYL LYNN
"Androgyny" — GARBAGE
"Jealous Girls" — THE GOSSIP
"Your Body Is a Wonderland" — JOHN MAYER
"I'm Really Hot" — MISSY ELLIOTT
"I Got It from My Mama" — WILL.I.AM
"Unpretty" — TLC
"Baby Got Back" — SIR MIX-A-LOT
"Low" — FLO RIDA
"My Humps" — FERGIE
"I Am Body Beautiful" — SALT-N-PEPA
"Work That Body" — TAANA GARDNER

Q&A:

A Lady Gets Dressed

The best part about creating this book has been the responses it's caused among the young women I've met at my book signings, over e-mail, and even on the street. There are some smart girls out there, and they've had some fabulous questions. I liked some of them so much I wanted to include them here.

Q: *Reveal your best shopping secrets!*

A: I've always thought, unless I see it in my dreams and it's torturing me not to have it at this very moment, I should never pay full price. Wait for the sales, always go straight to the clearance racks, and don't be afraid to ask for a discount if something is damaged. Keep an eye out for sample sales. And, truly, where I get the most stuff for cheap is vintage stores. Just make sure you give it a good washing first.

Q: *What should a lady never have in her closet?*

A: Anything plastic or so sheer you can see tan lines. And if anybody asks if you're a hooker or a stripper, you're going the wrong direction.

Q: *What modern celebrity do you think has the best taste?*

A: This could be a long list: I'm a fan of Gwyneth Paltrow and Nicole Kidman, of course; and if we want to talk about someone a little younger, I think Emma Watson (seen here on the red carpet of the last-ever Harry Potter premiere), always looks fabulous and age appropriate. But what I find more interesting isn't just having good personal style, but having self-expression and confidence. (Diana Vreeland once famously said, "We all need a splash of bad taste. . . . No taste is what I'm against.") I wouldn't suggest that anyone try to pull off some of Lady Gaga's outrageous ensembles, but I'm always curious to see what she has on. Style should be personal—or else you're just putting material on your body.

Q: *When in doubt, what should I wear?*

A: An LBD is always a foolproof fallback. It stands for little black dress, and it's what the entire house of Chanel was based on nearly a century ago. Here are two versions worn by two women I think have always been super stylish: actress Kirsten Dunst and fashion editor Lauren Santo Domingo. The good thing about something simple is that you can always dress it up with some jewelry or dress it down with a cardigan, depending on the situation or your mood. But remember: Whenever in doubt, it's always better to be overdressed than underdressed.

Q: *What should every woman have in her closet?*

A: Michael Kors, the King of American Style, once told me that every woman must have these three things in her closet: a pair of jeans that make her look ten pounds lighter, a flattering trench coat, and a giant pair of sunglasses that add instant glamour to any outfit.

Q: *How do you tell friends that what they're wearing is bad?*

A: Be careful how you word it, but it's certainly important you say something: If your friend can't tell you that you look ridiculous, who can? (And if you're the one who looks bad, be nice to your friend when she tells you!) I've always been thankful when someone tells me I'm wearing something that's too small or that I have spinach in my teeth, and you would be too. Just remember: Say it with a smile!

Q: *Who has had the best style in history?*

A: Tough question! But if I had to say someone, I'd say Jacqueline Kennedy, whose looks as the First Lady are just as chic today, more than half a century after she was in the White House. Audrey Hepburn and Grace Kelly run a close second, if we're sticking to the twentieth century. But historically speaking, fashion found its most inspiring muse in Marie Antoinette, the French queen whose sartorial excess ended up costing her her head, literally!

A Lady Receives an Invitation

"Good manners will open doors that the best education cannot."

CLARENCE THOMAS

I'M NOT ONE TO BRAG. (Ha! I can't even type that, much less think it, without blushing.) But I have to say, I've been to some pretty swanky parties since I've moved from rural Missouri to New York City: cocktail parties at Park Avenue mansions, gala dinners at the Metropolitan Museum of Art—hell, I've even been to Oscar parties in L.A. and traveled overseas for black-tie dinners at European palaces and sunset cocktails in South America. (See, I told you I'm not one to brag.) But let me be the first to say that it hasn't all been champagne and caviar. Living the high life—and doing the party-circuit thing—isn't as easy as it looks.

When I moved to the big city from a small town, I very quickly had to learn how to be a great guest. I had to learn—on the job, as it were—how to be a presentable dinner companion, charming escort, and witty conversationalist. Thankfully, I am pretty comfortable now saying that I am all three. (See my notes on bragging, above.) While it's not the 1920s anymore, and modern society's code of etiquette is nowhere near as rigid as it used to be, there are still some things that should be done when you're out and about (bringing a small gift for the host or hostess if you're invited to a party at a private home), and some things that should never be done (talking with strangers about your menstrual cycle over cocktails before dinner).

Whether you're attending a fashion-show after-party or hitting up a backyard barbecue with some ribs and a six-pack of Bud Light, the sooner you learn some basic rules of decorum, the better off—and more in demand as a party guest—you will be.

Good Guest Etiquette

I t's common knowledge that being a hostess is a skill (that's why there are so many millionaire party-planners), but attending a function or friend's fete is just as much an exercise in social graces. While it's important to remember the Golden Rule—do at a party what you would want someone to do at your party—there are a few other tips that pay to keep in mind.

The first thing you should do when you walk into a party—before sitting down or committing to a location in the room—is thank the host or hostess. If you don't know the host, be sure whoever brought you introduces you immediately. If you didn't come with someone—how the hell did you get there? (Mind you, this rule doesn't apply to raves and no-holds-barred house parties; but then, ladies shouldn't make a habit of attending too many of these.)

If you've brought a friend—which you should only have done if you've gotten permission in advance of the party—you should also introduce him/her to the hostess when you arrive. That will save the hostess the trouble of wondering about the complete stranger eating her food, drinking her drinks, and chatting up her guests.

Bring something—anything—as a party favor, even if the hostess says that she doesn't want anything. Flowers are always a nice choice. [See "Thank You, Come Again," pp. 158-59.]

"One does gather to talk, to be entertained, to be amused, and to be amusing. I think when you accept an invitation, you're taking on a commitment. You've got to be just as attractive as you know how to be—because you're not just another face or pair of legs. You're there to help the gang get cracking. I love dinner parties! And I love dinner parties in different countries where I meet a lot of people I don't know. I love to go to a dinner party and sit next to two perfect strangers."

NAN KEMPNER

Please note that wine should only come from those legally able to purchase it. Using a fake ID or robbing someone else's liquor cabinet in the name of proper guest etiquette probably won't fly, and showing up late to a friend's event because you were hauled to a police station after trying to buy a bottle of pinot grigio is terribly embarrassing. Sure, there are some cases when presents aren't nec-essary—if the party is not in a private home or if the event is so huge your gift will go unacknowledged ('cause if you're not getting the credit for your generosity, what's the point?)—but otherwise you should make like one of the Wise Men and come bearing gifts.

Once inside the party it's fine to devote yourself to a certain person or to a certain part of the room. But it's important to avoid being cliquish or mean. If you find yourself holding court over a group, be nice and invite any wallflowers or stragglers into your circle.

Similarly, if your worst enemy is there—that fat hag who stole your boyfriend or the skank with the audacity to show up in the same dress as you're wearing—remain civil. After the party, however, or when you next bump into the skanky home wrecker, feel free to be yourself and express your displeasure. Just remember to be a lady, which basically means looking civilized and using your inside voice while bad-mouthing the skank.

A few moral code rules should be obvious: If you spill something, don't just throw a coat on it or move a table over it. Take responsibility, grab a rag and some club soda, and clean it up. It's also crucial to know when to leave. I had a friend once tell me that the last people to leave a party are losers, loners, and the cleanup crew. Regardless of whether you're leaving alone or with someone, you don't want to be lumped in with any of those crowds.

If the party you're attending is a dinner party, remember to be gracious. [See "Table Manners," p. 55.] Don't complain if your food is cold, or if it's taking too long to get to you. And if you're a vegetarian, don't make a fuss if there's no vegetarian option or if the person sitting next to you just ordered a lamb's head for dinner. To be honest, a truly good party guest who has specific dining needs knows to eat before the

A lady **knows the most fun guest doesn't have to be the most poorly behaved.**

A lady **makes her bed when staying at a friend's house.**

dinner just in case there is no suitable menu option.

Before you go, you must thank a hostess or the organizer for having you. That's just common courtesy. (The only exception is if you have another engagement that requires you to leave rudely early—in that case, sneak out. But don't make this a habit!)

Finally, send a thank-you note to your hostess. (You may skip this step if the party was hosted by a best friend, as you will probably call her immediately the following day to gossip about the night's success.) A handwritten note is the most endearing; a call is still touching; an e-mail at least proves you thought about the party the next day. You must acknowledge your gratitude in some way, even if the party was terrible. Who knows? Maybe the next one will be good and you'll want to make sure you're invited back.

Classic Correspondence

A personalized note is still the classiest form of communication

GLENDA BAILEY   5ᵗʰ April, 2010

Dear Derek,
Coco Chanel said 'A
girl should be two things:
classy and fabulous' So I look
forward to reading the sequel...

VANITY FAIR

Dear Derek,
I thank you much
for everything —
Bob

THE CONDÉ NAST PUBLICATIONS INC. • 4 TIMES SQUARE, NEW YORK, NEW YORK 10036-6562
DIRECT LINE: (212) 286-2650 • FAX (212) 286-6707 • E MAIL: FFMAIL@VF.COM

HANDWRITTEN NOTES—especially when even toddlers have BlackBerries nowadays—are the best way to show your gratitude for everything from an evening of entertainment to an afternoon of cold cuts and free brew, as well as for favors, hard work, or just to be nice. Here are a few examples from editors (*Vogue's* Anna Wintour and *Harper's Bazaar's* Glenda Bailey), associates (*Vanity Fair's* Bob Colacello), interview subjects (designer Tom Ford), and friends (this book's covergirl Byrdie Bell). A friend of mine recently sang for the President of the United States, and a few weeks later she got a handwritten note on presidential stationary. So, unless you're busier than *the President of the United States,* you don't have an excuse.

ANNA WINTOUR

Have a great
holiday
AW

TOM FORD

February 6, 2007

Dear Derek,

Many thanks for the great piece in 10 Magazine. It made me laugh out loud and I loved reading it.

I hope that you are well and that that our paths cross again sometime soon.

Warmest regards,

Tom

Evelyn Byrd Bell

Derek,
You are the definition of a true
Friend. Just the idea of beginning
to count adjectives is exhausting!
Love always,
Byrdie

A Lady is polite about being a pescatarian, vegetarian, or vegan, even if a host or hostess hasn't accommodated her eating requests. By the same token, if a meat eater comes to a vegan's house for dinner, she feigns excitement at the tofu spaghetti and steamed asparagus.

A Lady always thanks her host or hostess first when attending a party.

A Lady knows when it's okay to crash a party.
Which is rare.

A Lady knows the best time to leave a party is when the party is absolutely pulsating. She's never the last to leave, unless the party is at her house (and even then sometimes it's okay to go).

A Lady eats carbs if she wants.

A Lady, if she is starving, eats before a social dinner. The quickest way to make a silk dress look like polyester is by racing through a meal.

A Lady can drink beer, but she better like beer.

A Lady knows not to answer her phone at dinner, unless it's urgent or she's planning an after-dinner drink for the table as a whole. But still, she must leave the table to speak on the phone.

A Lady can go to several parties in one evening, but she always fulfills commitments she's made to friends.

A Lady never asks who else is invited to a party before she accepts an invitation. While it's fine to want to make sure she will be in pleasant company, she finds a better way of getting this information.

A Lady knows it's okay to talk to one person at a party, or stay put in one place for her time at a fete. Remaining in a single corner all night makes it look as though you don't care about being seen. Elizabeth Taylor made this an art form.

A Lady knows to bring a gift to a house party—or else be really entertaining.
Or help clean up.

A Lady never asks someone directly who he or she is or what they do in an effort to see if they are rich or famous. While she can't be blamed for desiring either from a man or a friend, a lady gets this information in a more discreet manner.

A Lady has a strong, good handshake. Even if she's a princess, dresses like one or acts like one, a good grip is a must.

In the past century, table manners have gotten more and more lax. (Did you know that civilized men are still expected to stand every time a lady gets up or comes to the table? I suspect that's why Old Hollywood male movie stars had such sturdy thighs.) But even though dining rituals have largely chilled out, it's imperative that a lady knows a few basics before she takes her seat.

❯ Cell phones should not be visible at a dinner. It's downright gauche to give your phone more attention than your dining companions. One friend of mine has a rule: Unless you have a family member who is in the hospital dying or giving birth, keep your phone out of sight.

❯ Napkins belong on the lap, and should be placed there soon after sitting. (Don't even think about tucking a napkin into the top of your dress or blouse—unless you're at a BBQ.)

❯ Move your arms freely while eating. Your arm is not a crane, and you should be savoring your food, not shoveling it.

❯ Never put a knife in your mouth. And while you're eating, the knife belongs on your plate. You should not be clutching it in your hand as though you are a ravenous beast.

❯ Don't season your food, even with salt, until you've tried it, as it's insulting to the chef.

❯ Keep food in the center of your plate. Even if, like me, you hate it when food touches, it's beyond embarrassing when your food spills over the plate's

rim. When your plate is cleared, it will look like you performed a surgery—or modern art—on the tablecloth.

❯ You should not take two bites from the same forkful, or two sips from the same spoonful. Dinner is not a race. If you're that hungry, swing by a McDonald's on your way to the dinner. (Which I've totally done, by the way.)

❯ Do not use your fingers to put food on a fork. Not only will you have gross fingers, you will look like a toddler stuffing a kebab.

❯ Wipe your mouth before you take a drink from a clear glass. Doing this helps prevent that really gross mixture of saliva and undigested food that shows up on the rim of a glass.

❯ Butter should be removed from its serving tray and put onto your bread plate, and then applied sparingly to small sections of bread that you've broken off a larger piece. Do not smear butter over one whole side order of bread—butter is a garnish, not a food group.

❯ No food should go directly from the serving platter to your mouth. It should be taken from the platter and then put down on a plate, seasoned and split, and then consumed.

❯ There was a time when a young girl was supposed to "leave a little on the plate for Lady Manners." That's passé now. Eat as much as you want, and go for seconds. Leaving food on your plate as a formality is now considered wasteful and ridiculous. But don't lick the plate clean like a dog either.

❯ It used to be considered polite to wait for everyone to be served before you began to eat. This was fine when restaurants were well-staffed and everyone's meal came almost simultaneously. Now it's not considered rude to dig in after two or three people have been served, especially if you're eating something hot. But it's always nice to ask.

❯ Chew with your mouth closed.

❯ By placing your knife and fork together on your plate, you are signaling to the waitstaff that you are done with your meal.

Growing up in Missouri I was more likely to use paper napkins and plastic silverware at the table than good silver and china—and forget about trying to identify which fork should be used on the salad and which should be used on the pot roast. But my parents had the foresight to drag me away from fast-food joints frequently enough to teach me that there were things such as cloth napkins and plates you don't throw away. Those tidbits—and a few more tips I picked up on the fly once I was on my own in New York City—helped ensure that I only embarrass myself occasionally at dinner parties. So, whether you're a black-tie regular or someone who thinks Big Macs are fine cuisine, you should know a few vital pieces of information—like the difference between a wine glass and a water glass, a shrimp fork and a salad fork—before taking your seat at a dinner table. Remember: when in doubt, follow the host's lead.

a. Dinner Plate	g. Dessert Spoon
b. Salad Plate	h. Water Glass
c. Salad Fork	i. Wine Goblet
d. Dinner Fork	j. Napkin
e. Dinner Knife	k. Bread Plate
f. Soup Spoon	

NOTE: Some table settings can be slightly different; for example, if there is no salad course, the salad plate will not be laid. (Sometimes the salad plate is to the left of the entree.) But this is a basic setting, and the dinner plate, glasses, and silverware will always be where they are indicated here. The napkin can also be found on the plate. Immediately put the napkin on your lap but never put it on the table until after the meal.

GLASSES

a. Water Glass   c. White Wine Glass
b. Red Wine Glass   d. Champagne Glass

NOTE: Water glasses are filled to the top, wine glasses are filled only to the widest part of the glass, and champagne can be poured as liberally as a lady pleases.

UTENSILS

a. Teaspoon   d. Shrimp Fork   g. Steak Knife
b. Iced Tea Spoon e. Dinner Fork   h. Butter Knife
c. Soup Spoon   f. Salad Fork

NOTE: Utensils will be laid out in the order that they will be used: Start from the outside and work your way in.

HOW TO USE CHOPSTICKS

1

2

3

NOTE: Until you get this, don't be ashamed to use a fork!

Cell Phone Slaves

The joy of technology? Being constantly in touch. (But be warned: No one wants to touch someone who is always on the phone.)

My friend, a successful fashion editor, was once a very close confidant of the songstress Mariah Carey. (This was post-first marriage, pre-second quickie marriage in the Bahamas.) While she was perfectly lovely—all giggles and champagne glasses—the one thing he couldn't forgive was her relentless texting and e-mailing at the dinner table. It drove him nuts: Here was a girl, perhaps one of the most talented singers of our generation, with the entire world at her fingertips. What could have been so urgent that it couldn't wait for her, a self-confessed diva, to get to it when she was free?

For many people, the phone is an addiction. I can admit that I'm addicted. I'm relentlessly teased for the amount of time I'm on my phone, though many are impressed with my ability to type and message while holding a conversation or watching a fashion show. But even as someone who likes to be in touch 24/7, I acknowledge that at certain times everyone—even Mariah Carey and me—should be able to put the phones down. Here are three prime examples: at the dinner table; on a date; in a meeting.

> "A gentleman is a man who is only rude when he intends to be."
>
> WINSTON CHURCHILL

A lady never puts on makeup at the table.

This picture of two of my most lovely girlfriends was taken—this is not a joke—at my birthday party. Happy birthday to me!

It has taken me a long time to realize that it is extremely rare that an e-mail or phone call is so urgent as to require an immediate response. I was once almost fired for using my phone during a meeting. The fact that I was e-mailing someone about the meeting meant nothing to my editor. E-mailing and texting 24/7 is distracting, for you and the people around you.

Monitor your text use. Unless you are waiting on the news of a close friend or family member who is in the hospital, don't check your phone in mixed company, or while you're having dinner with friends. Never let new company—be it a new love interest or a soon-to-be-boss or a potential co-worker—know how much you rely on your phone, even if he/she seems to have a similar affliction. And when in any type of work or social situation, make sure your ringer is off.

If you absolutely have to use your phone, make an excuse to leave the room or table. Check your messages, make a call if it's urgent, and then hustle back to your companions, prepared to make up for your social lapse with some brilliant conversation.

Know your BlackBerry breaking point.

PLACES IT'S OK TO USE A PHONE

○ **Lunch:** Unless you're meeting with your boss or your mom, it's OK to casually check your phone at lunch. After all, it is a work day!

○ **Trains, taxis, and airplanes:** When you're on the go, one must keep in touch. But please, never be the obnoxious fool who has loud conversations in public places. (No one likes that person!)

○ **Expectant situations:** If you have a pregnant family member or a sick friend, by all means keep your phone close to hand—but be sure to tell the people you're with what's going on so they don't think you're being rude.

PLACES WHERE A PHONE IS UNACCEPTABLE

⊗ **In the big leagues:** If you're ever with a more senior boss or an elderly family member, it's a sign of respect to keep your phone out of sight. Bosses need to feel like they have all your attention, and newfangled technology will only confuse the family members.

⊗ **At a private home:** If you're having dinner at a friend's house, and they've gone through the effort of cleaning, cooking, and inviting you, focus on them and the party at hand, not your phone.

⊗ **Funerals, film sets, and weddings:** Not only is it a sign of respect, it's horrifically mortifying to be that girl who has her phone go off at an inopportune moment. (Trust me.)

A History of the Best Parties

From medieval feasts featuring court jesters and private dancers (I've seen the movies!) to modern-day blowouts, history is full of examples of great parties—though there have been some definite standouts. Here, I'll round up a handful of fetes I wish I had been invited to:

Alva Erskine Vanderbilt's Housewarming (1883)

Traditionally speaking, housewarming parties are civilized and muted affairs—maybe there's a bartender, probably a dress code. Not when Alva Erskine Vanderbilt, a new-money 19th-century socialite on a mission for social success, swung open the doors of her Fifth Avenue mansion, complete with a Versailles-esque ballroom. Every person in Manhattan was desperate to attend, even the stodgy old-money sorts, who were finally forced to allow Vanderbilt into their social circle.

Dîner de Têtes Surréalistes

At this intimate dinner for 150 of her closest friends (she had been known to invite ten times that number to her pad), which was announced by an invitation written backward, so that it could only be read with the aid of a mirror, Marie-Hélène de Rothschild dressed up like the kill at a shoot, antlers woven into her coif and pear-shaped diamonds—to represent tears—affixed to her cheeks. [See "A History of Hostesses," pp. 100-101.]

Truman Capote's Black and White Ball (1966)

Capote, riding a tidal wave of popularity after his genre-defining novel *In Cold Blood* was published, transcended the role of mere writer—he was a confidant to many, a social doyen, and the prince of society. [See "Famous GBF's in History," p. 173.] His Black and White Ball was the *ne plus ultra* of his social fetes, causing an absolute panic when his severely strict guest list of 500 (which included the likes of Diana Vreeland, Lee Radziwill, and Frank Sinatra) was issued.

The Met Ball (multiple years)

Alternatively called the East Coast Oscars and, appropriately enough, the Party of the Year, the annual fete that New York's Metropolitan Museum of Art hosts to fund-raise for its Costume Institute is the hottest ticket on the New York City social scene. In decades past, when the legendary Diana Vreeland organized the fete, it was a more casual affair—but when *Vogue*'s Anna Wintour sunk her teeth into the event, the star wattage exploded.

Woodstock (1969)

Every page before this one and every page after it emphasizes the importance of behaving like a put-together, controlled young woman—and attending Wood-stock, the infamous multiday outdoor concert that featured the likes of Jimi Hendrix and Janis Joplin belting out hits to a crowd of muddy, naked, drunk revelers, might not seem like the ideal activity for a classy lady. But every once in a while, it's important to push the limits and let your (freshly washed) hair down.

The Last Supper (a long time ago):

It didn't end so well for the guest of honor, but Jesus' last meal was no doubt a rager.

Oprah Winfrey's Fiftieth Birthday (2004)

I'm a huge Oprah fan. I used to watch her show way back in elementary school, even when she hosted shows on menopause and cheating husbands and I wasn't familiar with either. (I still don't have the firmest grasp on the former, to be honest.) But when I heard of her fiftieth-birthday party, that's when I *really* wanted Oprah as my homegirl. With a one-waiter-per-party-guest ratio, serenading violinists, and so many flowers it would put a botanical garden to shame, this dreamy night in Santa Barbara set a new standard for lavish entertaining.

The Boston Tea Party (1773)

This little political demonstration had it all: a scenic location (Boston Harbor), an important theme (down with English oppression!), and some of the best costumes ever—have you seen a traditional American colonist outfit? So cute! So while this wasn't a traditional party—there wasn't an open bar or a DJ booth—the day when Sam Adams and his Sons of Liberty associates infiltrated three ships to stand up against tax charges imposed by the British Parliament on their North American territory still deserves a shout-out.

French *Vogue's* 90th anniversary Masquerade Ball (2010)

Ever since Truman had his masked ball (see previous page), contemporary society has tried its hand at fancy dresses and masks. Some have failed, and some, like this rager in Karl Lagerfeld's former French residence, have left their mark. Gisele oozed sex appeal and Natalia reeked of danger. It was also a swan song for Carine Roitfeld, the fashion icon, who left the magazine not long after. What a way to say *au revoir*!

Are You Social Deadweight?

I've already said it doesn't only take a certain level of skill to throw a party—it also takes social grace to attend one. Too often, however, it seems that the girls who are the most unbearable in social situations are the most confident of their charm. So here, popular girls, take this quiz and find out if you're as cool as you think.

1. You've just received your seating assignment for a formal party. Your seat is:

(A) In the back, with the staff, or the most distant of relatives.
(B) With random other friends and family.
(C) Next to the guest of honor's mother.

2. You see a girl you know at a party. When you go up and say hi, she:

(A) Makes an excuse about a family medical emergency and leaves.
(B) Frantically looks around for someone else to talk to and looks disappointed when she can't find anyone she knows.
(C) Gives you a big hug and says how happy she is to see you.

3. It's suggested that everyone at a dinner party do something to get to know each other a little better. What do you do?

(A) Prank call your ex-boyfriend, then pass your phone around and urge everyone to yell obscenities into it.
(B) Demand to know, by a show of hands, who is from a broken home, who's wearing underwear, and who's drunk.
(C) Give your name, then provide one funny or random detail about yourself, like the fact that you wanted to be a fire engine until you were five. Suggest everyone do the same.

4. It's Thanksgiving and all the guests are going around the table saying what they're thankful for. When your turn comes up, you say:

(A) Thong underwear, breath mints, and birth control.
(B) Deodorant. Or rather, that the uncle you're sitting next to is actually wearing some this year.
(C) Friends and family.

5. Your favorite topic of conversation at dinner is:

(A) Colonics and other bodily fluids.
(B) Bad breakups.
(C) Current events.

6. There is a lull in conversation, so you:

(A) Take out your phone and text a friend to say how bored you are.

(B) Stare blankly at a wall until someone else brings up a new topic of conversation.

(C) Try and strike up a new conversation about the weather, sports, or recent movies.

7. Your cell phone starts to ring, so you:

(A) Answer it and have a loud conversation, mentioning how bored you are at the lame party you're attending.

(B) Don't answer it, but proceed to pull it onto the table and text and e-mail to your heart's content.

(C) Turn off the vibrator (the ringer was not on) and steal a glance at the screen; if it's urgent or an emergency, you excuse yourself from the table and respond to the message.

8. Another person spills cranberry juice all over her dress. In response, you:

(A) Point and laugh, then take a picture with your camera phone and e-mail it to your friends with the subject line: ROFL.

(B) Sit there and stare, holding back laughter.

(C) Quickly get some napkins and help the spill victim out, or indicate to the waiter that you have an emergency on your hands.

9. The hostess of the party is visibly tired and trying to get everyone to leave. You:

(A) Leave whenever you want to and don't say goodbye.

(B) Sigh exaggeratedly, grab your coat, and leave.

(C) Offer a few other friends a ride home and leave together after saying goodbye to your hostess.

10. You've been invited to a theme party. You:

(A) Wear whatever you normally wear. Themes are for wankers. Good thing you'll be able to spend the whole evening making fun of the lameasses who actually dressed up.

(B) Haphazardly dress for the theme, throwing on a cheap mask or some other accessory that requires the least amount of effort possible.

(C) Plan your outfit ahead of time and show up looking great. Theme parties are fun!

QUIZ KEY

Count up all your answers and see which of the three letters you had the most of. If you are:

Mostly A's. If there were a table in the restroom, that's where you should be seated. Even if your fellow partygoers haven't started rolling their eyes at you, even if your invites haven't started drying up yet—trust me—they will soon. Remember: It's a privilege to be entertained by friends—not a right. That means you have to earn it.

Mostly B's. When it comes to being a good guest, you're mediocre at best. While you're not the worst person at a dinner party, you're not exactly wowing people with your charm. There are very few people who can get through life by smiling and looking pretty—are you sure you're one of them?

Mostly C's. It's not easy being a great party guest or dining companion, but you've got the goods. You know how to behave in every situation and can count on always being at the top of the social pyramid—and one of the most popular girls at any party you attend.

Never, Ever Just Say Cheese

Posing for a picture is a serious matter. (Even if Mom's behind the camera)

It's completely shallow to talk about the ability to take a good picture as a "skill," but let's be honest here: Being photogenic can come in handy. In major cities, photographers attend all sorts of social gatherings—from dinky little store parties to black-tie galas.

And there is nothing more important to many young women than looking good in pictures; in fact, I know girls who have parlayed posing for D-list photographers at C-list parties into entire careers. Not that paparazzi shots are the only ones that need prep—it's just as crucial to know how to pose for a candid picture on a friend's digital camera as it is on the red carpet.

In New York, the girls who take this photo stuff seriously always say the same thing: When it comes time to stand in front of that flashing bulb (or digital camera), it's crucial to have mastered three types of facial expressions. The first is the big smile (see fig. 1), with which you must have already had years of practice; this is the expression parents are always asking you to display in family vacation pics and prom photos. This is the money shot (also known as The Tinsley, named after a contemporary Manhattan society swan, Tinsley Mortimer).

Another good look to have down pat has been described in a variety of ways: the Half Smile, the Smiling with the Eyes, and even the OTS (Over the Shoulder). (See fig. 2.)

As you venture away from the smiles—and into the realm of the Princess Coldstare (see fig. 3), which is for the girl too cool to smile—things get tricky. On the one hand, you want to

A lady isn't embarassed about perfecting her camera poses. We'll see who's laughing when she looks great and her friends look like sullen-faced hunchbacks.

look sexy and footloose; on the other hand, you want to look sophisticated and beautiful. Most importantly, you want to look nonchalant, like you're the type of person who is constantly being photographed.

This doesn't mean you should force a pout or stick your chest out like a stripper. Remember, you don't want to look like a skank, even in pictures you don't expect anyone to see but your dearest of friends. (You never know when your best friend might become your worst enemy and decide to pub-

licize the picture of your porn-star pose.) [See "The Big Bad Bloggers," pp. 176-77.]

Another rookie pose mistake: In an effort to look thinner, they will hunch their shoulders toward their ears and try to sink their chests back toward their spines, like Gwyneth Paltrow. Now, Gwynnie has this look down, but she's a pro. She's been doing it for years. But for us dilettantes, this pose can have the opposite effect, making a person look broader, sullen, or hideously misshapen. Keep it simple: Stand straight, shoulders back, arms at your sides—and you'll look thin and confident.

Here's another tip: Practice. It's perfectly fine to spend some quality time perfecting your camera face. Maybe you have a big chin and need to learn to tilt it down (lifting it will only make it look bigger). Maybe you have broader shoulders and need to angle slightly away from the camera to minimize them. Spend some time with the mirror, or practice with a digital camera at home. One caveat, though: You should never admit to spending your time puckering up in front of the vanity. It's one thing if you know you've spent hours perfecting your killer smile—but let everyone else believe you're merely naturally photogenic.

FIG. 1: The Tinsley　　　　FIG. 2: The OTS　　　　FIG. 3: Princess Coldstare

Here we have three basic types of poses, though there are thousands more used every day. (Tyra Banks says she has hundreds of different kinds of smiles alone.) Start with these, then feel free to expand your posing repertoire.

Please, (Carefully) Take a Seat

B ack in the day, good girls didn't show any skin but a hint of collarbone, and when ladies took a seat, they crossed their legs at the ankle. No exceptions. Today, things are different. But just because a lady can crisscross her legs ten ways till Sunday without getting labeled a jezebel doesn't mean she can perch any ol' way she pleases. (Especially in a mini.)

Sitting is like being on neighborhood watch, or preventing forest fires: It pays to be *aware*. Be aware of what you're wearing and what gets exposed when you take a seat in the cafeteria or the subway. Yes, the whole point of a short skirt is to show off the legs, but a short skirt can end up showing off a whole different part of your anatomy if you're not careful when you sit. I cannot tell you the number of times I've been sitting in the front row of a fashion show and seen a completely different presentation from a lazy lady sitting across the runway.

The trick is to keep a barrier between your lady parts and the outside world (and a slip of leopard-print thong is not sufficient). Lay a hand or a jacket on your lap. Slide your legs to the side and shift your weight forward, so a person who wanted to play peekaboo would have to see through the bodies of all the people sitting next to you (fig. 1). A more old-school pose? Sit down, place your knees together, then slant your legs to one side so that one leg is balanced on top of the other (fig. 2). It's not the sexiest way to sit, but it is

sophisticated. If you sit down in a short skirt and cross your legs at the knees, be careful—often a girl concentrates on covering her crotch, but forgets the part of her legs that goes from the back of her upper thigh to her rump, unintentionally flashing a whole lot of skin (fig. 3).

If this is all sounding like too much trouble, just don't sit down in public. Sure, it might sound silly, but I've had friends do that when wearing something particularly short. (Especially if seats have a texture to them—'cause then when you stand up, your legs will look like they've just gone through a waffle press.)

Sitting like a lady doesn't only apply to girls sporting minis. And the pitfalls of not sitting correctly don't only pertain to areas below the waist. It's important to sit up straight; I know that sounds like something your grandmother might tell you, but the reasons I think good posture is important have nothing to do with back problems. Slouching can make you appear to have a humpback, or (worse) a flat chest. Often when a girl wears trousers, she feels it

gives her the license to sit like a basketball coach (fig. 4). A piece of advice, ladies—*never* slouch. Sitting up makes you look taller, thinner, and more full-chested. Remember, there's a reason so many Renaissance portraits feature ladies sitting down—the way a lady sits can be a mark of her character and personality. (Well, that's one reason—another one is because those oil portraits took forever, and even Emma couldn't stand in a corset for days and days.)

The way you position yourself on the couch, or the way you slide into the dinner table, is a testament to the type of woman you are. Are you a self-conscious, lazy sloucher? Are you a girl who looks beautiful and classy even when she's just lounging around? Take a minute sometime to sit in front of a mirror and make sure everything you want covered is, in fact, covered, and you're doing your body justice.

And if you really want to expose your body parts, just put down this book and file an application at a local strip club. At least then you'll be making some cash for your shows.

FIG. 1

FIG. 2

The biggest rule to remember when sitting in a skirt? Make sure any areas of your body that don't tan naturally are completely covered, not like in the cases below. Furthermore, it's always best to err on the side of modesty, as in above. Trust me. (I've seen things I never want to see again.)

FIG. 3

FIG. 4

Say What?

Oversharing: the number one killer of dinner conversation and a lady's reputation

If you haven't heard someone say that the art of conversation is dead, you probably will sometime in the near future. That may be true, but it's not exactly news. While researching this book, I found that nearly every etiquette book from the 1940s, the 1960s, and even ones written more recently have all said the same thing: It's hard to find a good chat partner. But while not everyone is blessed with the skill to strike up and maintain a good conversation, you can ensure that you stay at the top of your friend's invite list by following a few simple rules.

No one wants to know about what came up when you vomited the last time you had the flu, or about that time when you thought you had gonorrhea but really it was just a urinary tract infection. [See "A Few Things to Make Sure You're Not Doing in Conversation," opposite page.] In actuality, no one wants to know the caloric value of undigested corn. No one wants to know about bowel movements in general, or really about any bodily fluids. Or deaths, or rape, or incest, or child abuse (except for your therapist—she wants to know). Good gossip is one thing; gross is another.

A Lady has an inside voice. Or she is smart enough to realize if she needs to develop one. (Ask a friend.)

A Lady only makes inappropriate jokes in appropriate company; and if she's not sure if she's in appropriate company, she waits.

A Lady never talks about dieting. She also doesn't talk about her own weight loss, no matter how drastic it is, in public or with mixed company.

A Lady is witty as hell.

A Lady doesn't whine or talk in a baby voice outside of a nursery, or a bedroom if she's desperate.

Here's a good rule of thumb when you're debating whether to tell the "hilarious" story about the time you got so drunk you climbed a telephone pole or made out with your taxi driver: Would you want to hear this story from an elderly family member? Chances are, you wouldn't. And if you do want to know about what your great-grandma vomited after Stacie's house party, you seriously need to overshare with a professional.

At the risk of sounding like an overbearing uncle (or aunt) here, allow me to say that I really think this particular condition is specific to modern generations. We live in a world where every single detail of our lives is seemingly important and can be transmitted onto the Internet via a variety of social networking sites. I can tell the whole world what I'm eating, while I'm eating it. Thrilling! I can tell the whole world what sick fetishes I'm into, just because maybe somewhere else in the world there's someone who likes the same thing. But just because you could find someone who shares your love of earwax, doesn't mean you should—or that it's appropriate to discuss the topic in mixed company.

The point is we live in a society where oversharing happens

A FEW THINGS TO MAKE SURE YOU'RE NOT DOING IN CONVERSATION

1. Standing too close. If you can smell the type of deodorant your conversational companions are wearing, you're probably too close. (Either that, or they've over-fragranced.)

2. Speaking too loudly. Use your inside voice.

3. Discussing money or personal finances. Do not mention your trust fund or your salary. Caveat: It is okay to talk about a good sale, but only if you've been to it first and laid claim to the good stuff.

4. Talking in graphic detail about medical issues. Words like *pus* and *placenta* should never, ever be used in social dialogue.

5. Divulging secrets about your sex life, or the anatomy of your friends or partners. If you're the kinkiest girl in the room—maybe you like to dress up in clown outfits and smear honey on your bottom, which is totally fine—you should let people find out for themselves.

6. Yawning or looking tired, even if you are. Especially if you are.

7. Talking exclusively about yourself. Ask someone else a question for once.

---

all the time. But just because it's common, doesn't mean it's not inappropriate.

Here's a tip: The next time you're interacting with someone, take a second and do this quick quiz.

1. Ask yourself if anyone is listening.

2. Ask yourself how many times you've used the pronoun 'I' in the past five minutes.

3. Ask yourself if anyone asked a question that prompted the story or anecdote you're currently telling, or if you're just speaking because you can't shut up.

Asking these questions can be difficult—indeed, the people who suffer from the worst cases of oversharing are so oblivious to the world around them, they could be reading this sentence right now and not know it applies to them (It does! It does!)

A Lady makes eye contact.

A Lady knows how to politely end a conversation.

A Lady knows the difference between being direct and blunt, and being assertive and aggressive.

A Lady says nice things about nice people in public; but she can be brutally honest about not nice people in private.

—but it's worth it to ask. I've been to dozens of parties where I'll meet someone who spills her guts to me, without any indication from me that I even care. I've actually sat down next to a person and not asked her a single question but have gone home knowing her sexual preferences, what she had for breakfast and lunch, what kind of deodorant she uses, that her parents are divorced, and that she relishes eating her own fingernails.

Now, I'm the type of person who loves to meet new people and talk about things and get to know a stranger—maybe that's why I am not terribly lacking for friends—but this young woman wasn't exactly what I would call a good dining companion. In fact, I kept thinking the truffles on my salad were her fingernail clippings. Gross.

Striking up a conversation can be difficult, especially if you tend more toward wallflower than social butterfly. Here are a few tips on striking up conversations on the spot.

1. Compliment someone on what he or she is wearing. When you can, turn your compliment into a question, like, "I love that vintage blazer. Where did you get it?" or "I've never seen a necklace like that. What's it made out of?" Just make sure you mean it—an insincere compliment is often very obvious and, for that reason, devastating.

2. People love expressing their opinions, so ask someone for theirs. Sure, some topics should be off-limits for a first time conversation—"What do you think about abortion?" is the wrong type of ice-breaker—but if you're at a gallery, it's a great chance to ask someone what he/she thinks of an artist. If you're partying at a fancy house, ask what other people think of the digs.

3. Go the simple route. Introduce yourself; ask for the other person's name, then remember it and use it with liberal abandon. People love to hear their names repeated. Seriously.

4. Show off that knowledge of current events. (A good reason to read the paper? Upping your social IQ.) This strategy has the added benefit of weeding out the idiots you don't want to talk to in the first place; if your conversational companion stares at you blankly, walk away.

5. Go the obvious route: What's with this weather? (L.A. version: Can you believe the traffic on La Brea?) What kind of music do you like? Have you seen any good movies lately? But use common sense: Don't ask a scruffy-faced stoner if he's heard about the new jewelry store that opened at the mall, and don't ask a pink-Juicy-Couture-track-suit-wearing mall rat if she's heard about the remastered Johnny Cash album.

When meeting a new person, the most important thing is to come off as friendly, genuine, honest, and interested. Not interesting—interested. Ask questions. Ask follow-up questions. Listen. Smile.

As someone who has suffered his fair share of abrasive, socially aggressive losers who think the loudest or most outrageous greeting is the most effective, I have to reiterate that you want to break the ice, not drive a truck through it.

Escaping an unpleasant conversation is not always easy. You don't want to be rude, and the person who is so unpleasant is no doubt also aggressive, really self-involved, and hard to shake. But remember: Even if you're talking to someone who has hurt your feelings, broken your heart, or really upset you—a social situation is not the place to discuss a serious issue or resolve a conflict. Excuse yourself like a lady, even if the conversation offends you, which will no doubt happen, or if you're bored, which will certainly happen. Generally speaking, it's a good idea to have the following excuses on internal preprogram:

The bathroom break
"Do you know where the bathroom is?" is a great way to simultaneously let someone know you need to excuse yourself, and flatter him/her by soliciting advice.

The phone call
"I have to take this—it's my mom. Ugh."

The fresh air exit
"It's so hot/smoky/cold/crowded in here, so I'm going to go for a stroll outside."

Get a beverage
"I'm so thirsty—be right back!" Feel free to add, "Can I get you something?" knowing fully well you won't.

I just remembered I need to give/tell someone something
"Oh, I just remembered that I had to tell Sally that her brother wants his iPod back."

Check the bag, get the bag, hide the bag
"I just want to put this bag down so I don't have to hold it all night." Or, "I put my bag down and need to get something out of it." Sometimes I've wanted to carry a purse just so I could use this one.

Check the coat, get the coat, hide the coat
Similar to the previous escape method. Just make sure you're using the right excuse at the right moment: More than once I've excused myself to get my coat when I'm already wearing it.

The hostess excuse
This is only applicable at a more formal occasion. "I really should say hi to Rebecca and thank her for having us—I feel rude that I haven't said hi yet."

The escape is not always as easy as it looks. I cannot count the number of times I've been at an event or cocktail party and found myself backed into a corner by a self-consumed jerk. These types can be hard to shake. Sometimes even the I-have-to-go-to-the-bathroom trick won't work—if I went to the bathroom every time I wanted to escape a conversation, by the way, people would think I was passing a kidney stone.

That's when the other excuses come in handy—but I want to get my coat from the coat check first, or put my bag down, etc. Indeed, sometimes you'll have to blow your whole arsenal on one pesky person. (After that, just leave the party.)

But trust me: You'll thank me when you've cleverly escaped that tedious conversation.

The Way Out of an Awkward Situation

Unfortunately for myself (but fortunately for you), I know a lot about awkward situations—namely because I have gotten myself into so many of them.

For some reason, asking a girl about her boyfriend when he's just dumped her is a special skill of mine. I'm also the king of inquiring after someone's job immediately after they've been fired and asking someone if they're going to a party that they haven't been invited to. And yes, in the past I have asked women if they're pregnant when they aren't, which is probably the most awkward situation to ever be in.

My only tip is this: feel like a complete jerk, and then move on. Smile, apologize for not knowing, and then quickly change the topic. Better yet: allow the other person to direct the conversation, even if that means they want to talk about it or complain about something. (Hey, you asked in the first place!) But never allow yourself to make your little gaff into a big deal. Don't start profusely apologizing, which will just make the person feel even more ridiculous. When someone suffers a big change, they will eventually need to discuss it—and if you've brought it up, it's your job to stick it out.

While I've created a few awkward moments in my life, I've gotten fairly good at cleaning them up. I've been a shoulder to cry on when I've mistakenly asked someone about a person in their family who has passed away, and I've confided personal stories about getting fired from all sorts of jobs to someone who has just lost their job.

The notion that getting fired is a new beginning can put a positive spin on the topic of job loss (I discuss this in "The Occasional Professional Mishap Can Turn Out to Be a Personal Triumph," p. 298).

If the person has lost a fam-

> "He seems to take his foot out of his mouth only for purposes of changing feet."
>
> JOHN DINGELL

ily member, let the person know he or she is not alone—but avoid relating their pain too much to your own. It's their loss they need to work out, not yours.

In the case of a friend's breakup, while you may be tempted to tell someone you always hated their significant other, don't say it until you're sure their split is permanent.

I once told a friend I thought her then ex-boyfriend was a pompous twit who wasn't good enough for her. Then they got back together, got married, and had children together. (Can you guess which wedding I didn't get invited to?)

Sadly, awkward situations abound. My biggest tip? Keep smiling. If you see your ex-boyfriend walk in with a new girlfriend, extend a warm greeting, even if it takes all your willpower not to cry or scream profanities at them both. (It'll make you look mature and confident!)

More times to smile and nod: when you walk into a room really late, and everyone is staring at you; when you're in a movie theater, and you drop something and make a big commotion; or when you're at the ballet, and you open a really noisy breath mint.

Lastly, there are some situations when you don't say anything at all: like, say, when a person is clipping their toenails on a public bus or playing an imaginary saxophone in the middle of Central Park. Or when a sophisticated older person secretes an odor that's unpleasant to the nose. In all of these circumstances, a very classy lady will keep mum.

Sometimes Partying Is Hard Work

Here's a statistic for you: Parties often diminish in fun-ness proportionate to the partygoers' age. Now, this isn't the case in every situation. (I'm still known to hit a dance floor with a vengeance, and I'm no spring chicken.) But it's true that the more parties you go to, the more they can seem like hard work.

There are so many factors to socializing: getting dressed up, putting on your party smile, remembering to say please and thank you, having to avoid so-and-so and not to ask someone else about their ex-boyfriend, remembering that your bread plate is on the left and your water glass is on the right, not actually *being* the drunk one, leaving at the right time to leave. It's exhausting! (Actually, let's be honest: Just looking good and smiling can be exhausting after a while.)

Fortunately for an avid partygoer and fashion fan like myself, I think it's all rewarding. It would be a tragedy to give up on going out. My good friend Daphne Guinness knows how to dress up for parties—and I mean *dress up*! (Google her for pictorial evidence.) She will leave the house in a veil and a diamond broach and a leather corset, even if she's just meeting me down the street for a tea. I love a girl who knows that getting dressed is a form of self-expression.

Staying sober and friendly at a party (instead of sloppy and flirty) can be tough. Parties are long, the drinks are flowing, and sometimes drinking can put you more at ease when you don't know everyone. But this

ME WITH THE FASHION MAVERICK DAPHNE GUINNESS.

can be a recipe for disaster. Let this be your goal: Do not be the drunkest girl at a party. If the only reason you're going out is to get drunk, stay home and drink by yourself. (Actually, don't do that. In addition to being unhealthy—see my essay on binge drinking on p. 262—it will make you bloated.)

Whether it's a big, fancy wedding or a small cocktail party with close friends—remember to put your best foot forward, and I'm not just talking about cute shoes. Don't go out if you're depressed or sullen: If you don't want to be there, the people there won't want you to be there either. Always err on the side of dressing up if you're not sure of the dress code. (I'd rather be friends with the only girl in a beautiful dress at a party than the only girl in jeans.)

I hope I'm not insinuating that socializing should be super serious. Quite the contrary: While having fun at parties I've made lifelong friends, done business, and met important editors who have helped me achieve success in this industry. Parties are hard work, but they're worth it. Andy Warhol once lamented to the writer and editor Glenn O'Brien at a fancy Manhattan soiree, "This is such hard work." He was right, but he was good at it.

To Tweet or Not to Tweet: That Is the Question

As my fashion idol pointed out to me, there are people in the world who may actually desire to keep the details of their private parties private. I know, I know—I was as shocked as you are.

The question of whether or not to put one's private interactions with others on Twitter came from a most unexpected source: Gwyneth Paltrow, probably our generation's most *Classy* woman alive, who once asked me my thoughts on whether or not it was acceptable for someone to Tweet or blog from a private residence or a very private party. This question had momentarily stumped me because, for the most part, I take pictures where I please and publish them without hesitation. (I've always taken a Warholian perspective on real-life experience, presumably.)

But she did introduce me to the concept that yes, there may actually be some people out there in the world who don't want their private lives to be viewed by anyone with a smart phone or Internet access. This may be an unfathomable idea to some people (at least it was to me), but it's true that I have met a few hosts and hostesses who would rather die than make public knowledge of their private entertaining schedules. There are those who, when they entertain at home, aren't too keen to have their guest list and menus up for review and judgment by their friends, peers,

and of course the faceless, anonymous commenters who make the Internet such a fun—and dangerous— place.

It makes sense if you think about it: If you were having a small dinner for close friends, would you want your not-so-

A Lady understands that once she says something on the Internet she can never take it back. The World Wide Web has a very good memory.

A Lady knows that everyone doesn't want to be mentioned on the Internet, even if she really likes it.

A Lady will acknowledge that the most menial details of her life will probably not entertain others.

close friends to know that they weren't invited? And to read that they weren't invited when someone else Tweets about it? Do you really want people to see what your home looks like and what was on your menu?

If someone is gracious enough to let you into their home, is it really your place to go off and Tweet an image of their baby picture or the sort of soap they use in the restroom?

When it comes to social networking—and that includes posting pictures on the Internet or Facebook or even something as simple as Tweeting—I always try to check myself before I upload or update. (I've learned the hard way that sometimes it's best to be cautious on the Internet, rather than send something and then be told off for it later. Yes, this has happened to me more than once!) The first question I ask is if the person who has organized the party is a prolific social networker. If so, then it's probably fine to mention the dinner, who is there, and the menu—and chances are that the hostess already has on her account anyway.

However, in the case of someone who is a little more reserved when it comes to social media, my thoughts are that it's better to err on the side of discretion and keep that camera phone picture to yourself. The last thing you want to do is upset or annoy your hostess, especially if she is generous and you want to be invited back. (For example, if Gwyneth invites you over, you want to make sure that the invitation comes back again! So keep those phones far from sight) If it does come up, and she says it's okay, be vague and overwhelmingly positive in your Tweet. Don't say anything disparaging, arrogant, or ridiculous.

Another thing to keep in mind is that there is such a thing as being really, truly obnoxious when it comes to social net-working. I know this because I have friends who have fallen into this category. (And, I will readily admit, I probably have been obnoxious more than once myself.) People who say things like, "Just hopped off a private jet and ready to go sailing," or "Great party with Wills and Kate—or the Duke and Duchess of Cambridge to the rest of you."

Self-deprecation is the name of the game on Twitter, my friends. Or, as another friend of mine put it, humble bragging. I speak to this personally because, as someone who has been invited to his fair share of fancy benefits, and as someone who has made his fair share of observations from these fancy benefits, I know how unappealing it can be to be a blowhard braggart. Sometimes I reread my old posts and think, *Shut up!*

Does anyone even care?

MY TIPS FOR TWITTER

While the Internet has made the world a much smaller place, it's also made it much more tedious. Since everyone now has the ability to pronounce their observations, desires, and experiences on the information superhighway, it's become much more difficult to sift through the news and the snooze. I wish that more people would ask themselves before they Tweet, blog, or post if they truly think what they're saying is valuable or inspirational information. (No, really, try asking yourself from now on.) The best Tweets are informative, engaging, and really funny—and a really good Tweeter can combine all three into one Tweet. And, oh, one last thing: People who are mean for the sake of being mean on the Internet need to find new hobbies!

A Stickler for Punctuality

Making chronic lateness a habit can lead people to think you're much worse than just plain rude

I take punctuality in social situations very seriously. Not only because I don't want to miss anything—little known fact: The best time to see what everyone else is wearing and catch up on gossip is at the beginning of an event (and, for the record, when it comes to Manhattan's biggest events, the cocktail hour is the most exclusive, before all the riff-raff comes in)—but also because it's rude and painfully egotistical to make everyone wait for you.

Still, ladies don't have to be *exactly* on time, either. Leniency—not laziness—is the word. Traditionally speaking, when you're meeting a single person or small group, you won't be considered rude if you make it to the rendezvous no more than five or ten minutes past the mutually agreed-upon time. For larger gatherings of five or more, a lady can be up to fifteen or twenty minutes late. You can show up to a cocktail party up until forty-five minutes before it's scheduled to end, and if you're heading to a big blowout, you can arrive up to an hour late, especially if you've dined beforehand.

The French, I've discovered, even have a term for being fifteen minutes late: There, being fifteen minutes late is called "being on time." Hostesses don't want you to start leaning on the buzzer at eight o'clock sharp. Fifteen minutes is typically the amount of time every host or hostess needs in order to tie up all the loose ends, take a last sweep of the apartment, hide the naughty lingerie, etc.

I know a girl who is always late. I finally told her to go to a shrink about it, and what she found out was shocking: She was told that it was a subconscious attempt to draw attention to herself. The shrink—whom I love for being so honest with her—also told her she was selfish. So just remember the next time you want to be fashionably late: You're a selfish tramp who just wants attention! And there's nothing fashionable about that.

> *A Lady* knows the only reason to be extremely late involves death—or at the least, lots of blood. If no ER is involved, she's on time!

> "Manners are a sensitive awareness of the feelings of others. If you have that awareness, you have good manners, no matter what fork you use."
>
> Emily Post

PUNCTUALITY REMINDERS

● Always strive to arrive fifteen minutes before you're supposed to. That way, given traffic, last-minute makeup emergencies, and unexpected phone calls, you'll probably be at most ten minutes late. Worst case scenario, you're early, which gives you time to reapply makeup (if you're on a date) or cruise the vicinity for hot boys (if you're meeting girlfriends—that way, you really did see him first!).
● Wear a watch. Duh. (Often the people who are chronically late have no way to tell the time.)
● Put a clock in every room of your house.
● Consult maps and get directions before you leave the house.
● Bring reading material: A book of poetry is always good to have on hand if you're waiting for someone (if you like poetry). Or sign up to have newspapers delivered to your phone, and brush up on your current events while you're killing time.
● Quit being optimistic! There will be traffic, you will have a hard time finding a parking spot, there will be a line to buy tickets, etc.
● Most importantly: Plan your outfits well in advance. Know that, despite these words of caution, you can get away with being late once in a while. And if you are late, don't waste it! It's like Holden Caulfield said in J.D. Salinger's masterpiece, *The Catcher in the Rye*: "If a girl looks swell when she meets you, who gives a damn if she's late? Nobody."

Q&A:

A Lady Receives An Invitation

The best part about creating this book has been the responses it's caused among the young women I've met at my book signings, over e-mail, and even on the street. There are some smart girls out there, and they've had some fabulous questions. I liked some of them so much I wanted to include them here.

Q: *Does stationary have to be expensive?*

A: While I've spent quite a few dollars on personalized stationary (and here's one of the fancy notes that Chanel's Karl Lagerfeld sent me), it's not vital. I've also written notes on hotel stationary, scrap paper, and even used napkins. What's important is the personal touch and the effort of actually breaking out a pen and jotting your thoughts down to a loved one. A handwritten note, to me, is still the epitome of class.

Q: *When is the right time to leave a party?*

A: Dita Von Teese, seen here when I was seated with her at the Sonia Rykiel show in Paris, once told me the best time to leave a party is when you're still having a fabulous time. The reason? First, you won't be disappointed if the party sours; and second, people will wonder what other fabulous party you left that one to go to.

Q: *What's your biggest party blunder?*

A: I've done some silly things, like showing up late to weddings and forgetting to turn off my phone's ringer at funerals. But probably my biggest blunder was when, at a birthday party, I was dancing with a friend on a table, which collapsed and sent us flying through the air and then sprawled on the floor. Arranging for an ambulance siren to blare over the music is never a good party trick! My biggest problem is getting carried away and lost in the moment, which can be really fun—and really not fun.

Q: *How do you say no to going to a party?*

A: It's always important to be polite, but it's okay to decline an invitation. I love this expression: "No is a full sentence." You don't need to provide a fantastic reason—and whatever you do, don't make something up. Always thank your host for the invite, and if you truly want to stay in the host's good graces, send a handwritten note of apology, or send flowers the day of the party.

NO

Q: *Do you really not look at your cell phone when you're eating with someone?*

A: Of course I've been guilty of checking a few e-mails or texts at the table, particularly if I'm waiting for an urgent message. But I never leave it out on the table, and I never whip it out when the person I'm with is in the middle of a story. Check your phone when you go to the restroom, or ask your companion if you can take a second to look at your messages—perhaps he or she needs a second to do the same.

Q: *Do you really always bring a gift to the hostess?*

A: Unless I'm coming from another event (or the airport), yes, I always try to bring something: flowers, a bottle of wine, a present. It doesn't have to be expensive. Being thoughtful and gracious will never go out of style, and after planning a party for weeks, a hostess will appreciate a little bit of kindness.

Q: *What's the best party you've ever been to?*

A: I'm not going to lie: I've been invited to some swanky parties. But the best? Madonna and Demi Moore host an Oscars after-party, which I have been lucky enough to go to. (No cameras allowed, and the door is tighter than a new pair of Spanx.) Once I got over the intense feeling of "I don't belong here," it was the most fabulous, glamorous night ever. Another party that stands out for me is the Louis Vuitton Bond Street store opening. Everything is more fun in London, and everything is more chic with Marc Jacobs involved (that's him, clowning around with Gwyneth Paltrow), but this one was extra special: there was a live interactive play and a special concert with disco queen Donna Summer.

A Lady
Throws a Party

―――――――――

"The attributes of a great lady may still be found in the rule of the
four S's: Sincerity, Sympathy, Simplicity, and Serenity."

EMILY POST

SINCE WE'VE DETAILED THE HURDLES associated with attending a party in the previous chapter, let's go a step further and discuss what it's like to throw one of your own. Be warned: Throwing parties requires a person to be fun, organized, attentive, creative, and charming, all at the same time. (If you don't have even one of those characteristics, feel free to skip this section and go straight to *A Lady Faces Temptation*, ch. 9.)

I've been to quite a few parties in my day, more than I'd care to remember. And I can pick out a good hostess when I see one. She's the well-put-together young woman who is simultaneously working the room and making sure that the behind-the-scenes magic (whether it consists of a staff of one hundred hired waiters or a single pizza delivery man) is running smoothly. It's a tough job—no, really—but somebody has to do it.

Not all parties need to be decadent. In fact, I have been to million-dollar balls so boring I've thought about putting a gilded toothpick through my eye—and I've been to just as many last-minute, super-casual soirees at friends' houses that have left me with some of my fondest memories.

This may seem simplistic, but the point is that people want to have fun at a party. They want to laugh, see friends, meet new people, maybe dance, and go home feeling good about themselves. So, sure, we can talk about the perfect table setting and where a bread plate should be placed, but even the ritziest parties can be a snooze if they're not fun. And a Hooters Hot Wings and Champagne party (I rang in a few of my birthdays with this party theme) can be just as fabulous as a black-tie extravaganza.

What makes a party memorable has to do with how much thought goes into its organization, and not how much money is spent on its realization. Take this to heart: The best party hostess isn't the richest. But the worst party hostess is definitely the one who half-asses it.

The Hostess: Pre-Party

The fun—and the hard labor— that precedes a lady's fete

Are you ready to throw a party? As you think about invitations, floral arrangements, and mood lighting, are you also thinking about broken lamps, spilled beverages, and a bathroom that looks like a high school boys' locker room? Because it's better to expect the best and prepare for the worst, especially if you're entertaining at home. If you're nervous about the consequences of your blowout, perhaps rethink the fete altogether (and just pile everyone into a car and go to a Domino's).

If you still think it's worth it to put together your own party, let's move on. First questions to ask yourself:

1. What is the point of the party?

2. Who is the celebrated guest? (You don't need a reason to party, but it's important to clarify that point before proceeding with the planning stages.)

3. Does the point of the party, or the person you'd like to celebrate, suggest a certain theme? Meaning, is this a birthday party? (Sweet 16? Anniversary? Parole?) Is it a party to celebrate your best friend's nose job? If there is a theme, ask yourself what you can do to make it more original. For example, a Halloween party might have a Japanimation-

ninja theme (I've actually been to one of these).

When it comes to proper entertaining, it's important to be creative. House parties can be fun, or they can be generic and boring. It's important to do something—anything—to distinguish your entertaining skills from some other tramp down the street who throws some

streamers up in her basement, sets up some folding chairs, and has the boys over for beer pong and keg stands. (Although, now that I think about it, that's the perfect setup for a White Trash party.) The whole point is to do something unique.

Recently, I helped a friend organize a party that featured a surprise visit from a gospel choir specializing in some delightful Beyoncé and Tina Turner medleys, which was wonderful. (But be aware that

this fabulous bonus touch was added only after all the basics were nailed down.)

Once you have a theme, it's time to pick a date. Confer with all the VIPs you absolutely need at the party, including significant others, loved ones of the honored guest, higher-ups in the organization that you're feting (if, for example, you are throwing a shindig to raise money for the school choir, it's important to, you know, make sure the choir can make it). You should pick this date well in advance, so you have enough time to send invitations (generally six weeks before the party) and receive RSVPs (two weeks before).

Decide on a menu. While it's considerate to have options for picky eaters—your vegetarian or vegan or macrobiotic food, or whatever the pale, skinny, unhappy people are eating nowadays—you needn't trouble yourself too much about it. Chances are that, if a person doesn't eat meat or fish or anything that has ever been alive ever, he or she is used to culinary disappointments. As a friend to many models and actresses with ridiculous eating habits, I can tell you that many of the people with special dietary obligations traditionally eat before a dinner party.

Music is critical. [See the *Dinner Party Playlist* on p. 74.] Don't leave this until the last minute; you'll wind up listening to radio commercials all night or scrolling through a friend's iPod for anything resembling good music. At cocktail and dinner parties, music should be lively but not overwhelmingly loud. People should be able to recognize the music, but not be distracted by it or tempted to sing along instead of carrying on a conversation. Of course, if the point is to have a dance party, you need a nonstop track of dance hits on your playlist. Be considerate of your peers: If you're the only person in the room who likes country, don't queue up a two-hour playlist of Garth Brooks' greatest hits.

Now we're on to the good stuff: decorating, and the fleeting moments leading up to the splendid event. First, take a sweep of the house and remove anything you don't want stolen or broken. If you're terrified about your beloved belongings being touched, fondled, mishandled, or broken, find and rent a venue. Or cancel the party. (In high school I had a party, and one of my friends, or one of my friends' friends—'cause there will always be stragglers and plus ones, be it at a house party or the Academy Awards—stole an iridescent Santa Claus soap dispenser from one of the bathrooms. My mother *still* talks about that. Be prepared for stuff to get stolen and broken. It happens.)

Cleanliness is imperative. Run a vacuum over the carpet, shake out the pillows, and clean

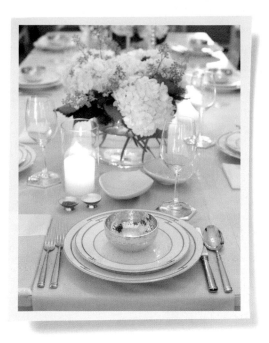

While these pictures were taken at a more formal setting, even paper plates and Dixie cups can be presented nicely. But that's the key: good presentation, like this one and the appearance of the simple veggie tray on the opposite page.

the windows. If you've rented a space, make sure the glasses are clean. Once I went to a fancy friend's Easter brunch on New

A lady thinks of everything!

York's Upper East Side; afterwards she called and asked if I had noticed the hundreds of lilies she had placed around her house. Of course I said I had—part of being a good guest is lying [See "Good Guest

Etiquette," pp. 50-51]—but in reality I hadn't even noticed. I did notice, however, that there was dust everywhere and my glass still had the previous drinker's lipstick on it.

This should all be done well before the first guests arrive. It is entirely not chic to be that frazzled lady running around, still not dressed and still not showered, asking the first guests to shake out a throw rug or polish a few spoons before the rest of the party starts. Give yourself enough time to prep the party, and then relax and get dressed before guests arrive. Panic doesn't look good on a lady.

The Hostess: Party On!

Lest we forget, the point of a party is to have fun, even for the person throwing it

Now, time for the party. You're sensibly dressed—and certainly in costume if it's a theme party—and diligently working the room, greeting friends and keeping an eye on both the moods of your guests and the physical safety of your valuables.

You're also making sure the refreshments are tasty and free-flowing. It's your job to make sure people are meeting and talking and bonding.

Even if you're miserable, you should act happy. No crying in bathrooms because a prospective significant other didn't show up, or freaking out because some skank arrived wearing the same dress as you. You've surely heard the song "It's My Party . . . and I'll Cry If I Want To." Well, that is a big fat lie. Only skanks, losers, and the emotionally unstable would literally cry at a party, especially their own.

No matter how much you've planned, it should always look like you've done nothing at all.

> "The best parties are gifts to your friends. The point of a party is to have fun."
>
> LUCIA VAN DER POST

Like you've spent your whole life circulating parties and keeping drink glasses full, and this party is just another ol' night at home for you. Nobody ever said being a hostess was easy; that's why it's so hard to find a good party, why party planners can make tons of money organizing successful soirees, and why people in cities like New York can be famous for doing nothing *but* throwing good parties.

The whole point, lest we forget, is to have fun. It's okay to let your hair down. A friend of mine recently threw a holiday party at a club in New York City and hired three severely obese drag queens to reenact Dolly Parton's "Hard Candy Christmas" number from *The Best Little Whorehouse in Texas*. It was an absolute surprise and totally festive. In the end, having a party should be somewhat simple: Humans have been doing it forever.

So remember to let loose—but not too loose, 'cause a messy hostess is *not* a good look.

PLEASANT DINNER MUSIC PLAYLIST

"Thursday" — ASOBI SEKSU	"Athene" — HERCULES AND LOVE AFFAIR
"In Anticipation of Your Suicide" BEDROOM WALLS	"Here in the Night" — KELLEY POLAR
"Speak Low" — BILLIE HOLLIDAY	"Heartbeats" — THE KNIFE
"Spring and By Summer Fall" — BLONDE REDHEAD	"Little Bit" — LYKKE LI
"Just Like Heaven" — THE CURE	"Long-Forgotten Fairytale" THE MAGNETIC FIELDS
"Baby Did You Hear" — DANGER MOUSE	"Little Girl Blue" — NINA SIMONE
"Under Pressure" — QUEEN + DAVID BOWIE	"Love Etc." — PET SHOP BOYS
"Jolene" — DOLLY PARTON	"Some Velvet Morning" — PRIMAL SCREAM
"Lips Like Sugar" — ECHO & THE BUNNYMEN	"Sweet Darlin'" — SHE & HIM
"Veronica's Veil" — FAN DEATH	"Fireworks" — SIOUXSIE AND THE BANSHEES
"Beggin'" — FRANKIE VALLI	"Big Mouth Strikes Again" — THE SMITHS
"Paris" — FRIENDLY FIRES	

○ **DATE** Pick a date that works for everyone. Dates are crucial. Consult the calendar of everyone you know, and an events calendar, and the lunar calendar if you want. You can never be too sure of your date.

○ **THEME** [See "Favorite Party Themes," pp. 92-93.]: A good theme is guaranteed to produce a good party. Not that a theme is necessary by any means. Sometimes it's nice just to dress up and feel fancy—call it a cocktail party theme, if you will.

○ **INVITES** Lots of girls lose their heads—and their wallets—when it comes to invites, getting over-the-top satin linings and embossed logos. Don't forget that the purpose of an invite is just to let people know the basics: the where, the when, the dress code. And don't be ashamed of sending an invitation via e-mail or the Internet—it's quicker, cheaper, and it's green.

○ **MENU** Food and drink are important at a party, but not the most important. There should, however, be enough for everyone to eat and drink. The second the bar runs out is the second a good party gets ugly.

○ **MUSIC** At parties, as in movies, the soundtrack sets the tone. Ask yourself: Do you want people to talk? Dance? In most cases, it's best to turn the task of mak-

ing a playlist over to a friend, preferably one who works as a DJ or is renowned for their musical tastes.

○ **DECOR** Cleanliness is the word. Sure, if you want to get festive and coat your walls in aluminum foil—I went to an amazing Andy Warhol-themed Factory party like that—that's great. But people will notice handprints on the wall and dirty panties in the hall if you don't take care of those first.

○ **ARRIVALS** If your party is at home, you should be the first person there (obviously). If it is elsewhere, you can be up to 20 minutes late. A friend of mine once took ages getting ready and showed up "fashionably late" to her own birthday, and everyone thought she was a drug addict. Happy birthday! Say hi to everyone, even the people you don't like or you didn't invite. Crashers are inevitable.

○ **THE PARTY ITSELF** Have fun. Remember, people will be taking their cues from you. It's important to look calm and collected—even if you're not.

○ **EXITS, OPTION 1** (a.k.a. Getting People Out): Liza Minnelli once told me that in the '70s Halston had dinner parties all the time but hated how people would always stay late and smoke up his house. Then he found a solution: At 10:30 p.m. a limo would pull up outside his house and drag everyone to Studio 54. It's a good lesson: The best way to get people out at the end of the night is to have a plan for afterward, even if it's going to a local bar or someone else's house. Another clever way is to have your best friend leave with a few people, to get the point across to clueless stragglers.

○ **EXITS, OPTION 2** (a.k.a. Seeing People to the Door): A good host will see to it that her guests have a safe and enjoyable departure.

○ **CLEANUP** This is when you find out the real victims of your party: the stains, broken glasses, and discarded napkins, the chicken bones, and (occasionally) the articles of clothing left as party litter. If you can't afford a maid, do half the cleaning that night and the rest the following day. Or have your friends over for a cleaning day and gossip session about the night before. Even better, when people ask if you need anything for the party, say yes—and tell them to hire you a maid for next-day cleanup.

A Lady realizes that the point of having a party is to bring friends together for a good time, not merely to impress them.

〜〜〜

A Lady knows not to criticize the table manners of her guests, no matter how bad they may be.

〜〜〜

A Lady knows that everyone looks much, much better in candlelight.

〜〜〜

A Lady knows that table decorations needn't be grandiose; fresh flowers on a white tablecloth are often a simple, easy way to lay a chic table.

〜〜〜

A Lady checks and rechecks her invitation to make sure the date is correct and every word is spelled correctly; sending a 'correction' for an invitation is painfully embarrassing.

〜〜〜

A Lady is aware that being timely with her invitations and RSVPs is paramount; she cannot expect people to change their plans at the last minute.

〜〜〜

A Lady knows how to keep a conversation flowing, which may mean changing the subject when a conversation gets too heated.

〜〜〜

A Lady knows when to take the keys away from a friend and call him or her a taxi.

〜〜〜

A Lady knows how to make a quick, effective toast to the guest of honor. She knows it should be endearing, and can be funny— which isn't the same thing as insulting.

〜〜〜

A Lady knows that some friends will have vices, like smoking. Thus, she has laid out ashtrays for her guests, or arranged for an outdoor smoking area.

〜〜〜

A Lady also knows that some friends don't have vices, so in addition to cocktails she should also have nonalcoholic beverages available.

〜〜〜

A Lady knows that dinner is served from the left and that plates are cleared from the right.

HOW TO LAY A BUFFET

START ➡

NOTE: Start from the left, fill plates, then retrieve flatware

"Be not forgetful to entertain strangers, for thereby some have entertained angels unawares."

HEBREWS 13:2

"A guest never forgets the host who has treated him kindly."

HOMER

Entertaining friends and socializing with others is supposed to be fun! And a well-planned setting only makes parties *more* fun. Don't be afraid to step up to the plate (literally) with a fancy table setting (above left) or do something outdoors, like host a beach picnic (above right) or garden party (left and below), which my friend, the chef Katie Lee, seen here, has done with great success.

"It is equally offensive to speed a guest who would like to stay and to detain one who is anxious to leave."

HOMER

How to Introduce People

O ld-school manners books devoted entire sections to the etiquette of introductions: like, if a girl was unmarried and under the age of twenty-five, she would be presented as a *Miss* to a young man under eighteen, who would be a *Master*. Yeah, forget it; seems like an awful lot of hoopla, no?

One valuable lesson to take from these guides, however, is the fact that the way two people are introduced is crucial, and it is the duty of a good hostess to know how to do it.

A hostess should try to make sure that the people she's bringing together have a good chance of getting along. Yes, sometimes this is hard to predict, but bear in mind that social occasions are not the place to stage an intervention or force former besties to start speaking again.

There are a few things to remember when you introduce two people. The first is to remain subtle about the introduction (no sense blowing up a friend's spot before she's had a chance to do it herself), and also wait for the right time to do it, when the situation arises organically. Even if you spent a whole night telling your girlfriend you can't wait to introduce her to your studly cousin, you don't drag her across the room to meet him as soon as he walks in.

Once you've found an appropriate time to introduce two peo-

Don't be afraid to introduce people twice. It's better than not introducing them at all.

ple, be sure to introduce them clearly. No mumbling. It's also common courtesy to interject a little fun fact about both people (which isn't the same thing as an insult), to get the conversational ball rolling when you walk away. Perhaps your friend Sarah grew up in the South, and has come to resent giant hair as a result, whereas another friend of yours spent her formative years in Florida and has been equally scarred by certain style tendencies.

Equally as important as the conversational prep work is to know when to walk away. Here's the thing about introducing two people—you're only meant to put them in front of each other, not monitor and guide them through every single step of the getting-to-know-you process. Or it wouldn't be called an introduction—it would be called a three-way. (And I'll go ahead and say it: A lady is not into three-ways. Especially in public.)

Guestlist & Party Vibe: Free, but Critical

To be completely honest, anyone with a fat wallet can throw a big party. If you have the dosh to rent out a baseball park or the connections to close down an amusement park, you will have no problem throwing a party—and people will come. (No lines at Six Flags? I'm there.) But what's important at a party isn't the damage it did to your bank account.

In fact, the whole spending-buckets-of-money-on-a-party-means-that-the-party-will-be-so-good mentality is so pre-recession. No, the two most critical things that distinguish a good party from a snooze-fest also happen to be free: the guest list and the party vibe.

This is one of the things I learned when I first moved to New York City for college: For my twentieth birthday I didn't get a table at an expensive night-club or rent a party bus for a pub crawl through the city. For one, I couldn't afford that kind of decadence on my student budget; and two, blowing part of my student loan on a white limo that I was only going to vomit in wasn't exactly how I wanted to ring in my twenties.

What I did instead was save up some meals on my NYU meal plan and host a black-tie dinner in my school dining hall. Everyone came: supermodels, socialites, heirs to millionaire Manhattan empires (basically, it was a bunch of people who had never set foot in a college dining hall in their lives, and

probably haven't since). But that party, where school friends and some of my more professional acquaintances mingled, was a major hit. People still talk about

A Lady doesn't
let a guest feel out of
place or ignored;
if she sees someone
alone, she joins her,
asks her to dance,
or tries to integrate
her into the group.

it. [If you're strapped for cash, see "Cheap Giggles," pp. 96-97.]

The vibe at the party—a bit of absurdity mixed with the unique—was something that didn't cost me a penny. In fact,

all in all, the whole party cost me a few dozen swipes on my card and the few dollars I blew on the kimono I wore. I brought my own stereo and begged the cafeteria staff to let me play it; I put white sheets on the tables to make it look fancier—and we had a laugh!

These are the things that a lady should remember when it comes to throwing a party: Some of the most important aspects can't be rented or bought at a store. Invite some of the coolest, most interesting people you know, strive for an atmosphere that will keep people entertained and excited to be there, and the party will be a success.

Ask yourself if you would want to come to the party that you're throwing. If you're just having a party to show off, or flaunt the fact that you have money to throw down, you might want to reconsider the fete.

QUIZ

Do You Know How to Throw Down?

No one said throwing a party was easy, and no said it was for everyone, either. (That's why the role of the "wedding planner" is often played in movies by a neurotic, anal-retentive freak. And, having met a few in real life, I can tell you the cinematic version isn't too much of a stretch.) To see if you have the skills to throw a successful blow-out, here's a simple quiz.

1. So you've decided to throw a party. What's the first thing you do?

- **(A)** Send out a mass e-mail a few hours before you want people to begin coming over, put out whatever leftovers don't stink too badly, and dust off your couch.
- **(B)** Check some dates with your friends, making sure that everyone's schedules line up. Then send out a save-the-date e-mail.
- **(C)** Call everyone you know to ask about a date, send out a save-the-date e-mail, panic about color coordinating, and immediately start to curse out friends you know won't come in theme.
- **(D)** Sweat profusely, tremble. The mere *thought* of having people over makes you want to crawl under the couch.

2. The RSVPs for your party are fewer than expected. You think:

- **(A)** *Oh, well. More drinks for me.*
- **(B)** *What a perfect excuse to throw a smaller, fancier party. Maybe I'll finally try out that soufflé recipe my granny sent me.*
- **(C)** *What? Why is no one coming? Do my friends hate me? Can I rent some male models to fill the room?*
- **(D)** *Thank God. Now I have an excuse to disinvite the rest of the guests.*

3. The party has begun, and more people have come than you expected. Your reaction?

- **(A)** You don't notice. You've been parked on the couch, making snarky comments about people's outfits all night.
- **(B)** Bust out the small cups and start serving smaller snack portions.
- **(C)** Start crying, ask people to leave, have a panic attack, and end the party alone, snuggling a pillow drenched in your own tears.
- **(D)** Are shocked; you didn't think you had half this many friends. The party might be kind of fun if you weren't locked in the bathroom having an anxiety attack.

4. Someone has just come up to you and said there's been some red wine spilled on your couch. You:

- **(A)** Flip the couch cushion over. Your "rents" will never know.
- **(B)** Politely excuse yourself from whatever conversation you're having, find the stained cushion, and apply some seltzer water.
- **(C)** March up to the asshole who spilled the wine, kick him in the nuts, and then torch the pillow in the backyard to make sure there's no evidence of the damaged goods.
- **(D)** Ignore it, ignore it, ignore it—and it will go away.

5. The caterer doesn't show up, or the food that you've prepared turns out to be inedible, so you:

(A) Don't put any food out at all. People only came here to pick up boys and drink anyway.

(B) Quickly run to the store and buy some cheese, crackers, and olives, or call a local diner for last-minute delivery.

(C) Begin to cry, order a pizza, and then try and cut it into decorative pieces and pass it off as a gourmet appetizer. When that doesn't work, start crying again.

(D) Put every single piece of food in your refrigerator—including a half-used bottle of mayonnaise—out on a table. Then go to sleep.

6. It's late, food and drinks are running low, and it's time for the party to end. How do you conclude the festivities?

(A) Throw a bunch of dirty sheets and pillows on the floor and turn off the music, yelling, "Shut up and sleep or go home."

(B) Turn down the music, subtly remove the drinks and the food from the party, and start politely walking people to the door and wishing them a safe journey home.

(C) Call the cops on your own party, and then make a big deal about how devastated you are that everyone has to go home. You don't want to seem rude by being the one to suggest that people leave!

(D) Lock everyone outside, turn out the lights, and act like no one is home—even when your friend begs to be let back inside to retrieve her bag.

7. As your guests arrive you notice that someone has shown up in the same dress as you. In response you:

(A) Trick question. You're not even wearing a dress—you and the other girl are actually wearing the same dirty hooded sweatshirt.

(B) Politely excuse yourself and change into your plan B outfit.

(C) Kick the bitch out. How dare she.

(D) Lock yourself in the bathroom, shivering with embarrassment.

8. Another one of your friends is also throwing a party on the same night as yours. Your response?

(A) More food and booze for me.

(B) Trust that the people most important to you can come to yours and hope that everyone else manages to attend both.

(C) Sabotage the other party, spreading rumors about the rival hostess and telling your friends that you will never speak to them again if they even think about stepping foot in that tramp's house.

(D) Cancel your party. No one will come over if there's another option for the evening.

QUIZ KEY

Count up all your answers and see which of the four letters you had the most of. If you are:

Mostly A's. Lazy Linda: You should not be throwing parties. Since you primarily want to get drunk and talk with your close friends, you should stick to being a guest at other people's fetes.

Mostly B's. Responsible Rita: You know your way around a casserole. You're calm under pressure and have a natural gift for getting people together for a good time.

Mostly C's. Crazy Carol: You have some serious control issues and aren't the best in intense or high-pressured situations. It's true that when you plan a party, you never leave a stone unturned—but a big part of celebrating is *having fun*. Learn to chill out.

Mostly D's. Henrietta Hermit: Having fun isn't a sin, and it shouldn't make you so anxious. Sure, you shouldn't be throwing parties if the thought of human interaction makes your EKG spike, but it's important to learn to relax.

Let's be honest. Most theme parties are just an excuse for boys to feel macho (think: military costumes or tool belts and hard hats) and girls to dress like sluts (silk nightgowns and some variation on kitten or bunny ears). Seriously, the only time a luau-themed party is acceptable—when girls prance around in coconut-shaped bikini tops and ask every boy in the room if he wants to get lei'd—is, well, at an actual luau on a beach in Hawaii. (Okay, okay, full disclaimer here: Sometimes tacky themes can actually be fun. I mentioned a White Trash theme earlier, and I'm still thinking about how great a party that would be.) If you decide to go down the theme-party route, here are some great ideas that will allow you to feel sexy without looking skanky. [See "A History of the Best Parties," pp. 60-61, and "A History of Hostesses," pp. 100-101.]

⊕ Arabian Nights
This is a great theme if you like the look of a turban or gilded, heavy fabrics and lots of gold jewelry. (And who doesn't?) It's also fairly easy to decorate for an Arabian Nights party: Make the venue look like a harem tent, with lots of candles, scarves, rugs, and pillows all over the place.

⊕ Cannibal Feast
This one will be particularly popular with the kids who like vampire books and movies. It's pretty easy: get some fake pointed teeth and fake blood, serve some blood-themed cocktails and maybe some red velvet cake, and we've got ourselves a theme. Stay up late the night before for those extra convincing bags and dark circles under your eyes!

⊕ Masked Ball
Truman Capote's Black and White Ball, held at the Plaza Hotel in New York City in 1966, is without a doubt the most memorable masked ball of the second half of the twentieth century. Capote planned the party for years and used the invites as social weapons—many friends were made and lost as a result of this shindig's yearly VIP list. The point is, everyone wanted *in*: Dressing up and wearing masks made the party exciting.

⊕ '70s
If you're using it as an excuse to wear an Afro wig and smoke hash, a hippie theme can easily slip into cheesy territory. The trick is to take your look seriously, searching out legitimate costumes from thrift stores or older family members. I once went to a '70s-themed birthday party in a small coastal town in Italy. The birthday girl was in a peasant dress with a tambourine, and all her friends wore fringed dresses. Everyone looked so chicly '70s it was easy to embrace the wonderfully tacky hits of the era, like Gloria Gaynor's "I Will Survive."

⬆ Toga!

Although toga parties are famously popular on college campuses and the frat scenes, I'm not suggesting you wrap yourself in stained bedsheets and encourage your male friends to smash beer cans on their foreheads. I'm talking about a civilized toga party (yes, they exist), where men wear Roman battle dress and the ladies slip into their favorite Lanvin or vintage Pierrot dresses. Set out a few bowls of olives and grapes, maybe some feta and Greek dips, and you've got a party on your hands.

⬆ 1920s or Great Gatsby

F. Scott Fitzgerald's 1925 masterpiece has become an icon of American literature. But more important—to me at least—it captured black-tie decadence and has continued to inspire amazing parties. Throw on a drop-waist sequined frock, style your hair in a bob (or buy a wig), and make the guys starch their white shirts and slap on their black bowties—and get ready to dance around until the sun comes up (or the rents come home).

⬆ Halloween

The last day in October is one giant theme party. People expect some kind of costume will be necessary, which shuts up the lazy spoilsport demographic. Your creative friends will come up with something ironic or comical, while your trampy friends can wear black silk lingerie, throw on some little cat ears, and go as pussy cat. (I must say that the "smarter" costumes are always a bigger hit. If a guy wants to see a half-naked girl dressed like a slutty idiot, he can go on the Internet.) If you're really into themes, you can take your Halloween party a step further by giving your soiree a mini-theme, like Surrealist Ball.

⬆ Come as You Are (And Beyond!)

Elsa Maxwell, the legendary party hostess, threw an ingenious Come as You Are party in the first half of the twentieth century. The idea was that guests had to come to the party in exactly what they were wearing when they received their invitation. Were they in their PJs? Completely nude? In a winter coat? Maxwell, along with Truman Capote, went down in history for being the type of person whose party you never missed, precisely because of this creativity. Don't be afraid to get creative with themes, or if you're feeling particularly creative, create one of your own.

⬆ Heaven and Hell

This party is good for venues that have an upstairs and a downstairs: decorate the below as a fiery dungeon and the above as a cloud-covered wonderland. Then pick your costume—something modest, white, and angelic if you're on the top floor, or something red, revealing, and devilish if you're on bottom—and then find out if it's good to be bad, or bad to be good.

Printed Invitations

It's not exactly green to insist on sending paper invitations—but they sure are fancy! Here are a few of my favorite invites, which I've kept as mementos, including a handwritten invitation for a secret Courtney Love concert in Paris, an invitation to the White House Christmas party, an invitation to a fancy twenty-first birthday soiree in New York, an invitation to a Chanel fashion show in Miami (featuring a watercolor by Karl Lagerfeld), an invitation to dinner at the US embassy in Paris, and an invitation to Alexander Wang's first store opening, which had a most intriguing font.

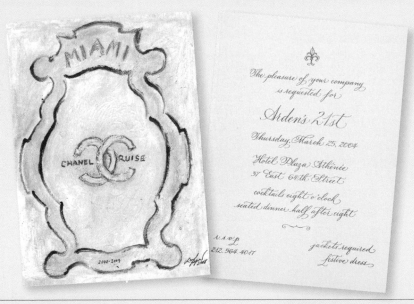

The Joy of a Place Card

Marjorie Gubelmann is the famed New York City hostess with the mostest. Her Upper East Side house has played venue to some of Manhattan's best soirees, and every time she has had me over for dinner or brunch I've swiped my place card. Sure, making place cards takes some effort, and a monogrammed, gilded card isn't cheap, but they're an easy way to introduce people and make sure everyone is making new friends!

YOU ARE INVITED TO

A Holiday Party

AT THE WHITE HOUSE
SATURDAY, DECEMBER 20, 2008
AT EIGHT O'CLOCK

BARBARA BUSH
JENNA AND HENRY HAGER

EAST ENTRANCE

*Courtney Love will be performing
a private show for givenchy at July 4th*

*givenchy Haute Couture Salon
3 avenue george V
Paris 8e*

Champagne reception at 10.30 PM

...ue to limited place this invitation is not transferable

Charles H. Rivkin
Ambassador of the United States of America
and Ms. Susan M. Tolson
request the honor of the company of

Mr. Derek Blasberg

at a cocktail reception followed by a seated dinner
celebration of the 30th Anniversary of fashion designer Michael Kors

on Monday, March 7, 2011
at 9:00 pm

Ambassador's Residence
41, rue du Faubourg Saint-Honoré
Paris 8e

Festive Dress
R.S.V.P.

Please present this strictly personal invitation and personal identification at the entrance

*Alexander Wang Invites
Derek Blasberg
To an Intimate Celebration of the Opening
of our first ever Flagship Store*

February 15th, 7pm to midnight

103 Grand Street

Please bring invitation

RSVP fashiongps.com/kco

RECESSIONISTA Cheap Giggles

The trick to having a good party is not to blow the bank. Sometimes the best memories can be created on the tightest budget

My father is one of the thriftiest men I've ever met. His coupon-clipping and penny-pinching afforded me many opportunities later in life—like being able to attend college in a city as expensive as New York—but it did throw a wrench in my teenage party-throwing ambitions. My dad was always afraid we'd break something, or that he'd be buying soda, then later beer, for all my friends, and that the cost of food and other party favors (my mom always liked fresh flowers in the house when we entertained) should outweigh social considerations.

Now that I'm an adult, however, I know that his worries were unfounded. Yes, I've been to some swanky parties in my day—white tablecloths, real candles, waiters in white jackets, a half-dozen glasses for a half-dozen beverages per person at dinner—but that doesn't mean that every single enjoyable party I've gone to has cost a fortune to produce. Quite the contrary: Some of my favorite social events have been casual, last-minute fetes at friends' houses. So if you want to organize a little get-together with friends, don't think for a second that you'll need to take a loan out at a bank.

Disposable dishware—as opposed to handmade china—is totally suitable. (But don't make this a habit—it can't be good for the environment to be constantly tossing your party discards.) No matter what Martha Stewart tells you, you don't need to decorate your house with fresh flowers, throw pillows, silk tablecloths, and other decadent decorations. As long as your house is void of dust and clutter, it will be fabulous for a party. (Just knock down those lights

A lady knows that a good time doesn't have to be expensive.

~~~~~~~~~

a few notches, and nobody will notice the mismatched couch cushions. People look better in candlelight anyway.)

There's nothing tacky about encouraging your guests to bring a beverage (unless you're throwing a party at a restaurant), or something to eat. That's called a potluck, and it gives guests a great opportunity to bring something that's actually useful to the party. If you insist on doing the menu yourself and preparing your own food, it's not like caviar and foie gras have to make an appearance on the menu—well-prepared veg-

gies and a shrimp platter have always done the job. What's important to remember here is the way it looks, however: If you're skimping on price tag, don't skimp on presentation, which means if you're using pre-catered foods, you can take them out of the plastic trays.

Themes come in handy when you're trying to be thrifty. [See "Favorite Party Themes," pp. 92-93]. If you're doing a Greek party, all you need is grapes, olives, and some dips. One year my birthday party was a Hooters Hot Wing and Champagne party at Billy Joel's New York townhouse. I lured friends in with the bubbly, but kept them content with an unlimited supply of cheap fried chicken products.

Just because dinner parties are often associated with prim ladies with lots of time on their hands, showing your friends a good time is not a luxury of the wealthy. Sure, it might be easier for the über-rich—with their butlers and maids—but you can have just as much fun doing something affordable and chic at home. Remember, the company is always much more important than the commodities. You don't need a centerpiece and a silver serving tray. Give me a good friend and fried chicken any day.

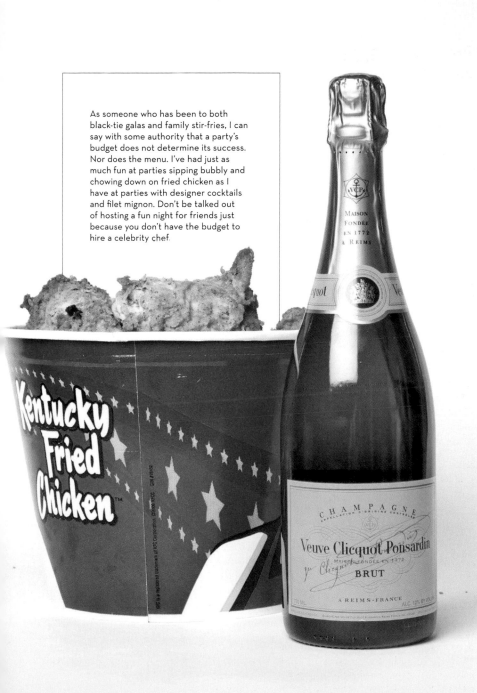

As someone who has been to both black-tie galas and family stir-fries, I can say with some authority that a party's budget does not determine its success. Nor does the menu. I've had just as much fun at parties sipping bubbly and chowing down on fried chicken as I have at parties with designer cocktails and filet mignon. Don't be talked out of hosting a fun night for friends just because you don't have the budget to hire a celebrity chef.

What to Do with Persnickety Eaters?

Is she a vegan, a vegetarian, a raw food dieter, or your basic pescatarian?

These are trying days for the modern party hostess who's trying to plan a menu. It can be downright impossible with these new picky eaters, pesky nutritionists, and a whole new slew of diets, some of which I can't even pronounce. Some people can't have their food cooked above a certain temperature, some people don't want to eat anything that has ever had a head, and some people prefer only to eat things that belong in the green color scheme.

So what is a hostess supposed to do? In the nicest way possible, my suggestion: Screw 'em.

I'm not saying you should serve a leg of lamb at a PETA dinner, but what I'm trying to get at is that at the end of the day, the point of a dinner party is to enjoy and indulge in the company of friends and new acquaintances. The food is, basically, a very generous bonus. What should be the focus are the guest list, the party vibe, and the good time—and then we can think about the menu.

All of that said, even though your friends will probably not starve if they don't each have their ideal dinner put in front of them, it's kind to ask what they would like to eat, and what they

A lady never points out that someone has not eaten a meal she has prepared, even if she's furious.

~~~~

A lady makes sure everyone is full, but she doesn't shove second helpings down their throats.

~~~~

A lady encourages her guests to go home with some leftovers, but she doesn't force a doggy bag on anyone. There's a difference between a goodie bag and a doggie bag.

~~~~

A Lady wants her guests to be happy and full, but she knows the most important thing at a dinner is spending time with each other. Entertaining is not done merely for sustenance.

~~~~

would not like to eat. If it's a very, very formal dinner, you'll need to have a vegetarian option, which could (and probably should, if you don't have one) also double as the vegan option. That means nothing that was ever alive and nothing that was taken from a live animal—so no eggs, cheese, or milk.

If the dinner is smaller, you'll want to ask about food allergies, which are common and can keep a person from partaking in the good food. You want to make sure you respect those allergies too—I once went to a dinner and the hostess didn't tell a girl who was allergic to shellfish that there was shrimp in the sauce, and the night ended with an ambulance siren. (It wasn't the desired dessert course, that's for sure.)

Something to remember, however, when it comes to food: The only reason that a person should refuse food or make a big deal about not eating something that is served to them is because they have a serious medical condition that prevents them from eating it, or a moral or religious conviction. If you're serving pasta and someone says they've reached their carb limit for the day, they're a wanker and they deserve not to eat in the first place.

Some people are so particular about what they eat I imagine they're on a prison diet. But never fret too much about a menu. There are more important things to worry about.

Also, if you find yourself entertaining someone who has serious food allergies, don't take it the wrong way if they're picking around their food. Chances are, someone who is a vegan and has serious issues with their diet is used to going to dinners and restaurants with limited menus, and thus not being able to eat what their friends are having. In fact, I have several friends who fall into this category of VDEs (Very Difficult Eaters), and they're smart enough to eat their own dinner before they go out at night. (But if they show up hungry, just throw some uncooked lettuce leaves and vegetables on a plate and they'll be happy.)

All this said, don't get offended if someone doesn't take everything off the buffet or doesn't serve themselves something when it's passed around the table. They're not being rude, and you probably don't know why they're passing on it. It's not because it tastes bad—maybe they have an allergy to pesto and their throat will swell shut if they have that dish. Or maybe grilled asparagus reminds me them of their recently deceased grandmother, who knows? Don't even give it a second thought.

A good hostess will strive to make sure all her guests are well fed, but she will not harp on it. And a good guest knows not to make it a big deal—attracting attention to the fact that they cannot eat anything that is being served is terribly rude and the hallmark of a person who is wholly unclassy.

(Tell them to read the previous chapter!)

At the end of the day, these are not prehistoric times! People don't come together to eat because they'll go back to their caves and die of hunger otherwise. Yes, you should think about the food and encourage your guests to enjoy themselves and partake in the food on offer, but the most important thing for them to do is enjoy themselves with fabulous conversation and a witty host. So pay less attention to your menu and more attention to what people are saying. And then, maybe you'll have some fun!

The art of civilized socializing is, presumably, as old as humanity itself. Surely back in caveman days at least one buffalo-fur-clad hostess organized a feast or two, and even in biblical times major events were commemorated with a dinner. (Reference: a certain Leonardo da Vinci painting called *The Last Supper*, which can be found on the back wall of the Santa Maria delle Grazie convent in Milan?)

The point is, people have been partying forever. But looking back on all of the events and galas of the past century or so, there are a few hostesses who stand out.

Marie-Hélène de Rothschild

Marie Hélène de Rothschild was the hostess—nay, the baroness—with the mostest. She didn't so much throw a party as meticulously prepare a feast, gala, and dance, launch them into a catapult, and hurl them over all of European aristocracy. Perhaps the most famous of her fetes was her Dîner de Têtes Surréalistes. The invite set the tone; it was written backward so it could only be read with the aid of a mirror.

Sao Schlumberger

Born in Portugal, married to a Texan, with mansions in Houston, New York, and Paris, Schlumberger left a trail of Dalí and Warhol portraits (of herself) and couture in her wake. In fact, she is believed to be John Galliano's first-ever couture client. She lent the then-fledgling designer her Paris home for his Princess Lucretia show in 1993.

Elsa Maxwell

A self-taught party expert, Elsa Maxwell was unrivaled in her hostessing abilities, pioneering many parlor tricks (scavenger hunts) and themes (Cross-Dressing party!) that have become commonplace for adventurous party throwers. Perhaps my favorite was her Come as You Are party. [See "Favorite Party Themes," pp. 92-93.] Not the most outstanding beauty of her day, Maxwell was also extremely honest. Of her life, she said it was "not bad for a short, fat, homely piano player from Keokuk, Iowa, with no money or background, [who] decided to become a legend and did just that."

Peggy Guggenheim

The life of Peggy Guggenheim, the American heiress and art patron who was instantly recognized for her bat-shaped sunglasses, was as populated with aesthetic genius as her walls and gardens. Jean Cocteau, Man Ray, Marcel Duchamp, Max Ernst (whom she married), Henry Moore, Alexander Calder, Pablo Picasso—these weren't just the names on the canvases and sculptures in her home. They were friends she made, loved, and supported in London, Paris, and Venice, mainly from the small fortune she inherited at twenty-one. Her artistically minded spirit lives on, presumably, in her house in Venice (currently a museum). It's still a hot party venue, especially during the Italian Biennial. Peggy would be proud.

Nan Kempner

R.S.V.P.: Menus for Entertaining from People Who Really Know How, a book written by Nan Kempner, is a bible on party planning. But Kempner was more than a hostess; she was an inimitable member of New York society. Slender as the cigarettes she smoked even while on the treadmill (and even toward the end of her life), she kept her passion for fashion no secret. The famous socializer—who admitted she would attend the opening of an envelope—once remarked that she would like to be buried naked, adding, "I know there's a store where I'm going."

C.Z. Guest

C.Z. Guest filled her life with men as impressive as the flowers in her garden and the horses in her stables: Truman Capote was a confidant; the Duke of Windsor a houseguest; and Ernest Hemingway the best man at her wedding. She was the reigning queen of Newport, Rhode Island society, and a woman who embodied American chic for over half a century—from her early modeling days to her eighth decade, when she continued to inspire the likes of photographer Bruce Weber.

Vicomtesse de Noailles

For Marie-Laure de Noailles, life was art and art was life. She was one of the first patrons of the surrealist artists, including Man Ray and Salvador Dalí. She counted Luis Buñuel and Jean-Michel Frank as close confidants, and was even the lover of Jean

Cocteau. The great-great-great-granddaughter of the Marquis de Sade hosted these men in her Paris *hôtel particulier* (now the Maison Baccarat, whose original interior was designed by Jean-Michel).

Duchess of Devonshire

The Duchess of Devonshire, or Georgiana Cavendish to her friends, died more than two hundred years ago, but her relevance lives on. The Keira Knightley film *The Duchess* was based on Cavendish's life, and the ill-fated saga of her distant niece Princess Diana is well-known. The Duchess had much in common with Diana—she was involved in a much-publicized love triangle, for one, and had a penchant for handling her own political press. Diana may have been the queen of hearts, but the Duchess was one of the first women to enter into the political sphere, and—famously in 1784—traded kisses for votes.

Alva Vanderbilt

Alva Vanderbilt gets props for hosting the best housewarming in New York City history. When Caroline Astor, her rival society

queen, barred Vanderbilt from attending one of her celebrated galas for the Four Hundred elite, a list of Manhattan's most well-to-do that still exists today, Vanderbilt decided to swing open the doors to her new mansion at 660 Fifth Avenue by throwing a masquerade ball that rang up a $3 million price tag—in nineteenth-century money. (Astor ended up coming, admitting the fete was not to be missed.)

Lauren Santo Domingo

How could I not be partial to my beloved friend, Lauren Santo Domingo, or the LSD, as some know her? Not only is she the chicest thing on two legs, she has played hostess to my birthday parties and even hosted the swanky dinner party for the launch of this book. Classy indeed! I'd be hard pressed to find a better example of the modern contemporary hostess. The gorgeous blonde, who grew up in picturesque Greenwich, Connecticut, married music executive Andres Santo Domingo in a 2008 ceremony in Cartagena, Colombia, which *Vogue* dubbed the Wedding of the Year. In addition to being wonderfully gorgeous and effortlessly chic, she also conquered the fashion industry as a model, an editor, and most recently as an online entrepreneur.

Q&A:
A Lady Throws a Party

The best part about creating this book has been the responses it's caused among the young women I've met at my book signings, over e-mail, and even on the street. There are some smart girls out there, and they've had some fabulous questions. I liked some of them so much I wanted to include them here.

Q: *What's the best theme party you've ever been to?*

A: French *Vogue* had a fabulous masquerade ball for their ninetieth anniversary. I went as Zorro (including the sword), but everyone went wild with their costumes (there was lots of lace), including Gisele in a Phillip Treacy eye mask and Tyra Banks in a hairnet she stretched entirely over her face. Talk about fierce. But my favorite spotting—and she's my favorite spotting at any party, theme or not—was Kate Moss, seen here with my pal Alison Mosshart from the band The Kills.

Q: *What's the best music to have at a dinner party?*

A: While every group is different—I have been to dinners where hardcore techno music was played over the appetizers—I personally think that it's good to start a party with instrumental music or something soft and almost inaudible. And then when the party gets swinging, you can pump up the jams with music people can sing along to. (Early on, you want people to talk to each other—not do karaoke in their heads.)

Q: *How do you handle a party crasher?*

A: Talk about an awkward situation. Without fail, someone will show up at a party who wasn't invited (please make sure that this someone isn't you), and it's simple: Be polite and gracious, and act like you're happy to see him or her. But if the crasher starts making a scene—or worse, eating all the food and drinking all the drink—there's nothing wrong with discreetly pulling him or her aside and explaining you wanted to keep things small and intimate tonight.

Q: *Do you ever get pre-party jitters?*

A: Of course I do! In fact, in the days leading up to every single party I've ever thrown, I've regretted the whole thing and wanted desperately to shut down the entire operation. It's normal to get worried, but it's always senseless. (But mind this tip: Whatever you do, don't drink to calm your nerves. No one wants a sloppy party planner around.) Your friends want to have fun just as much as you want them to!

Q: *What's the nicest invitation you've ever received?*

A: While I love a little pomp and circumstance in an invite (I once received an invite that was so luxe the envelope was lined with crocodile skin), there are two things that are most important: thoughtfulness (I once received a wedding invite that was merely a Polaroid of the happy couple holding a sign that said, "We're Getting Hitched") and clarity, which I have a few examples of here. After all, you don't want people showing up at the wrong place at the wrong time.

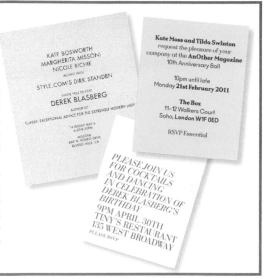

Q: *Who do you think is contemporary society's best hostess?*

A: That's easy! My friend Lauren Santo Domingo, seen here after we went to a gala at the Metropolitan Museum of Art, who hosted this book's launch with a sit-down dinner at her house for sixty people.

Q: *Is it déclassé to send Evites?*

A: I've sent just as many Evites as I have paper invites. Evites are smart because they save paper, save postage, and arrive more quickly, and you can check to make sure they were delivered. But I do prefer paper thank you notes!

Q: *What's a flower you always send?*

A: Interestingly enough, both *Vogue* editor-in-chief Anna Wintour and provocative fashion photographer Terry Richardson's favorite flower is the peony. (Talk about a spectrum of tastes!) So if in doubt, send those!

A Lady Decorates

―

"I believe in plenty of optimism and white paint."

ELSIE DE WOLFE

TO SOME PEOPLE, HOME FURNISHINGS are a matter of life and death. An unreturned chintz pillow can end a friendship. Whole days can be lost debating the right shade of blue. (Is it too robin's egg? Or too sky?) While I admire (and adore) these sorts of aesthetically minded people, I'd like to encourage them to look beyond this book to cultivate their visual desires.

The type of person I hope to reach isn't the one who knows the integral difference between a duvet and a throw blanket. I want to connect with that girl's slightly messy best friend: I'm talking to the young lady who's never linked home décor to her personality—the girl who doesn't think her environment can impact her life.

The way someone decorates her personal spaces speaks volumes about her person. Chances are, if your house is a mess, so is your character —and probably your hair. On the other side of the coin, someone who can keep her dirty laundry in a basket and her milk in the refrigerator probably can also keep a boyfriend and a job. I will never understand the sort of woman who spends a fortune on her wardrobe but lives in squalor.

I'm not suggesting that to be a lady, a young woman must iron her bed sheets every night before she goes to bed. (Although once I went to Valentino's house and his maids ironed the sheets twice a day, and it was like lying on a cloud.) And I'll be the first to point out a few too many stacks of papers and magazines I have lying around my apartment. But remember this: There is pride in making rooms a little prettier, and one's life a little nicer.

The Importance of a Lady's Dwelling

I 'm not going to lie: I am not the most organized person in the world. I'm the first person to accept a complimentary gift with purchase (a trait I got from my mom), and I often have a hard time throwing anything away (a trait I got from my dad). But I cannot say enough about simplicity when it comes to personal space.

First, chic living isn't the privilege of the wealthy. I've gone to the houses of girls who had billionaire parents and seen panties hanging off their chandeliers, and I've been to community college dorm rooms with such meticulous organization you'd would think there was a full-time assistant under the bunk bed. While you can tell a lot about the way someone decorates their lives, monetary wealth doesn't have to do with decorating.

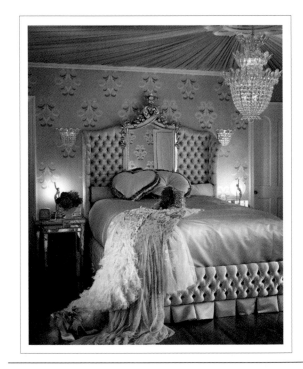

A truly chic young woman acknowledges that the world she creates for herself is just as important as the world she hopes to one day live in. We all need to start living the life we want now. Think about setting precedents: A tidy childhood means a tidy adulthood, a tidy studio apartment could lead to a tidy mansion. If you want to become a super-successful businesswoman, you don't need to transform your dorm room into a conference center, but I don't know a single successful businesswoman who has old fast-food wrappers around her bed or decaying French fries under her pillow.

Here's the thing: If you're reading this book, chances are you care about how you interact with the world. Right? Well, the way your dwelling space decorates your life will set the tone for the way you live your life.

A Room Should Have a Mood and a Theme

I used to suffer from this: I would buy so many things at jumble sales and vintage stores that my house started to look like a doctor's waiting room with multiple personality disorder. It doesn't matter if you're decorating a whole house or just a room; figure out a general sense of décor to help streamline your design and decoration process.

This can be as simple as choosing a color. The famed fashion editor Diana Vreeland once described her red and brocade sitting room as a "garden in hell." The artist Terence Koh has his entire Chinatown townhouse decorated white, from the floor and walls to a giant albino peacock in a glass box in the middle of his kitchen. The designer Tom Ford has homes almost entirely decorated in blacks and grays (he even had the tractors on his New Mexico ranch hand-painted midnight black).

Not that a theme has to be as simple as a color. Maybe it's a sport, or a print, or an exotic location, or even a book. My friend Margherita Missoni has a family home in Paris, and the whole place is decorated in her family's trademark knitwear—so everything is brightly colored and full of textures and zigzags and wild prints. Also in Paris, I've been to other houses that have a Venice theme (lots of mirrors, Murano glassware, and blues to mimic the water in the city), and still to other houses with outrageous themes like taxidermy or the Wild West.

Because a theme should also say something about you; it shouldn't be a giant contradiction for the person you are. If you're a Goth girl who wears black lipstick and Victorian-era funeral garb, don't have a house that is decorated with ponies and rainbows and pink walls. (People will think you're a schizophrenic.) And likewise, if you dress like a good girl and wear pearl necklaces and cardigan twin sets, don't have a dungeon-themed bedroom. (Although this may attract a few gentleman callers, they probably won't be the sort of man you want to spend too much time with, you kinky freak!)

I spend a lot of my time looking at all varieties of interior decorating, and the ideas and inspirations are never-ending. There's never an excuse to be uninspired nowadays! Sure, many people may find it difficult to pick just one, but it shouldn't be hard to get stimulated: Look at magazines, look at decorating blogs, and find some rooms you like. Find your aesthetic, and then decorate. Impulse shopping is never a good idea when it comes to home décor.

HABITUALLY CHIC:

Here are four super stylish women who understand that how they decorate their living spaces is just as important as how they decorate an outfit.

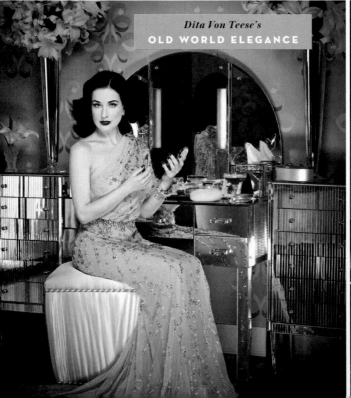

Dita Von Teese's
OLD WORLD ELEGANCE

Tory Burch's
COUNTRYSIDE CHIC

Tamara Mellon's
METROPOLITAN GLAMOUR

A House Should Be a Home, Not a Department Store

Here's a little problem with a lot of young people when they try to decorate, especially their first place: Like a rookie athlete, they burst into the game trying to impress everyone. With very few exceptions (an ambitious reader should Google "Diana Vreeland red apartment" to see how hard it is to make overdone look good), when it comes to decorating anything, there's a general rule of thumb: Go easy on the eyes.

I had a friend who inherited her grandmother's house when she passed away, and then shoved it full of brand new "fancy" stuff that a bunch of decorators told her she had to buy. It was the ugliest house I had ever been in. She replaced all her grandmother's classic, aged pieces with a bunch of new, fancy stuff that was meant to impress a visitor. How gauche!

It's like when you're getting dressed for your first gala or school dance: You don't need to put on a pound of makeup, a gallon of hairspray, and some brand-new, trendy frock to look beautiful. In fact, the most elegant person at a party is the one who looks nonchalant and naturally gorgeous.

Remember this when you're decorating: You don't need all new stuff, you don't need every single wall to be filled with some piece of art or a poster, and you don't need something newfangled to impress a visitor. It's just like when you're getting dressed: You don't have to have logos and name brands to look fabulous.

When I go to someone's house, I think it's gratifying to see that some of the pillows were purchased from Hermès and Ralph Lauren, and some of the others were bought at a Pottery Barn or wholesale liq-

A Lady knows a room can say a lot more about her than what comes out of her mouth.

uidation. At the end of the day, it's the exact same thing as with your wardrobe: You don't have to spend a lot to look nice.

Kanye West once told me (and then later Tweeted, much to the Twitterverse's entertainment) that fur pillows are really hard to sleep on. And I've seen his place, and maybe he should have read this essay before he started decorating. That's exactly what I'm talking about here. Yes, fur is luxurious and rich, but when it comes down to it, what you really want to put your head on is something soft and comfortable. So remember to err on the side of simplicity when it comes to home design.

But for the record: Kanye, I love your house.

A House Is Not a Museum

T he trick with nice stuff is to actually use it. Don't let the fear of ruining something prevent you from enjoying it.

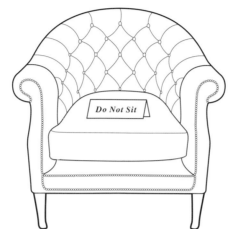

A Lady buys things she loves, not what's trendy or expensive.

Do Not Sit

A Lady doesn't need to spend a lot to look like she has a rich life.

This is a lecture I've had to have more often with older people than I have with people our age (particularly my mother, who didn't even let me set foot into the two "nice rooms" of our family home until I was old enough to drive), but I've seen a few young women who suffer from it too. The fact is: there is no point to having nice things if all you do is look at them.

Clearly, I don't advocate using cashmere towels to clean the bathroom floor, but the fruits of life are made to be enjoyed. If you have a big house, open it up to your friends and have a party. If you have a big dining room table, put down some plates and have the family over. If your mother gave you an expensive blanket, curl up with it and watch the TV with your dog. If you've just moved into your first apartment,

order some pizza and watch *Mean Girls*, the seminal 2004 film I've seen too many times. Bond, have fun and be merry! Like I mention in my chapter on throwing a party (p. 80), I am nostalgic for the days of dinner parties and intimate

A Lady lives in her house. She doesn't treat it like a museum.

times at home with close friends.

Use your room—buy a nice chair so you can lounge around in it with a good book. Make use of your things and enjoy your life! Turn up the music when you have people over. Dance all over the new carpet.

I would never suggest throwing a rave complete with glow sticks and a DJ booth and a bunch of people doing drugs in your bathroom—I've been to those parties and you might as well burn the house down afterward because it's so wrecked. But if you do have a nice space, invite people over. When I moved into my first apartment in New York that could actually fit a dining room table, I had dinner parties with pre-prepared meals from a local supermarket. It wasn't expensive or rowdy stuff, but it was marvelous fun. There's truly nothing better than a small dinner party with friends in a cutely decorated home. A friend's mother explained it best: "If you want to go to a museum, go to the Met, not my living room."

Don't Stutter with Your Clutter

A lady does not clutter: She doesn't clutter her outfit with unnecessary and distracting accessories, she doesn't clutter her life with bothersome and unflattering boys, and she certainly doesn't clutter her house and her closet.

I used to love shows on hoarding. For the people on those shows, their sense of reality is twisted and material objects become obsessions. (I can relate to them because my family had some problems with hoarding—but, thankfully, never bad enough to need a TV intervention.) Things like newspapers and old bills and household products bought on sale become all-important.

The way to get past that obsession is easier said than done for some people: Don't feel guilty about throwing away sentimental souvenirs, especially if they're starting to take up more room than the people who gave them to you. Unless it's something practical, don't feel bad about giving it to someone else or tossing it in the trash. When it comes to magazines and newspapers, which have always been my biggest problems (my friends used to call my magazine collection the Archive, and I still keep my collection of *Vogue*s—every issue from 1986 to present—in a friend's basement), keep only the ones you think you'll truly need—and take solace in knowing that everything else is probably Google-able.

As for clothes, a common obsession, only keep the things that you've worn in the past year. The rest you can give away to a friend or donate to a charity. That feels good for two reasons: first, because you're doing something for someone else; and second, because it means you have room in your closet to buy some more stuff!

I know a thing or two about hoarding: I grew up in a house where my parents kept every single report card, artwork, school paper, and teacher's note. While this was no doubt because they loved me and were proud, in my head it made it seem typical to make large collections of stuff. As I grew older, however, I realized I didn't need every single piece of mail I received and didn't need to save every single catalog. It was hard to purge, but with tips like this, I managed to sift through the keepables and the trash.

⊗ Start gradually: If you give yourself a few minutes every day—even if it's while watching your favorite TV show—you'll be shocked by the amount of stuff you have edited, sorted, and gotten rid of after a few weeks.

⊗ If you're overthinking it, chances are you don't need it. If you can't think of when you wore a piece of clothing last or what that gadget actually does, donate it.

⊗ Scale down when items start to take over. If you have a mound of love letters from your ex-boyfriends, why not save only the ones that are truly moving, and from the guys you don't hate?

⊗ Reward yourself—but only when you deserve it: Consider installing a one-in-two-out rule, which means every time you bring something home, you have to pitch two things.

⊗ Just because it's useful, that doesn't mean you'll use it. I've known people who have had boxes of tools in their house—but didn't know how to use any of them. The same goes for household appliances. If you don't drink juice, get rid of the juicer.

⊗ Less is more. This is true for makeup and home clutter.

⊗ Beware of freebies. I love a goody bag more than anything, but who really needs another ugly mug, mouse pad, or cheap T-shirt? Get rid of free gifts with purchase and junk mail as soon as you get it.

⊗ Cleverly disguise everything else in neat storage spaces. I love those cheap plastic storage bins, which come in all sorts of colors, to discreetly organize my stuff. What makes the cut should look well contained.

Décor Affects Mood

When it comes to the importance of a room's humor or disposition—and how mood-altering a room can be, for better or for worse—you don't need to look further than a hotel room. They are a fabulous example of how decorations can make or break a room. Since I travel so much, I can tell instantly when I walk into one if I'll get a good night's sleep. I can remember one painful experience in Miami, when the hotel lobby was pumping techno music and there was a line of scantily dressed locals trying to get into the hotel bar, and the rooms had concrete floors and what I can only describe as porn star lighting fixtures. (That reminds me of one very important tip: Never, ever put a mirror on the ceiling in a bedroom. Go to page 129 for more on what never to have in your house.) It was a case of abominable decorating, and it killed my mood—and my ability to sleep.

The first step to putting a room together is asking what the room's purpose will be: If it's a bedroom, presumably you want to sleep in it. You'll want to think about curtains that will block out the early morning sun on the weekends, and you probably will want to steer clear of fluorescent wallpaper. If it's a dining room, presumably you'll want to eat there, maybe even with friends. So don't hang up fashionable pictures of skinny models, and make sure the chairs are comfortable and there's a nice warm feeling to the room. If you're doing a living room, make sure you have room for a nice couch and a few comfortable seats for company.

While it's true that a room should ultimately please the owner, guests shouldn't be horrified at the view. For example, if you're single and ready to mingle, don't leave out your Barbie collection. Or if you're having colleagues over, maybe you don't want a bunch of pictures of yourself from college doing beer bongs. (In fact, you don't want to have too many pictures of yourself anywhere, which I talk about on page 128.)

> "I don't care if you pick up something off the street or pick up a rock on the side of a hiking trail—you have to combine items of different ages and different styles. Otherwise, it gets really boring."
>
> NATE BERKUS

Sadly, that *Sex and the City* episode when Mr. Big goes through a midlife crisis and paints his wall crimson red and then can't sleep isn't uncommon. Putting together any sort of living space should be a fun activity that offers you an outlet to express yourself. So don't waste the opportunity by haphazardly painting or hanging just any ol' thing on your walls. Or even worse, don't be the person who does nothing with a room or a house, whose house always looks like you've just moved in or are about to move out. No one wants to live with a hospital décor!

Sprucing up a room is all about self-expression, self-representation, and finding another way for people to articulate how they feel. Don't waste it. Just do me this one favor: Think a little before you start decorating.

I've always been drawn to bold colors, and I love the vibrant red of this bedroom. I would find it hard to be in a bad mood with all these joyous tones surrounding me!

A Lady Knows Her Way Around a Garden

I was very close with my grandmother before she passed away, and one of the things that we would do together was work in her garden. She had a very green thumb, and she grew the best-tasting tomatoes I had ever eaten. Before I get lost in my nostalgic trip down memory lane here, let me clarify that I'm not trying to get you to learn how to grow award-winning produce. But I will say this: The benefits of knowing how to keep a plant alive are manifold.

Even from the most basic perspective, being able to keep something alive is good training for harder life tasks (like having a pet fish or a newborn baby). A plant teaches responsibility. And horticulture—and the ability to nurture and water something until it blossoms— can give you an amazing sense of accomplishment. There's great pride in making something beautiful. In fact, that's what this whole book is about!

To get back to decorating, allow me to say this: Fake plants are repulsive. I have an Aunt

> *A Lady* attends to the flowers in her life, not the weeds.

> *A Lady* can keep things alive.

> *A Lady* respects Mother Nature. She's quite a lady herself!

Mary* who has more fake plants in her house than she knows what to do with, and every time I come over, I try to shake the dust out of a few of them because they're starting to look like decorations in a bank's conference room.

A little green something in the corner is a nice addition to any decorating scheme. It doesn't need to be an exotic plant species that eats live bugs or something—there are plants that need nearly zero love and attention, like cacti. I even have some small plants in my bathroom (air plants) that don't even need dirt—just a little sprinkling of water every few weeks. But something alive and growing adds a lively element to a room.

The plants can be a small accessory in a home, like a standing plant in a corner, or they can be an entire theme of a room. A woman who has a well-tended, thriving garden is outrageously beautiful. In fact, I once went out to legendary supermodel (and Playboy bunny) Stephanie Seymour's house in Connecticut, and when she offered me a salad made with vegetables from her own garden, I almost dropped dead. She looks good naked, and she knows how to garden? Wow.

HEALTH

And on a healthy note: According to NASA research, these plants clean indoor air of harmful pollutants:

* Aloe vera
* Gerbera daisy
* Philodendron
* Bamboo palm
* Peace lily
* Spider plant

---

* My Aunt Mary would like me to say she no longer uses artificial plants. (But that's a lie. They're very addictive!)

Every bloom is not created equal. So while we're on the all-too-important topic of plants, let's have a look at what each one means:

⊘ The ivy: These aren't as easy to grow as the cactus, but they're still pretty foolproof: they don't need much light, and depending on the species, they can be left outside or even hanging in a window. They're easy to move—and easy to get rid of.

⊘ The cactus: I start with this one because these desert-loving plants need little water and can be forgotten about for long stretches of time. (Read: they are probably the hardest to kill.) Thus, they are good starter plants. Among other things, the cactus symbolizes endurance. While they can be very pretty and they give off a no-nonsense vibe, the cacti aren't the most endearing for obvious reasons: They hurt like hell when you touch them.

⊘ The orchid: This fancy little plant isn't for the faint of heart—or the faint of wallet. Orchids are very expensive, very exotic, and difficult to keep alive. While gorgeous, orchids are high maintenance. They're for people who really love beauty at any cost.

⊘ The sunflower: Who doesn't love these big ol' plants with giant heads that literally follow the sun from rise to set? And they also provide wonderful snacks. The sunflower, it is said, symbolizes wishes and loyalty.

⊘ The rose: Roses are great for a garden. They require sweat and hard work, but they reward you with such beauty. In the house, different roses can mean different things. Red roses, of course, mean romance; yellow roses symbolize friendship; and white roses suggest purity. (When in doubt, send pink roses, which are just pretty.)

⊘ The tulip: When I was a little boy, my mother used to bring me home tulip bulbs from her work trips. Since then, I've loved planting tulips and watching them emerge in the spring. They're so bright yet so simple in their beauty. I have been told people who are optimistic like them.

⊘ Anything growing grass: If you have a Chia Pet, you're probably lighthearted and fun. (And a little bit ridiculous. It's hard to take a freakin' Chia Pet seriously.)

Quality Decorating Doesn't Have to Be Expensive

Two rules to live by: credit card debt is never attractive; and anything less than 40 percent off isn't really on sale. Now that we have that settled, let's talk more specifically about affordable home decorating.

My first apartment was decorated entirely by junk shops, from the furniture to the dinner plates to the lamps. And in most cases, I preferred the things I found to things I couldn't afford. (Besides, isn't the hunt half the fun when it comes to thrift shopping and bargain binning?)

When I lived in Brooklyn with a few roommates, there was an entire warehouse of discarded furniture and home goods—I think it was literally called The Junk Store—from which we bought goods to decorate our entire apartment. I found a charming little desk to put in my room, and a few old buffets that we used as bookshelves and as an entertainment center. Just clean it up, slap on some paint, and voilà!

Just remember the same thing goes when you buy an antique piece of furniture as when you buy a piece of vintage clothing: Scrub that thing within an inch of its life.

If you're buying old pillows (and there's nothing wrong with that), make sure you replace the stuffing and wash the case or have it dry cleaned. Anything with wood should be doused in strong cleaning solution and polished. Dishware or glasses can be run in the dishwasher

a few times, just to be sure. Believe me, it's much cheaper—and chicer—to buy a few cans of paint (and save the rest for a pair of shoes or something truly important) than it is to splurge on a brand new table. Wood can be re-stained or repainted, surfaces can be polished, and old materials can be cleaned up.

I always think that it's fine if things are a little nicked up or downtrodden. Mind you, there's a difference between a few scratches that give an old wooden desk some character and a couch that has a burn mark on it.

The true recessionista decorator has no quarrels finding things anywhere, even if it comes off the street. Yes, I have taken things out of the trash, and I'm proud of it! (This is one of those times when it's a literally case of someone's trash being another person's treasure.) I'm not saying to hop into a dumpster behind an office building if you're looking for some new printer paper, but one of the joys of decorating a room is putting together things from all walks of life: Maybe you found a poster of your favorite childhood movie discarded, so why not frame it and hang it on a wall? Maybe you need a chair, and you walk

by a broken one outside a restaurant; why not take it and pay a handyman a few bucks to fix it up?

Every town has a Salvation Army, and you'd be surprised what you can find there. A simple online search can provide local charity shops, church resale stores, and larger warehouse-sized charitable bazaars.

The modern decorator looking for something new and affordable is spoiled for choice. Entire specialty shops that make high-quality products at low prices now exist, like Ikea and Habitat. My tip here: only purchase very plain looking things. A black lacquered table looks like a black lacquered table almost anywhere you buy it, but when discount chains try to get fancy, things start looking cheap. In addition, most impressive interior decorators and designers have branched out into diffusion lines: TV's favorite decorator Nate Berkus has a QVC line; Phillip Staerk does things with the store Design Within Reach. When it comes to decorating your house, the same idea as stuffing your wardrobe applies: You don't need to spend a bunch of money to look rich.

THRIFT GETS

The great thing about an antique shop is that you literally never know what you're going to find. A perfectly aged leather chair, a just-like-knew Art Deco lamp—or maybe you'll find nothing at all. But what my eyes are trained to look out for when I go on the vintage home wares hunt is the following:

- BOOKS
- LAMPS
- CHAIRS
- CHINA

- DESKS
- ASHTRAYS
- CLOCKS
- GLOBES

- GUITARS
- MIRRORS
- ARTWORK
- NEEDLEWORK PILLOWS

* Please note, you must wash EVERYTHING
** What to stay away from: Mattresses, shag carpets, or anything else that can trap other people's years of grossness

"When I go to a country, I go to flea markets, antique stores. I am always looking for something."

URSULA ANDRESS

BILLY BALDWIN SAYS . . .

In the history of home décor, the twentieth-century decorator Billy Baldwin is an icon. Resolutely modern with his work, he somehow blended classicism, modernism, and comfort. But even more powerful than his list of clients (which included the likes of Jacqueline Kennedy and Diana Vreeland) was a list of bon mots he dispelled on the topic. Here, some of my favorite Baldwin quotes:

- Be faithful to your own taste because nothing you really like is ever out of style.
- If I find that something I am doing is becoming a trend, I run from it like the plague.
- Decorating is the art of arranging beautiful things comfortably.
- There is one fundamental fact about lighting: Where there is no light, there is no beauty.
- When you want to transform a room into a entirely different animal, change the color.
- The best decoration in the world is a roomful of books.
- Nothing is in good taste unless it suits the way you live. What's practical is beautiful . . . and suitability always overrules fashion.
- Stick to the things you really love. An honest room is always up to date.
- The first rule of decoration is that you can break almost all the other rules.
- Comfort is perhaps the ultimate luxury.

Sometimes, even after a room has been tastefully decorated, it needs a little oomph! Don't be afraid to add an adornment that is bright or personal or loud or that smells nice. (But, just a word to the wise: Don't add all things at once, or else it will look like a circus!) Here are some tips I've used to add an extra touch to a room that may otherwise be a tad drab.

⊙ Picture frames:
Colorful or kitschy photo frames are a great way to pep up a windowsill or unadorned table.

⊙ An interesting pillow:
The quickest way to add some excitement to a couch is with a fun pillow! In Nantucket, I bought a needlework pillow that was stitched with the slogan "You Can't Be Too Rich Or Too Thin," and it's become my favorite thing in my house.

⊙ A throw:
While a quilt or homemade afghan may remind you of your grandmother's house, fabulous throws add some excitement to a bland room. I have an iridescent throw that I bought in Graceland with Elvis's head on it. (But if you can, get cashmere so you can snuggle up to something nice on the couch.)

⊙ Let loose on eBay:
I love doing online auctions—they're a great place to find affordable antiques, in addition to being a thrill. (Feel free to lie and say that the old trunk you bought on eBay came from your great-great-grandfather's Civil War farm.)

⊙ Hang something up:
Put anything up on the wall, as long as it's hung straight and isn't profane.

⊙ A bright wall:
Paint it bright red or a shocking shade of blue. But don't go overboard—it's hard to sleep inside a neon jewelry box.

⊙ Trays, boxes, and bowls:
I'm always on the lookout for something to put on a shelf or a table—and it's a bonus if it can help organize loose change, TV remote controls, or pens. I have a solid silver tray in the shape of a herd of elephants (my favorite safari creature)

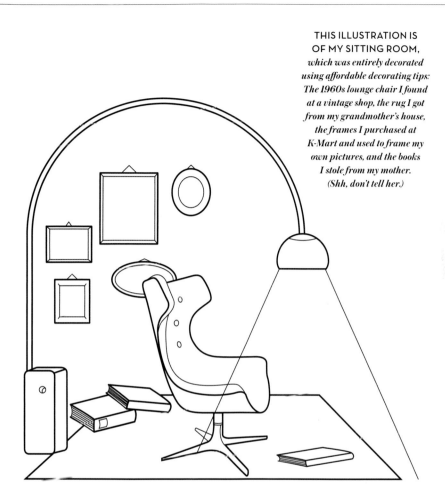

THIS ILLUSTRATION IS OF MY SITTING ROOM, *which was entirely decorated using affordable decorating tips: The 1960s lounge chair I found at a vintage shop, the rug I got from my grandmother's house, the frames I purchased at K-Mart and used to frame my own pictures, and the books I stole from my mother. (Shh, don't tell her.)*

that I bought at a Hamptons yard sale for ten dollars, and it's one of my favorite things. Other good yard sale finds? Book ends, mirrors, and tchotchkes.

○ **A colorful rug:** An interesting or bright rug is a great way to fix a bland room, but be careful not to get anything too crazy—you don't want someone to get vertigo looking at it. I have a divine leopard print throw rug in a muted gray color scheme—it's kitsch but subtle.

○ **Lamps and sconces:** There's nothing worse than having to squint when you're reading a book in your bedroom or sitting area. If you have the space, invest in a beautiful lamp or hunt for some old wall sconces. Light is literally a great way to brighten a room.

○ **Incense or a scented candle:** Don't forget about the rest of the senses! Make sure your home smells good too.

Investment Dressing for Your Home

E arlier in this book, I devoted quite a few pages to the importance of investment purchases when you stock up your wardrobe. We talked about how it's best to spend the most money on a good shoe, a smart coat, and handbags that you'll use forever. The exact same goes for when you're decorating: Don't blow your wad on an ashtray and have to put your couch on layaway. And don't go wild in the pillow store before you've bought paint for your walls.

I once had a friend who was putting together her bedroom and had her heart set on a small cameo engraving of a beautiful woman in a very small frame. To her credit, it was a divine piece and it was truly beautiful. Problem was it was so ridiculously expensive: Her entire budget for the room grouped into this itty-bitty portrait. Being passionate and bull-headed, she bought it, blew her budget, and had to go cheap on the rest of the contents in her bedroom, like her bed. She set up the entire rest of the room for disappointment, and because she couldn't afford any other nice things, the girl in the fancy small portrait is now sitting on top of a desk that wobbles and is made of artificial wood.

Pull back on the frills at first, invest in the big stuff, and then work your way down. If you're decorating a bedroom, buy a nice bed since presumably you'll get a lot of use out of it, and then the other furniture. Save the frills for the end. Finding a great poster at an affordable price is much easier than finding a nice mattress for cheap.

Trust Your Taste More Than Anyone Else's

I've been to so many homes that have been entirely decorated by someone who doesn't live there. (That person is typically an overpriced decorator or an overbearing mother.)

Here's the thing about decorating: If you're going to live in it, and if you're going to have to look at it, you're going to want to like it. So even if you're rich and you've hired some fancy-pants designer to outfit your entire home, you need to weigh in on a few things—like what your favorite color is, for example. If you hate the color blue, don't go for a nautical theme.

For the rest of us who aren't rich, getting second opinions can be a more complex exercise: Maybe it's a family member or friend offering too many unsolicited suggestions, or the classic case of too many cooks in the kitchen. Barring a few extreme circumstances (like, if you want to paint all four walls of your room and your ceiling black, and your mom objects), how you decorate your space is your business.

The easiest way to diffuse this is to explain that while you're grateful for suggestions, the decision is ultimately yours. You're the one who will have to look at your place every day, so if you want wallpaper with bows on it, then that's your perogative. I can't say this enough: Don't let yourself be talked into things that you don't like. Not only will you not like the décor, every time you look at it you will be reminded and annoyed. (Trust me!)

The annoyance isn't limited to just pushy friends and family.

Salespeople can be the most suggestive of all, and I've had friends walk into a furniture store and before they know it, walk out with more pillows than a sorority slumber party.

Never be bullied, never be pushed, and never buy something that you're not sure about. Even if it's on sale!

TIPS FOR PERSONALIZING YOUR SPACE

At the end of the day, the most important person to impress when decorating a space is the person who is going to live there. (That's you, silly.) It's ultimately you who needs to be happy with your dorm room, bedroom, house, or apartment. It should be an expression of you and it should be a place where you feel comfortable. So here are a few tips for making your home look like it's your own.

◉ Sentimental tchotchkes: I have a dachshund called Monster, so people have given me all manner of things bearing a wiener dog's likeness. But heed this warning: There's a big difference between choice crafts and an overload of knickknacks.

◉ Plants: A green thumb adds a very personal touch, and I'm a sucker for anyone who can keep a plant alive. [See "A Lady Knows Her Way Around a Garden" on pp. 116-117.] A few flowers add multitudes of appeal to a room.

◉ Books on interesting topics or your favorite hobbies: I have stacks and stacks of books on artists, fashion designers, and entertainment legends. (I have entire sections devoted to Marilyn Monroe, Coco Chanel, and the Kennedys.)

◉ Photos: My house is full of pictures of my friends and family. In the digital age, there's no excuse not to have a few choice photos around.

◉ And lastly, keep your space organized: Especially if you're a scatterbrain, knowing how to easily find your own stuff is a truly rewarding exercise.

◉ Scented candles: A nice aroma and a little candle-light can go a long way.

◉ Holiday decorations: I will admit that my family holiday decorations have left me with some mental scarring. But it's a nice touch to have a little something in a room devoted to the holidays—maybe a miniature Christmas tree, or some bunny-shaped chocolate around Easter. But even with (or maybe especially with) holiday decorations, remember this: Less is always more.

Your Grandma's Trash Could Be Your Treasure

E ven before I moved out of my parents' house, I was digging stuff out of my basement. I was constantly surprised by what was down there—and not just my own basement, since I'd also hit my grandparents' basement and the basements of friends.

When I was finally allowed to move out of my brother's room, which was the living situation my parents insisted upon for reasons that are still unclear to me, I asked my parents to dig out an old bedroom set instead of purchasing whatever children's imitation-wood series furniture was on sale at the mall. Who wants to sleep in a racecar bed when there's a nice 1960s oak bedroom suite collecting dust in the basement?

This is one of my biggest tips when it comes to home decorating: Before you go shopping, see what you already have. Especially if you're decorating your first house, or your first bedroom (which means you probably don't have a lot of money to play with in the first place), ask around and see who is trying to unload some junk. If it's something particularly nice or in good condition, offer to trade it for something. Family and good friends probably won't accept cash, but maybe offer some manual labor or a home-cooked meal in your new place as payment.

If your grandmother doesn't have anything good, try a stranger's grandmother: Hit up the vintage shops and antique markets. But not the fancy-schmancy antique markets, which have stuff that is oftentimes more expensive than at a furniture store. (For more on-a-budget decorating tips, see "You Don't Need to Spend a Lot to Look Rich" on page 118.)

With the exception of grumpy old people who want to hold on to everything, most people are happy to see someone young want their old stuff.

To take something that has been hiding away in someone's basement is to vindicate him or her for having kept it down there for so long. I can't tell you how particularly proud my father is of these moments: He has been known to keep cardboard boxes for decades on the off chance that, at some point, someone will need to mail something large. So you can imagine how happy he was when I asked for a desk that had been buried under years of accumulation.

Art Is Everywhere—but Not Nowhere

My living room wall, seen here, currently showcases the following: a painting a friend did of a penguin when he was in elementary school; a postcard from the Pablo Picasso Museum in Switzerland; a beloved picture I took of Kylie Minogue, Mary-Kate Olsen, and Alison Mosshart walking down the street in London; Polaroids of Karl Lagerfeld in Paris, Richard Prince in his New York studio, and my brother and his wife on their wedding day; a painting I made of my dog, Monster; two Mario Testino photographs I got when I worked at *Vogue*; a letter from the designer Tom Ford and a letter from the White House when (the second) President Bush was in office; a picture of my friend from when he was in his college a capella group and performed for (the first) President Bush; and a sketch of my face a friend did on a napkin one night at dinner. They are all nicely framed and grouped like a collage over my couch.

The point of this blabbing is that, apart from the professional photographs (and maybe that sketch if my friend dies an important artist one day), nothing on that wall was either hard to find or worth much money. I wouldn't go as far as to say I wouldn't trade some of the things on that wall for an Andy Warhol silkscreen of Elizabeth Taylor, but until someone makes me that kind of deal, I'm very content with this display.

"You may hang your walls with tapestry instead of whitewash or paper; or you may cover them with mosaic; or have them frescoed by a great painter: all this is not luxury, if it be done for beauty's sake, and not for show: it does not break our golden rule: Have nothing in your houses which you do not know to be useful or believe to be beautiful."

WILLIAM MORRIS

"What is Art?" is a discussion too complex to tackle here, but when it comes to decorating one's house, the only person that needs to be pleased with their art is the person who lives there. But while art can be almost anything, it cannot be nothing. A blank wall is detestable—it reminds me of hospitals and storage spaces.

Think out of the box, and don't assume you need to spend much money. If you are not in the financial position to traipse through New York's Chelsea art galleries, that doesn't mean you can't put something entertaining on the wall. Perhaps you have some fun pictures of friends on a night out, or a landscape you photographed on vacation—blow it up and frame it.

My brother is a big fan of Salvador Dali's work, but since he can't exactly afford any important Surrealist works at this time in his life, he found a great vintage poster on an online auction and hung it in his den.

Art and home décor are all around us: personal pictures, souvenirs, old prints, or even a letter from an important person in your life. I took a painting class one year, and while my finished project isn't going to give Pablo Picasso a run for his money, it meant something to me—so it's framed. Let your walls reflect you.

A Lady lady knows to keep clothes off the floor—she doesn't want her precious clothing to be ruined.

A Lady knows a new shower curtain can pep up her bathroom.

A Lady uses skinny hangers because she knows crowded closets are ugly and can damage the clothes.

A Lady understands how flattering candlelight is.

A Lady knows a home should look nice and smell nice too.

A Lady is responsible with her electronics and remembers to turn off the lights to conserve energy when she's out.

A Lady splurges on her sheets.

A Lady has a green thumb.

A Lady puts safety first: she doesn't give out her address, and she remembers to lock her doors.

A Lady isn't afraid of a little color in her home.

Say No to Narcissistic Home Dècor

It's a hard thing to explain, but you know it when you feel it: that forced sense of being impressed, or when you go into someone's house and you can tell they want you to think everything is really fancy, and really expensive. The same thing happens when you meet someone at a party and they do nothing but drop famous people's names to impress you, or when you see someone walking down the street and everything they're wearing has a logo on it—we get it, we get it. You spent a lot of money to look like that. (Ha, that reminds me of a fabulous quote from Dolly Parton: "It costs a lot of money to look this cheap.")

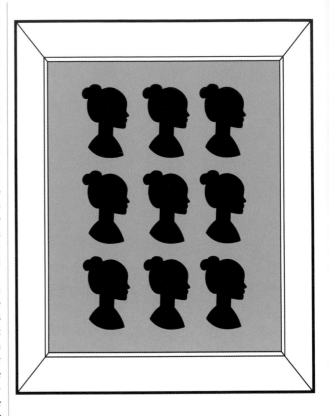

The ultimate worst is when you walk into someone's house and there are a million pictures of that person. I've seen this sort of narcissistic home décor in all variations: from supposedly sophisticated people who have walls devoted to pictures of themselves posed with famous people and world leaders to another sort of narcissistic decorator, like my beloved Aunt Mary, who has bunches and bunches of framed pictures of herself through the years throughout her house. (Aunt Mary even has a wooden bust sculpted in her likeness in her room. Though to her credit, because we have teased her relentlessly over the years, she's replaced many of the framed pictures.)

I'm not saying there's anything wrong with a few tastefully placed and arranged pictures of the owner of a house around a room. I also hope I'm not insinuating that a few personal artifacts shouldn't be spread around the house. A multitude of imagery that glorifies yourself is tacky.

A few pictures of you with the president, your mother, and maybe a handsome actor you stalked on a family trip to L.A.? Yeah, that's fine. But a dozen self-portraits is overkill. Once, in London, I went to a party where the owner of the place would sit on his couch and methodically stroke his chin—whilst sitting in front of a portrait of him on the very same couch methodically stroking his chin. It was shocking and unnerving.

To me, there is nothing more fulfilling then entering a house that looks lived in yet decadent, something sophisticated yet approachable. And this is in all home décor styles: just because a house is minimal doesn't mean it has to be cold. Just because you want your bedroom to look quaint doesn't mean that it needs to look run-down.

What Never to Have in Your House

I've spent the last few pages talking about what looks great in a house and where to find that great stuff, but let's take a few minutes to discuss the things that no respectable lady would let litter her house.

Yes, there are the obvious unattractive items: dirty undergarments, nasty clumps of hair extensions or false eyelashes, pregnancy tests, expired dairy products, and general rubbish. But there are a few other choice objects that are almost guaranteed to leave a nasty impression. For example: a lava lamp. Or a black light. Or a bong. Even if you're living in a college dorm, it shouldn't resemble the film *Animal House*. (If you're too young for that reference, Google it. It's a classic.)

Some other no-no's: a mirror on the ceiling, which is grotesquely tacky and off-putting, and disrespectful taxidermy. I know someone who has a deformed stuffed dog in their foyer, and someone else who has an elephant hoof with ivory toenails. I actually like taxidermy—but only when it's certified as a natural-death animal and its life is respected.

Think about what you have on display and what it says about you. My friend once gave me a *Book of Panties* as a funny gag gift. It was actually really funny to look at, until I realized that if a visitor saw it, they'd think I'm either really kinky or a secret transvestite.

Another friend of mine had a book called *High Fashion Crime Scenes*, which was all photos of dead people looking super stylish—no doubt an interesting read, but perhaps off-putting for a visitor.

An overabundance of chick flick movies can ward off a gentleman caller. (While I love Kate Hudson, the prospect of watching her entire oeuvre of work on a Friday night makes me want to run for the hills.) Anything too babyish may bore your more mature friends or, worse, attract the wrong sort of man. Trust me, the sort of boy who wants to watch *How to Lose a Guy in 10 Days*—or play with dolls and hair bows—isn't someone you should plan a romantic future with.

Are You an Interiors Guru or Grump?

QUIZ

The way you treat your belongings says a lot about you. If you don't know how to use a hanger or a vacuum you're going to have a hard adjustment to real life and relationships. But, on the other side of the coin, if you're obsessive about your space, you might be missing out on other things in life. Take this quiz to see what your interiors say about you.

1. When you walk into your bedroom, your floor consists of:

- (A) A cute little rug by the door, and then another vintage carpet by my bed. And there are some shoes neatly laid out by the door.
- (B) Um, everything I own. Here's the outfit I wore yesterday to the gym (still sweaty!), and there are some of the McDonald's French fries I in a late night binge (so good!), and somewhere around here is my dog.
- (C) Absolutely nothing. It is spotless, bare and so clean I could eat dinner off of it or perform heart surgery. It shines like a mirror.

2. Where did you get your desk?

- (A) I found it for an affordable price online and built it myself!
- (B) What's a desk?
- (C) I use a stainless steel butcher's table as a desk. Less germs.

3. If your grandmother suggested you take an old table of hers for your first apartment, what's your instinctual reaction?

- (A) Old things can be just as good as new ones—sure, it may need a little elbow grease and a new coat of paint, but it will look as good as new in no time. And I like that there's a little character and a story behind it.
- (B) Yeah, sure, I'll take it. Just clear a path, move that pile of trash and oversized sweatshirts into the corner, and put it over there. I needed a new surface to display my shot glass collection anyway.
- (C) Old? Oh no no no, I don't do old, darling.

4. Does your house have a theme?

- (A) Of course it does: I'm doing minimalist and modern, so I have a lot of glass, dark wood, clean surfaces and framed photos.
- (B) Maybe. Would you consider 'overrun youth hostel' as a decorative theme?
- (C) Are you kidding? Every single room of my house has a theme: The bedrooms are Moroccan, the kitchen is 'country weekend,' the living room is Art Deco and I turned my entire basement into a tribute to Versailles' Hall of Mirrors.

5. What's on your walls?

- (A) I have a few family photos, amateur artworks and vintage movie posters.
- (B) Well, I think that's ketchup over there. Or, you know, blood.
- (C) In my minimalist rooms there is nothing but white walls.

6. Is there anything in your house that you don't let people touch?

- (A) There are a few things that I would hate to see broken, so I've put them on shelves and would take them down before I had company.
- (B) You can touch anything you want at my house, honey. Anything.
- (C) You mean like my collection of crystal vases? Or do you mean the white silk brocade lounge chair I bought at a Sotheby's auction and haven't let anyone sit on?

7. What's your theory on clutter?

- (A) If things are particularly crazy for me, I'll let my stacks of papers and magazines get a little unmanageable.
- (B) Clutter is like butter: the more the merrier!
- (C) If everything is not in its appropriate place by the end of the night I can't sleep. No, really, I have nightmares that old newspapers and taxi receipts will come get me in my sleep!

8. Who helped you design your place?

- (A) I spoke to a few people—my friend, who's a decorator, and my mother—but ultimately I went with what I liked and what I thought would look fabulous in my place.
- (B) I got all this crap by myself, thankyouverymuch.
- (C) Only the best for me: I hired the leading decorator in my town, had him over, and then rented another apartment for four months while he decorated my entire life.

9. Who's your ideal houseguest?

- (A) Everyone is welcome here: my family, my friends, someone I work with. But I'm also happy just being home alone with my favorite things.
- (B) Honey, I'm going to need a can of gasoline and a match before I ever have company in this place.
- (C) The Queen of England.

QUIZ KEY

Count up all your answers and see which of the three letters you had the most of. If you are:

Mostly A's. Organized Olivia: It's nice to see a young woman who knows her way around her house. While a house is your personal showcase, it doesn't need to be as meticulous as a hospital and as stuffed as a department store. You want to live in your space, and enjoy it. You know the value of keeping a clean house, and making sure a visitor feels welcome. I'll come over for a visit anytime!

Mostly B's. Messy Molly: Get it together, girl! While it's ultimately much easier to live like a slob (and yes, I'll agree that people who actually like to clean are a little freaky), it's very unhygienic and can lead to very unhealthy life choices. You don't need to scrub your whole house with a tooth brush (assuming you have one of those), but make small steps to start cleaning up and de-cluttering your house. It will reflect in your life too.

Mostly C's. Spoiled Sheila: This is sort of tricky territory: While I admire a clean, organized and disciplined young woman, there's a fine line between organized and having obsessive compulsive disorder. Houses are meant to be lived in, to be used as entertainment space, and enjoyed. No one wants to visit a friend if they live in an overly polished, uptight, fragile castle. Come down from the tower and have some fun!

Q&A:

A Lady Decorates

The best part about creating this book has been the responses it's caused among the young women I've met at my book signings, over e-mail, and even on the street. There are some smart girls out there, and they've had some fabulous questions. I liked some of them so much I wanted to include them here.

Q: *What's the ugliest thing you've seen in someone's home?*

A: My pet peeve in personal décor is an overabundance of pictures of the person who lives there: It's rather gluttonous and embarrassing. Beyond that, I once went to the home of a person who had taken nude pictures of their mother, which were graphically displayed everywhere. I didn't know where to rest my eyes!

ME ME ME

Q: *What's an easy way to decorate a wall?*

A: I have always thought that if it's nicely framed, you can convince someone that almost anything is art. A childhood sketch, an old movie poster—anything that is framed nicely can be a chic wall cover.

Q: *What's the craziest thing you have in your house?*

A: Hmm, with all my trips to vintage shops and antique stores, I have acquired my fair share of ridiculous knickknacks. But perhaps the most ridiculous is my collection of ashtrays—I don't even smoke! And cigs are strictly *verboten* at my house.

Q: *Is there one thing in your house you'd never want to leave?*

A: For the past few years I've been going through an embroidered pillow phase. I think they're so funny and old school, and quite ridiculous. Here are two of my favorites: one that says, "You can't be too rich or too thin," which isn't the best message to put out there but still a funny one; and then another one that reads, "Too much of a good thing is simply wonderful," which is an old Mae West quote that puts a smile on my face.

Q: *What's the most beautiful home you've ever been to?*

A: The fashion designer Valentino has a chateau outside Paris, seen here, that is so luxurious and so exquisitely decorated that it makes your eyes melt.

Q: *If you have surprise company, what's the most important thing to have cleaned up?*

A: This is bound to happen to all of us: the unannounced visitor. The first thing I do is try to hide the dirty dishes—there is nothing more unsightly then filthy dishes with caked-on, dried-up food. Gross! And then—this is a good tip— I scoop up all the clothes on the couch, chairs, and floor, lay them as flat as I can on the bed, and then make the bed over them. (If someone asks, just explain you have a really fluffy duvet!) Then, stack up any papers, put them on a desk or the side of a table, and break out the Lysol! Voila, a clean house!

Q: *What do you love to see when you go into a house?*

A: While I'm a major fan of minimalism, blank walls drive me crazy. (Note: there's a major difference between the clean lines of minimalism and a neglected white wall.) Your house should be a form of self-expression, so dress it up! Put out your favorite books and your personal photos. And while you don't need to keep your place as polished as a hospital, take pride in your personal space—or no one else will.

Q: *Is it annoying to bring a pet to someone's home without asking?*

A: This can be tough, and it ultimately depends on how badly behaved your animal is. If it routinely makes a mess or makes noise, don't bring it to someone's home, especially if you have ever been asked not to. Always ask first, but also be aware of your dog's temperament—Is he a good boy like my dog Monster, seen here? (OK, he's not always a good boy.) Is he used to new places and people? Or will he be frightened by a crowd and pee everywhere? (It's never a good look to be that person whose dog left a special "present" in someone's shoes.)

A Lady
Goes Abroad

―

"The world is a book, and those who
do not travel read only one page."

SAINT AUGUSTINE

TRAVELING WAS ONCE A LUXURY enjoyed only by the wealthy. Then it was a pastime shared by all classes, and increasingly it has become a necessity. Whether you're packing up the station wagon to visit Aunt Sue across town, or filling up the Range Rover for a weekend camping trip with friends (best of luck to you, if it's the former), or jetting to South Beach for spring break, or trekking around Europe on a museum tour, the fact remains: You will at some point in your life have to pack up and ship out. And although a taste for spontaneity is a crucial part of the travel experience—in my mind, the best thing about leaving home is breaking away from the familiar—it pays to do some prep work long before you ever buy your tickets, or fill up your gas tank.

The modern young woman knows that travel is beneficial; she also knows how to get herself from point A to point B with ease. She knows what to wear when she's traveling, and she knows how to behave when she gets to her final destination. Whether she's traveling to L.A. for the Oscars, or flying to Missouri for Mother's Day, she knows it's important to honor certain travel conventions. Most important, she knows that traveling—on budgets both big and small—is a critical part of a rich and fulfilling life.

The world has never been smaller than it is now. Planes are faster and safer, trains run on time (well, some of them do), and bigger and better highways are being completed every day. So do yourself a favor and go somewhere new. Who knows? Maybe you'll even like it.

See the World!

The world today is smaller than ever: Find out for yourself

When I was a young man— I'm talking middle school here— my parents decided that it would be a good idea to pack me up and send me off with a bunch of other brats to the United Kingdom for a month. (Their rationale had something to do with encouraging my independence—the bonus was being free of me for a few weeks, no doubt.) I was, of course, excited about seeing a far-off land, but I was also absolutely terrified. Questions raced through my mind: How would I make it in England alone? Would I make new friends? Would I actually have to learn stuff? Would I be forced to call French fries "chips"?

As so often happens (but not always, as I will happily point out to them when given the chance), my parents were right. My first trip to Europe ignited in me a passion for European history, for experiencing different cultures, for meeting new people and being open to new ideas. Everything from Shakespeare to Doc Martens seemed different and better to me after that trip. I came back with a renewed appreciation for paintings, for good books, for street fashion, and for the sacrifices my parents had made for me.

To be completely honest, I can't say that if they hadn't pushed me on that trip I would be the same person that I am today. I might not have had the motivation to save up my money in order to send myself back to Europe nearly every subsequent summer; I probably would not have had the courage to introduce myself to new people, a skill that has served me well ever since; and I definitely would not have had the courage to move from Missouri to New York City to attend university without knowing a single person in the big city.

> "He that travels much knows much."
>
> THOMAS FULLER

> "Laziness travels so slowly that poverty soon overtakes him."
>
> BENJAMIN FRANKLIN

Not that learning new things and meeting new people are the only benefits to be gained from traveling. You might benefit from spending a few days alone in the Canadian wilderness with your thoughts and a good book (for the record: This sounds like hell to me), or maybe you're into yoga and might benefit from a hatha retreat on a beach in Mexico (this sounds only slightly better).

That's the good thing about getting out of the house and trying something out of the ordinary: Maybe you'll find something new—or someone new—that you really love. Or, at the very least, you'll discover something you really hate, which is equally as useful. (I've learned, for example, that I don't like muddy music festivals, and that I can't relax in the ridiculously fast-paced cities in the Far East.)

I have to acknowledge that not everyone will love traveling as much as I do. Indeed, I have met people who are much better off staying within a three-mile radius of their homes, who are afraid of planes and cars, who get claustrophobic at the mere thought of sitting next to a stranger on a train. For those people, traveling to Asia to see the real-life geishas or taking that bike tour of France's Provence region might elicit nothing more than a severe panic attack.

But for the rest of us, for any adventurous and passionate people out there: Trust me when I tell you that there's nothing more exciting than experiencing in person the places that we typically only read about in textbooks and novels and blogs. So see the world. Believe me: It's a beautiful place.

INDIA

GREECE

SYDNEY

EGYPT

SOUTH AFRICA

SWITZERLAND

Some Notes on New Places

Whether you're crossing the street or crossing the ocean, it's good to keep a few things in mind when you've changed your location

When I was studying and living in London, I had the oddest exchange with a local Englishman on the Tube (that's *subway* in American). I had been talking to a friend, in my American accent of course, when this gentleman came over to strike up an initially pleasant conversation about (as Winston Churchill once described it) our two countries separated by a common language. Suddenly—I'm still not really sure what set him off, though I'm sure booze was a factor—he flew into a rage and started chasing me through the train's carriages and onto a platform. It scared the tea and crumpets out of me.

Ever since then I've been a responsible (and careful!) traveler.

I don't mean to discourage you from talking to strangers or taking public transportation. But the lesson I learned was that it pays to be cautious when in a new place—whether visiting a family member a town over or moving to a foreign country to go to college. Make some mental notes about your new environment. Stay alert, aware, and on guard.

Obviously, a good idea is to make as many accommodation and travel plans as you can in advance (so you're not trolling the streets of a new city for a youth hostel) and to accumulate facts about the place you're going to (so you're not walking around Brazil speaking Spanish, which I did once for about a week, embarrassingly enough).

Another thing I always do is print maps off the Internet of the location of my hotel and any restaurants, museums, event spaces, or clubs I know I'll be visiting. (It's easier to fold up a piece of a paper than it is to bring a map if you're going out at night.) Likewise, if you're in a foreign city and have the inclination to take a late night stroll, ask the concierge of the hotel you're staying in, or the owner of the house at which you're lodging, what a safe, well-lit route might be. If you're going abroad, go ahead and jot down the address and number of local embassies—just in case.

If you want to go out and party, keep your wits about you. If you're walking to the venue, try and make a mental map of the route you've taken to get there. Remember that you made a left at the store with the green letters and a right just past the boutique that had the funny-looking transvestite mannequins in the window. I once had a few too many drinks in Venice and had to walk home; I didn't know much else, but I knew the street two down from the building with skull-door handles was where I would find my hotel. If you want to get absolutely trashed, do so in your hotel's lobby or at a friend's house. Worse comes to worst: raid the mini bar. You'll get screwed on the prices, but at least you won't wind up in a gutter.

Basically, the best advice is pure and simple common sense. Don't get into a car with a drunk person (or a stranger). Don't split up from your friends if you're wasted. Don't lose your wallet and don't flash cash around. Don't mouth off to a local or get into fights because, um, people who live in another city probably have more friends there than someone that is just visiting. I know, I know: When you're on vacation it's really easy to let loose, but we've all heard horror stories about people being robbed—or worse—on spring break. (Not to mention, you want to be able to remember spring break when it's over.)

And, for heaven's sake, if someone tells you it's not okay to drink the water—seriously, don't drink the water.

While it's true that English is a very common language around the world, especially in touristy locations, it is 100 percent not true that everyone speaks English. Pronouncing words more slowly or screaming louder won't help a person understand a language they don't speak, and repeatedly asking questions like "How can you not speak English?" not only makes you look foolish, it makes you look rude. (I have to bring this up because when I go abroad I see this happen at least once a day, without fail.)

If you find yourself in a situation when you can only speak English to someone, be polite. Either wait to talk to another person who does speak English, kindly ask a passerby to play translator, or get really good at talking with your hands. If you're buying something, chances are the vendor wants the business and will be patient.

In the same vein, if you've studied another language and think you have some mastery of it—even a small amount of fluency—don't be afraid to use it. It's the only way your proficiency is going to get better, and no matter how badly you speak, there will always be someone who speaks with an even worse accent (like me). Yes, there's a good chance that the person you're speaking to won't understand you, but in nearly every case the person with whom you are speaking will be impressed—or at the very least, amused—by your attempts. (Just don't be offended if he or she answers your questions in English.)

Even the Parisians, the notoriously snooty group of Frenchmen, are often amused and delighted when their despised American tourists try their hand—or vocal cords—at the local language. Though they have a hard time showing it.

A Lady has a valid passport at all times. Who knows when a travel opportunity will arise?

A Lady knows the best things to bring with her abroad are a smile and a positive outlook.

"Many shall run to and fro, and knowledge shall be increased."

DANIEL 12:4

Travel Etiquette

Airports and train stations are not playgrounds, so don't act like a kid

I can remember the very first time I saw images of a pornographic nature. I was a teenager escorting my grandmother to a family reunion at my aunt and uncle's house in Little Rock, Arkansas. We were sitting on the airplane, minding our own business, when the person sitting across the aisle from me produced a plastic-sheathed magazine of a most suggestive nature. Porn! On a plane!

I couldn't look away. But I wasn't looking at the large-breasted women touching themselves in the weirdest of places. I was trying to sneak a peek at the guy who had actually bought porn in an airport and thought it appropriate to whip it out on an airplane—when he was sitting next to a fourteen-year-old kid and his grandmother!

Since then I've always been curious about what other people are thinking when they travel. (Computers have only made matters worse—I've actually seen people sneakily trying to watch dirty movies on their laptops.)

The perverts aren't the only ones who annoy me. I can't stand people who act like they've never seen a security line, who act surprised when their belts, telephones, or other metallic objects set off the metal detec-

tor. Security procedures are completely degrading—people root through your things, pat you down, run a metal detector across your body—and it's common courtesy to ensure this process is as quick and painless as possible.

Remember this: A lady knows how to go through a metal detector with ease. Please keep the studded belts, giant nose rings, and dozens of metal bracelets

> "Not all who wander are lost."
>
> J.R.R. TOLKIEN

in your bag until you've landed safely at, presumably, whatever Gothic conference you're going to. (It's also a good idea to keep medications and jewelry in your carry-on bag: If you check them and either get lost, it could be a fatal tragedy indeed.)

If you're on a train or bus, please keep your cell phone conversations to a minimum, and if you have to be on the phone, don't scream. Chances are, the whole bus doesn't have a vested interest in what Billy did to Susie at homecoming. If you're

sitting by the window on an airplane, don't wait until the person next to you is almost asleep to ask to use the bathroom—and if you have a small bladder, quit requesting a window seat.

Be polite to the people sitting next to you (especially if this is an overnight flight and you plan on sleeping), and respect others' personal space; this means no sparring over the elbow rest. Keep the volume on your headset or your computer at a decent level. Not only because listening to headphones at high volumes can permanently damage your eardrums and affect your ability to hear later in life, but also because the person next to you probably doesn't want to watch whatever questionable films you're into secondhand.

And last, while this isn't exactly an etiquette issue, it's something all ladies on planes should be aware of: drink lots of water to stay hydrated, and don't drink caffeine so you can rest and wake up looking great. [See "Tips on Jet Lag," p. 147.] Try and steer clear of very salty food before getting on a long flight. The body swells enough at that altitude, and salt will only worsen the situation. Trust me, no one wants to touch down in paradise with a newly sprouted pair of cankles stuffed into her shoes.

Lady vs. Tramp: At the Airport

The all-important airport chic: because your travel outfit might be your most important social asset

Tom Ford, the legendary designer who brought sexy back to the Gucci brand before leaving the company to start his own successful menswear company, once told me that he's never more disgusted with the state of fashion than when he's at an airport: the terry cloth and velour jumpsuits, the sneakers, the dirty T-shirts, the nappy hair. To be honest, I never realized what a crisis the aviation industry was in until he pointed this out. If he hadn't, I probably would have continued (mistakenly) thinking the real crises of international travel were gas prices and airline bankruptcy, and not the way more pressing issue of the shabbily dressed masses. No, really—next time you're at the airport have a look. For every power suit or chic skirt you see, there will be at least a half dozen poorly dressed layabouts schlepping around a Diet Coke, a pack of gummy worms, and the newest issue of *People* magazine.

I'm not suggesting that American Airlines enforce a dress code (or should I?), but it's important to look nice when you travel. Think about it: Now that the entire courting phase of a young person's dating life has gone out with hoopskirts (there are fewer debuts and cotillions every year, and church mixers

A Lady knows to pack an evening look—or at least something to wear to dinner—in her carry-on baggage. What if her luggage is lost?

A Lady can put on mascara in the back of a car and on an airplane.

A Lady knows that planes, trains, and buses are the only places in which she can sit mere inches from a stranger and not say a word to him or her for the duration of their time together.

A Lady looks presentable at an airport. Those leisure jumpsuits are for being at home. The airport is one of the last remaining places to meet eligible men who can afford to travel.

are harder and harder to find), the airport is one of the few remaining places where you might randomly meet a good guy. You should want to look your best.

Look at it this way: Chances are, the people in airports come from stable families and have, at the very least, enough money for a plane ticket. Which, in this day and age, is already a giant pro.

> "To a wise man all the world's his soil."
>
> BEN JOHNSON, VOLPONE

It's not too difficult to put together a sensible look: well-tailored jeans or trousers, a nice jacket, a cashmere sweater, something that flatters your figure, and a very little bit of makeup.

Your future boyfriend might be right there at the Chicago O'Hare Airport, bored off his tail on a layover like you are, but he doesn't pay any attention to you because you're trolling about the Hudson News kiosks smelling like McDonald's with ketchup running down your Juicy Couture jumpsuit.

At the Airport

Given that the venue is teeming with single men, you'd think girls would put more effort into their appearances. But no, you see far more skanked-out, PJ-clad hoochie-momma's trolling the terminals than you do chic, put-together young ladies. For tips about how to dress chicly on the move, see this visual.

MENTAL STATE
With a smile on her face and a zip in her step, a lady like this is more likely to get that complimentary upgrade than the moody, drunk mess.

EYEWEAR
Sunglasses to cover superficial signs of tiredness are a good idea.

THAT'S YES CLASSY!

LADY

LUGGAGE
Most flights allow one carry-on bag and a personal item like a purse. These bags are chic and functional.

WATCH
A lady is always on time.

COMFORT CLOTHING
It's hard to get comfier than a plain white T-shirt (which can be layered under the sweater packed in your carry-on) and relaxed high-waist jeans. The jacket is tailored and chic, but baggy enough so it doesn't constrict movement.

FOOTWEAR
Simple boots that slide on and off—with a bit of a sexy heel—plus no-fuss, easy-to-remove jewelry are a must when you're going through security.

MENTAL STATE
Travel can be stressful, so please show up to the airport rested and alert. Not exhausted, sleep-deprived, or worse, drunk.

GROOMING
While there's no reason to call in a professional hair and makeup team for travel, you don't want to look like you've just woken up from a hibernation either. At least use a rag on your face and run a brush through your hair.

PAJAMAS
Even if you plan on sleeping on the plane, you don't need to show up looking like AirFrance is one big slumber party.

READING MATERIAL
Airplanes are one of the few remaining times you're safely away from your cell phone (well, for now). Why fill your head with something trivial? Try a book! [See pp. 312-15.]

TRAMP

THE THONG
If you're in big boots, flannel pants, and a stained sweatshirt, don't even try and be sexy. Besides, how can you sleep in those things?

ORGANIZATION
Getting from the entrance of an airport to your seat will require following basic protocol, including showing your ID and boarding passes. You know this, so don't act surprised when the airport personnel asks to see your license.

UGG BOOTS
Yes, they are comfortable. Yes, they are warm. But do you really want to parade onto a plane full of businessmen surrounded by the ugliest shoes in the world?

Big Trip, Big Bag, Big Decisions

There is nothing more stressful—and important!— than packing for a long trip

I've read my fair share of travel articles, most of which have provided predictably sensible and boring advice when it comes to packing for long trips. Like, "bring enough medication for the duration of your stay, since pharmacies are hard to find in foreign lands," or "bring detergent so that you can rinse out personal garments in the sink."

Occasionally I find these eminently practical lists are, well, too practical, particularly when the advice provided is: "Don't bother to bring any high heels or cocktail dresses for academic or business trips abroad." Here's the thing: You never know where your adventures are going to take you, so it's best to make like a Boy Scout (a heel-and-cocktail-dress-packing Boy Scout, anyway) and always be prepared.

Once a friend of mine and I went backpacking through India—which is typically not the most glamorous terrain, as the north is mainly desert and the south is all raves on the beach—but something told me to bring at least one smart garment. So amid cargo shorts, comfortable T-shirts, and gallons of bug spray, I threw in a spiffy Calvin Klein tuxedo jacket.

It's a good thing I did. While stopped in the city of Udaipur, we were randomly invited to have cocktails at the palace of the town's maharaja. My friend put on some jewelry and a floaty cocktail dress that she had also packed—just in case—and I put on a collared shirt, the cleanest jeans I could find, and that tuxedo jacket. We were wined and dined in decadent Indian form, before hitting the backpacking trail again.

Adventures take you to bizarre and unexpected places: That's the whole point of an adventure. So, yes, while it's important to make sure that you have the basics (a few pairs of jeans and trousers, sensible skirt, blouses that go with everything, and a few jackets), you want to make sure that through some clever styling of your own you have something for every occasion. [See "Vital Packing Tips" p. 146.] Pay attention to the necessities—especially when it comes to the important stuff, like first-aid kits and a needle and thread for buttons on the loose—but you want to make sure that you don't confuse *sensible* with *hideous*. Sure, you shouldn't bring anything you could absolutely not stand to lose—but that doesn't mean you should only bring what you

wouldn't mind throwing away. (It's better to just be responsible and not lose anything.)

The trick for shrewd, stylish packing is putting things together that can be dressed up or dressed down. Yes, pack a comfortable cardigan for your trip—but not that old, worn-in comfortable sweater that has holes at the elbows. The cardigan should be tailored, soft, and easily paired with jeans or belted over a cocktail dress. You should bring at least one pair of good, basic heels anywhere you go in the world. Throw in a little bit of statement jewelry—which doesn't have to be expensive— so you can pep up an outfit if you need to.

Maybe you'll meet your future husband while you're abroad, or at the very least enjoy a summer romance. Or maybe you'll find yourself in a situation when you want to go to a fancy restaurant that has a strict dress code. Even if you're following a specific itinerary, you never know whom or what you'll stumble on while traveling. That's another thing to remember to pack: an open mind for adventure.

Because, when opportunity knocks, you'll want to look cute.

"Nothing can take
the place of practical
experience out in
the world."

A. B. Zu Tavern

Suitcases should be well-made, which
unfortunately often means expensive. You
don't need designer luggage, but you want
a sturdy case that can withstand airport
abuse. One time, I bought a cheap suitcase and nearly had a heart attack when
it split on the journey home—and all my
precious material objects came out one
by one (um, underwear by underwear) on
the conveyor belt at JFK Airport. But the
case doesn't need to be pretty, and it definitely does not need to be flashy. Save
that kind of showiness for your purses,
handbags, and other accessories,
which people will actually see.

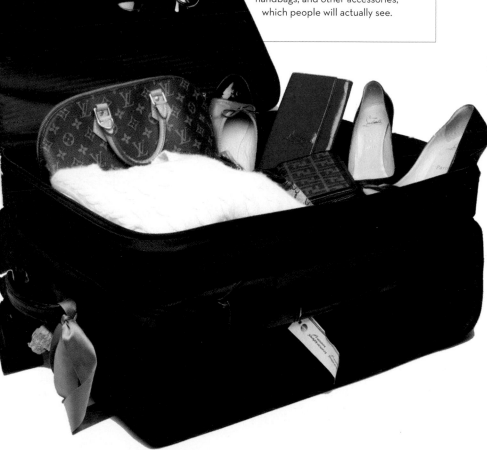

● **TOILETRIES**
When it comes to lotion, less is more. Unless you plan on wrestling with other girls in a bathtub filled with the stuff to pay for your hotel room, you won't need loads of fragrant lotions and body sprays. One trusted, favorite product—along with a simple facial moisturizer—should do.

● **BATHROOM ELECTRONICS**
Find out if your hotel has a hair dryer in the room; most do, even the less expensive hotels, which saves you the hassle of bringing one. If you must bring a curling iron or a flatiron, keep in mind you might also need a voltage converter, depending on where you are going. If you have to buy electronics abroad, prepare to be gouged on the prices.

● **MAKEUP**
Bring only what you use. Traveling is not the time to try out a slew of new lipsticks or a new palette of eye shadows. A girl should always travel with makeup,

but keep it basic: a favorite lipstick, some mascara, and powder.

● **OUTERWEAR**
Depending on the climate of your destination, bring a coat—or a trench coat at the least. Also, wear it on the plane to save room in your luggage. (If you're going to a cold destination from a hot one, hold it under your arm at the airport.)

● **DRESSES**
Always bring a little dress that can be dressed up or dressed down. Translation: no prom dresses. You want to wear something that is light and easy for a day of bumming around, but with the right accessories can also be jazzed up for a dressier evening, like a simple black wrap dress.

● **ACCESSORIES**
Brooches, a funky necklace, a hat, a belt that can go on top of everything and spice up an outfit—these are good things to have with you. But just because they go with everything doesn't mean they need to be expensive. If you do have a few expensive pieces, however, be

sure to pack them in your carry-on and store them in the hotel safe (along with your passport and other important items).

● **PAJAMAS**
Especially if you're staying with a friend, make sure you haven't packed inappropriate sleepwear. That can mean anything from stained shorts to smutty lingerie.

● **SHOES**
Yes, be sensible about your footwear. Sandals, flats, and even tennis shoes are good when abroad, but squeeze in a pair of nice, versatile heels (like classic black pumps) just in case.

● **MEDS**
Don't forget to bring enough medications for the duration of your trip, and a few extras in case of an emergency or an unanticipated extension of your journey. Be sure to pack these in your carry-on.

● **EXTRA SPACE**
Leave room for stuff that you're going to buy, or pack a collapsible travel bag that you can use later.

TIPS ON JET LAG

Jet lag is the worst part of travel. (Well, it used to be—now customs interrogations, bag searches, and security can be pretty infuriating as well.) It took me a little while to get the hang of it. Here, after years and years of research—which included trials of herbal sleeping pills and staying up all night at bars until flight time—and some conversations with a few professionals, are the best ways to beat changing time zones:

⊘ Be nice to the body before you fold it up like a lawn chair for a gazillion hours. Get a good night's sleep the night before you travel and drink lots of water. Also, do not drink alcohol at the airport. (And, just 'cause no one told me: Don't show up drunk to the airport, even if you're scared of flying.)

⊘ Try to adjust your schedule in advance. In the days before your flight, try to stay up later or go to bed earlier, depending on whether you're going to a time zone that is ahead or behind your own. This will help your body get on schedule right away when you arrive.

⊘ Don't drink anything with caffeine. The point is to sleep on long flights.

⊘ Come prepared. Put a pair of warm socks in your bag if your feet get cold (especially if you're dressed up, as you should be, in an airport). If you're a very light sleeper, bring earplugs and a sleep mask in case it's still light when you take off. Bring a big scarf to wrap around your shoulders— while the airline might have blankets available for lending, they are probably very, very skanky. I quite happily use airline blankets to warm my legs—but they don't get near my face.

⊘ If possible, don't eat before you fly—no matter how tasty the Sbarro, McDonald's, and Chevy's look in the terminal. When you wake up, have a big breakfast. Soaking up some sun can also trick the body into thinking it's your usual morning time.

⊘ Medications can be dangerous. One time, I took a sleeping pill and was forced to drag my bags, while I was drooling and half delirious, through the airport after a last-minute gate change. Another time, my aunt fell asleep next to a stranger and (humiliatingly) curled up in his shoulder nook. The body should be awake and alert when it lands. You'll have a hunch of silly paperwork to fill out and a rude customs official to talk to. If you do take a pill, try the natural ones, like melatonin.

PLAYLIST FOR CHILLING OUT

Song	Artist
"Waiting for the Miracle"	LEONARD COHEN
"Universe"	SÉBASTIEN TELLIER
"A Tour in Italy"	BANDAID
"Haiti"	ARCADE FIRE
"God Only Knows"	THE BEACH BOYS
"Fantastic Voyage"	DAVID BOWIE
"Starry Eyed"	ELLIE GOULDING
"Sands of Time"	CUT COPY
"Mahalo"	RATATAT
"Your Voice"	SANTIGOLD
"Never Forget"	FLEETWOOD MAC
"Mer du Japon"	AIR
"It's a Wonderful Life"	SPARKLEHORSE
"In the City"	CHROMATICS
"House Jam" (Hot Chip Remix)	GANG GANG DANCE
"Asleep at a Party"	MEMORY CASSETTE
"Dear Miami"	RÓISÍN MURPHY

RECESSIONISTA Travel on the Cheap

Let's get this straight from the beginning: You don't have to be rich to see the world. Even when I was a student, even when my budget was so tight I couldn't afford to live in a parking space in a New York City garage, I did a pretty good job of seeing the world on the cheap. And I wasn't just traveling to Third World countries where you can pay for things in cigarettes or barter farm animals for silver. I was hitting up cities like London and Paris, and traveling to places like Northern Africa and Brazil.

I now have more frequent-flier miles than I ever thought I would—I've been to every continent apart from Antarctica—but I still employ tricks to keep the cost of my travel reasonable. The first thing I do when I get to a new place is find a local grocery store and fill my hotel room with fresh fruit, water, and snacks. Hotel menus are often loaded with surcharges. On the rare occasion that I forget something, like a voltage converter or toiletry, I never get it in the hotel lobby. Prices there are always jacked up, and often there will be a store nearby that sells those items at a more affordable price. On my first trip to Europe, I bunked at a local family's house in order to keep expenses down. (I will never forget the lacy pink bedroom of my homestay in Scotland.)

Other tricks? Fly coach. Stay in a youth hostel. Ask a friend if you can sleep on his or her couch for a few nights. (But only for a few nights. Don't abuse your houseguest privileges.) [See "Staying with Friends, and Staying Friends," pp. 156-57.] If you're lucky enough to be staying in a hotel, don't even

A Lady can
fit in anywhere.

"See one
promontory,
one mountain,
one sea, one river,
and see all."

SOCRATES

think about touching the mini-bar, and bring your own DVDs so you're not tempted to pay-per-view. If you can't afford a hotel, try backpacking and camping. Research the subway and bus systems on the Internet before you arrive, and figure out how to use them. Remember to bring student IDs for discounts at museums and never turn your phone on unless it's an emergency to avoid outrageous long distance bills. Yes, being a

jet-set playgirl is an expensive vocation, but we no longer live in a society where trust-fund babies are the only people who can move around the globe.

Look for special airfare promotions and for discount packages. Try traveling on less high-volume fly days (during the week) and avoid traveling on popular holiday weekends. I always browse the travel section of the newspaper, just in case there's a good article on a place I'm interested in seeing. The *New York Times* wrote up a discount guide to Croatia a few years ago, which I clipped out and stored. Now if I ever get my act together and get to Croatia, I'll know where to find a cheap hotel and how to score some cheap eats (of, um, whatever they eat over there).

Something else: Make sure you don't get schnuckered by a dodgy travel salesman or representative. Only fly legitimate airlines and please use common sense: Don't buy a travel package from someone who is selling "funtime" packages out of a cardboard box in the mall, or from an organization that doesn't have a phone number or a secure website. If it seems too good to be true, it probably is.

Remember: Just because you have the money to stay in a five-star hotel doesn't mean you'll have a five-star time. (Though, I'm not going to lie: It does help!)

There's a possibility you don't know what kind of vacation suits you best. (Or perhaps, like me, you're the type who enjoys any type of travel.) This short diagnostic quiz will help ensure you don't find yourself in any situation— or country, or strip club—you don't like.

1. Your favorite drink is:

    (A) Anything containing vodka (but no juice or full-fat soda—ew, calories!), preferably served at a swim-up bar or beach rave.
    (B) An expensive specialty martini, preferably carried to you by a waiter in white gloves and a traditional jacket with tails.
    (C) Tea, homemade, from the chamomile growing in your window boxes.

2. Your idea of paradise is:

    (A) Dancing until sunrise on the beach.
    (B) A walking tour of the historic art district in a foreign city.
    (C) Doing sunrise yoga on the beach, alone.

3. Your favorite weather is:

    (A) Sunshine, baby. Bring on the baby oil!
    (B) Nothing too bright, but nothing too cold.
    (C) Cool; perfect for hiking or cross-country skiing.

4. The suitcase of your dreams contains:

    (A) One sarong, four string bikinis, baby oil with SPF O, and a box of condoms.
    (B) Books, books, and books, a travel set of encyclopedias, and SPF 45.
    (C) A yoga mat, organic granola bars, and lots of breathable layers.

5. The ideal travel mate would be:

    (A) Whatever hotties I meet at the pool!
    (B) My long-time boyfriend.
    (C) My portable Buddha statue.

IF YOU ANSWERED

Mostly A's. You are a One-Woman Wet T-Shirt Contest: Book your holidays somewhere warm, preferably where swimsuits are optional. Just be sure to stay safe. And at least read a book on your way to Cancun.

Mostly B's. You are a Lady and a Scholar: You should look into a European tour. Read up now about what museums to check out. But don't be afraid to let your hair down while you're away.

Mostly C's. You are at One with the Universe: You might enjoy yoga retreats, hiking trips in the mountains, and horseback-riding adventures out west. But try to get a friend or two to join; there is such a thing as too much alone time!

There's Something for Everyone

There isn't a rule that says every vacation must have beach time, museums, or family fun. No, the point of getting away is finding something that you actually want to do!

Different types of people like different types of vacations. People with body issues may not be rushing to showcase their skin on the beaches of Cannes; they might prefer to trundle around in London's West End in mid-autumn, wrapped in all the body-concealing scarves and jackets they could ever desire. My literati friends might like to visit the homes in which their favorite early 19th-century British writers lived. Other friends of mine, who don't have body issues (and, coincidentally, don't care where Shakespeare lived), might prefer to go to tropical destinations near the equator packing nothing but tiny bathing suits, and spend as much time as they can damaging their skin with harmful UV rays. (For the record, because I fancy myself a Renaissance man, I can do both the English-writer book tour and the Mexican-beach retreat. I'm an all-seasons travel kind of man, myself.)

So the good news is this: No matter what you're into, you can find a trip or an excursion that is sure to tickle your fancy.

But just because you think you've found a place you'll enjoy doesn't mean your work is done. Read up on your destination, buy a guidebook, and either print off a map of where you're heading or, at the very least, GoogleMap it. It doesn't matter if you're just going to Miami for a week of clubbing (if you can make it the whole week—trust me, techno music and fluorescent lights get really old really fast), make sure that you know what else is going on in the area. Specifically Miami, for example, has more than just a bunch of tanned hot bodies in skimpy Lycra outfits; it also boasts several great art galleries and a newly fledging Design District with great modern design exhibition spaces and great shops.

Don't let yourself get talked into taking trips that don't interest you, even (or especially) if it's a good friend doing the talking and persuading. I can't emphasize this enough. If you love fancy cruises where the most you exert yourself is hoarding shrimp cocktail and champagne at the all-you-can-eat-buffet, don't agree to go with a friend on a budget backpacking tour of the Scandinavian Peninsula.

On the other hand, you have to keep an open mind. As a child I traveled a lot. We're talking the entire travel spectrum: I followed my mother on work trips to the West Coast. (She was the one that instilled in me my hatred and fear of overpriced hotel minibars.) I went with my grandmother on fishing trips to small creeks throughout America's Midwest. My father liked to visit his brother in a little cabin in the middle of nowhere; for the first few years of my uncle's tenancy, the place didn't even have electricity. For a time my brother lived in Switzerland; when I visited him, he introduced me to a whole new world of veal and sausages.

To be honest, these places might not have been my first choice for travel destinations—give me a fashion show in Paris any day—but the experiences I had on these journeys, and the memories I cherish as a result, are irreplaceable. Even though I like electricity and hate fishing, I credit my sense of adventure with these early travel experiments; and I like my sense of adventure even more than I like the Ritz Hotel in Paris during fashion week. (Well, almost as much.)

My parents packed me up and sent me on my first tour of Europe when I was just in eighth grade, tapping into my nascent desire to see the world and try everything once. Maybe you're not especially adventurous, but surely there's something in this great big world that suits you: like a traditional English football match, which I enjoyed with Emma Watson (a), or an NYC bike ride, which I watched Kanye West do with Joy Bryant (b). My friend Evan Yurman and I did a road trip down to New Orleans and saw a whole array of American landscapes (c), and further south I met some new friends in Rio de Janeiro (d). Whether sailing close to home with Byrdie Bell in Connecticut (e) or venturing to the far corners of the world—like Moscow, here with Barbara Bush (f), the Great Wall of China, with Eugenie Niarchos, Olympia Scarry, Elisa Sednaoui, and Tatiana Santo Domingo (g); or India with Jacquetta Wheeler (h)—I have yet to find an adventure I didn't like. And sometimes, going home can be just as festive. That's me back home in St. Louis, hanging out under the city's famous Arch, with my friends Christopher Bollen and Chloe Sevigny (i).

Cameras: Perfect for Memories (and Blackmail!)

Without fail, the moment that you'll want your camera the most is when you've forgotten it at home

There are two types of people in the world: Those who take pictures, and those who don't.

I am very happily in the first category (witness some of my handiwork on the opposite page). But the number of people who venture camera-less into the world routinely shocks me. I've been at birthday parties where no one—not even the birthday girl—is packing a digital device with which to record the special moment. It confounds me: We live in a day and age when cameras are so small they can fit into the palm of your hand (or on the tip of a ballpoint pen, if you're into that spy store stuff).

I can't imagine life without my photo album. Not to pat myself on the back here or anything, but I love my pictures: I love to take them, I love to look at them, and if they're particularly good, I love to print them out big and give them away as presents. [See "Thank You, Come Again," p. 158.]

As I am often the only one with a camera, I often receive some much-appreciated attention as a result of my tendency to photographically commemorate important moments (being the sole person in possession of a fabulous group picture has a way of making you very popular). More good news? If you're the only one with a picture of a friend standing next to the guy she's crushing on, you have an excellent bartering tool in your hands. (Now what was that she said about refusing to lend you her new sundress?) In the same vein, a really bad picture can easily become great blackmail!

Not every camera has to be fancy or expensive. I have some friends who cannot make their newfangled, swanky cameras function—and their pictures are worse than dodgy camera-phone photos. (Plus, they freak out when they leave their gazillion-dollar cameras in taxis or nightclubs, which unfortunately happens all the time.)

When I was living in London not long ago, I used disposable black-and-white cameras pretty much exclusively—and the pictures turned out great. Now they have disposable digital cameras, so there's no excuse not to have one.

Since you can print photo albums, greeting cards, and digital frames from the comfort of home nowadays, even the laziest photogs in the world should have no trouble preserving their memories in convenient digital and print format. (It's hard to imagine that our parents had to—gasp—wait a whole three days to get their film rolls back. Life was so hard back then!)

Sure, there are a few things everyone should know about taking pictures. Most of it is common sense: Don't take pictures in museums or nightclubs that specifically prohibit photography, and when you get a new camera, do yourself a favor and at least scan the manual. Also, it's great to try to get candid shots, but make sure you're doing your friends a favor by trying to catch them on their good sides.

Etiquette-wise, when you're taking a picture of someone you don't know (for example, someone famous), be courteous about it. Don't try and be sneaky and get a picture of him or her chowing down on a slice of pepperoni pizza; be polite and ask. In most cases, the person will say yes, so snap away quickly to avoid generating interest from a posse of people who will want to do the same thing. If he or she says no, the person is probably a jerk. And there's no need to take pictures of jerks; it only gives them the right to be bigger jerks.

As a person who routinely looks back on his pictures with pride, nostalgia, and a sense of accomplishment, trust me when I say that toting around a camera is a gift, not a burden. (And oh, if you do shoot digital, don't forget to back up your hard drive!)

I very rarely leave home without my camera, a trusted device I use to make a record of all my memories. And I've captured a few choice memories in my day: Like the time a few friends and I caught Joan Rivers at a live stand-up comedy routine in New York (b), or when Leigh Lezark tried to get Blake Lively and Penn Bagley involved in a game of charades (c). Some experiences just don't happen more than once, like the time I busted Heidi Mount and Liv Tyler in the men's room in Paris (h), or when I randomly found myself at a dinner with Mary-Kate Olsen, Kylie Minogue, and Alison Mosshart (e). There have also been a few fabulous nights out, like this picture of Kate Moss, sitting on Mario Testino's lap, admiring Natalia Vodianova's beauty at a party in London (i), and when I went clubbing with Brandy, Jessica White, Nicky Hilton, and Serena Williams in Miami (a). Sometimes it's just nice to take some snaps of the beautiful people, like Beyoncé, here with my friend Marjorie Gubelmann at a Grammys party in LA (f), and Florence Welch and Karen Elson, in New York (d). But the moment when I was so happy I had my camera on me? When Courtney Love struck up a conversation with my father at an Elton John fundraiser in New York (g).

Check In, But Check Yourself

Many people have learned the hard way that hotels are not fun houses

I have a very good friend who is a very bad hotel guest. In fact, she has been entirely banned from a very posh hotel in West London after leaving some candles burning in her room and nearly incinerating the entire place. The bellhop will call the police if she so much as walks by on the street.

You don't have to be a rock star (or a cockroach) to be an undesirable hotel guest. I have stayed with fancy friends who eat in bed, stain the sheets, throw cigarettes out the window and into the courtyards (or just stub them out in the sink), and berate the staff. This is most definitely not sophisticated behavior. It reeks of entitlement and bad manners, and it's not a good way to behave when you're relying on others for a good time and smooth service. [See "Never Be Rude," p. 180.]

I think that one reason people let themselves behave badly when they stay in hotels is because, well, that's the point of vacation: You don't have to worry about making your bed or cleaning up after yourself. Even if you don't want to flush the toilet—which, for the record, is disgusting—you can rest assured that at least once a day someone will make sure the bowl is fresh for your next visit.

Relaxing on holiday is fine; treating your place of temporary residence like your personal opium den, or festering brothel, is not. Whether you're staying at a five-star hotel by yourself or sharing a common room with a few other backpackers in a youth hostel, make sure that you treat your space with respect. You don't have to give yourself the white-glove treatment, and make your own

A Lady doesn't make maids cry, and neither should her hotel room.

bed and put a chocolate on your own pillow, but remember: Hotels aren't playgrounds.

Respect the people who work in the hospitality industry, particularly the maids. It is customary to tip the bellhops and busboys, though it is not required. (Do so if you think the service is worth it—otherwise carry your own stuff, which I do if I'm strapped for cash.)

Don't steal things. Don't be obnoxious to fellow hotel guests. Don't host raucous late-night parties or prank call strangers

in other rooms. (They'll get you back, trust me. Maybe they'll be louder the next night, when you're dying to sleep, or charge $200 worth of drinks at the bar to your room. I have been the victim of these revenge techniques and much, much worse.)

Full disclosure: I'm not telling you this just because it's nice. I'm not telling you all this to make you a better person. (But, yes, those are bonuses.) I'm not worried about whether or not the staff likes you, whether you'll get a free upgrade on your next visit, or whether your travel companions think you're a courteous person. I'm telling you this as a warning.

Think about it this way: There are countless things an angry maid can do to you when you're not around. You think that towel is clean? Or that those are freshly laundered sheets? Only if you've been a good guest, I would say. If you've left a particularly nasty room for a maid, what do you think she'll do if she has a few moments alone with your toothbrush? The mere thought makes me want to avoid hotels forever! And the dangers don't stop with the maid service: Mistreat a busboy, and you can go ahead and expect that the vase you bought grandma will be "mysteriously" crushed in your bag.

So, ladies, listen up: If you want to make sure your material possessions stay safe and the hygiene of your toiletries isn't compromised, you have to play nicely.

Perhaps as a kid you read the story of Eloise, the precocious

"One travels more usefully when alone because he reflects more."

THOMAS JEFFERSON

toddler who lived in the Plaza Hotel in New York City; she got away with a lot of bad behavior. But remember: Unless you're an adorable fictional storybook character living in the 1950s, you can expect that the hotel staff just won't put up with much nowadays.

Staying with Friends, and Staying Friends

While it's often cheap and comfortable to stay with a friend or loved one, it's not necessarily easy

There is nothing better than a slumber party. And I'm not just talking about the ones you had as a little girl when you'd do your friends' hair and makeup, gossip till dawn, and prank call boys (man, those were some good parties).

As you grow up, chances are that you'll continue to be invited to spend the night with friends or that you'll be invited to a fancy fete in a far-off land—unless you haven't followed my advice about being a gracious guest or oversharing.

I'm lucky enough to travel a lot, and I generally prefer to stay at a friend's house when I'm in a new city. It's the most effective way of living like, and pretending to be, a local. Sure, hotels can be fun once in a

"Never lose sight of the fact that the most important yardstick of your success will be how you treat other people—your family, friends, and coworkers, and even strangers you meet along the way."

BARBARA BUSH

while—I love twenty-four-hour room service as much as the next person—but after a while, it's nice to have a family room, cable, and the security provided by being in a real home with a loved one.

But being a good houseguest requires some consideration. The first thing to keep in mind is that when someone tells you to make yourself at home, he or she doesn't actually mean that you should make yourself at home. Don't trash the place, leave your clothes on the floor, eat all the food in the fridge, or spend hours in the bathroom. In fact, it's always best to check before polishing off the Chinese takeout in the fridge or getting into the shower. (I once forgot to ask if anyone needed to use the bathroom at a friend's apartment before I began my beauty routine. Turns out my host needed to use the restroom just as I was taking over and had to drive to the gas station to relieve herself. Needless to say, I haven't been asked back.)

It's also a good idea to know when to leave—you should tell your hosts of your departure date before you settle in, and unless there is an emergency, you should keep to that date.

Going in together on flowers can make a housewarming cheaper, like I did here with Karolina Kurkova and Jaquetta Wheeler at a house party in New York.

The amount of time you may comfortably stay varies depending on your host's temperament and your relationship with him/her: You should be able to gauge whether you've been invited for a weekend or for a month.

Some other general rules: Keep the same hours as your hosts—if they get up early, you should get up early, or at least act like you're trying to. If they go to bed early, get used to tucking yourself in right after dinner. (No one wants to be kept up by someone staying in his/her house, and no one wants a houseguest who sleeps until four p.m. either. It's quite rude.)

Another tip: Bring a pair of pajamas. I made this mistake once, assuming that since I wasn't sharing a bed with my friend, it would be fine if I slept in an old T-shirt and a pair of short shorts. Let me tell you, there is nothing more humiliating than being caught in your underpants making a peanut butter and jelly sandwich in the middle of the night by a friend's father. Not only do you feel silly, you then have to sit there and have that late-night chatter while still in your panties.

Remember to show gratitude to your hostess. When I show up at a friend's house I often already have a present with me—

maybe some champagne or a houseplant. If you don't bring a gift, be sure to leave one, or at the very least a nice note that you leave on the bed or on the kitchen table. [See "Thank You, Come Again," pp. 158-159.]

Last, be fun and be grateful. I say *fun* because no one wants to invite a Debbie Downer or Sad Sally to spend the weekend. Even if you don't feel like mingling or chatting, too bad—when you agreed to stay at your friend's house, you agreed to socialize. Locking yourself in a room, or the bathroom, is extremely rude, and will guarantee that you will never be invited back.

In addition to drinking from a friend's milk carton, here are a few things to never, ever do when being a houseguest: snore loudly, walk around not wearing clothes, steal stuff, sleep in, go to bed late, make noise, be a remote control Nazi.

Thank You, Come Again

Make sure your host thinks you had a grand time (even if you didn't)

When I show up at a friend's house I usually have a present with me, whether it's a nice candle or some fresh flowers. Once, I brought a friend a fish as a thank-you, but apparently it died soon after I left. (So while I got points for originality, it kind of put a damper on the festiveness of the present when Goldie the Goldfish went belly-up.)

These little mementos don't have to be expensive ('cause nowadays, those designer candles can set you back). Without getting too Suzie Homemaker here, there are other great ideas, like a nice potted houseplant, or a garden herb, or a picture frame. For a long time I used to bring along framed pictures I had taken of my friends.

I also went through a phase when I would get people unconventional teapots. Not the ones that you find at a mall, but the quirky, odd ones you can find at antique stores or in cheap knick-knack stores. Don't be afraid to try something unconventional: The best present is one that the recipient wouldn't have bought him or herself, and one that they'll remember.

Gourmet coffee beans are great if the host or hostess is a caffeine-fiend, and cookies will endear you to friends who have a sweet tooth. You can even leave a fancy kitchen gadget, if your friends are into cooking.

Coffee-table books are also good, but make sure you know what you're looking for (and at). Don't give a large book of Robert Mapplethorpe's graphic nudes to someone extremely prudish. Bonus points for proving to the host that you actually know what he or she is into.

A Lady knows it's the thought that counts, but she makes sure it's not a second thought.

You can't go wrong with a book of beautiful fashion photography—and remember to sign on the inside of the book, so they remember who sent if for years to come.

If you don't feel like getting creative—or if you're cramped for time—you can always fall back on the tried-and-true presents: bottle of champagne, chocolates, or a nicely worded note you leave on the bed or kitchen counter to be discovered once you're gone. While it's nice to show up with something, it's not necessary: You can send thank-you presents after you leave too (the traditional thing to do is bring a present and leave a note). And the good thing about something like flowers is that they can be ordered and sent conveniently from your computer—and can make you seem much more thoughtful than you actually are.

Even if you never plan on visiting your host or hostess again, even if you have a miserable time, you should always leave a home confident that you will be asked back. And these little mementos, in addition to making you look like a nice girl, will ensure that that happens.

A Lady **leaves a token of appreciation behind her after staying with friends.**

ALTERNATIVE THANK YOU PRESENTS

1. A book *for the intellectual*
2. Coffee beans *for those needing stimulation*
3. Flowers *for the aesthetes*
4. Picture frame *for the nostalgic*
5. A handwritten note *for the sentimental*
6. Champagne *for the boozers*
7. Or something crazy (like this fish) *for the creatives*
8. Something monogrammed *for anyone who's hard to buy for*
9. Candy *for a sweet tooth*

What's Your Travel Style?

It isn't surprising that different people favor different sorts of vacations and have different travel habits. For some, paradise is Sex on the Beach on the beach. (I'm talking about the drink here, you perverts.) Other people prefer guided educational tours; still others might prefer to stay home and catch up on their TV shows. But for those wondering what their travel style is, and which sort of vacation best suits their personality, there's this handy quiz.

1. A friend asks if you would like to accompany her on a trip to Cancun for a long weekend in the sun. Your first thought is:

- (A) *I'll need SPF 60 to go anywhere near the beach, and a can of pepper spray in case a drunk frat boy tries to talk to me.*
- (B) *A long weekend with a good friend? Sounds like fun. But it's too bad that Cancun isn't known for its cultural events.*
- (C) *Absolutely. Booze is cheap there.*

2. Ever since you finished E.M. Forster's novel *A Passage to India*, you've wanted to see this distant, exotic land. So you:

- (A) Buy every guidebook about India you can lay your hands on, and then implore any of your Asian friends to take you with them on the next family reunion.
- (B) Buy a guidebook, read up about the country, and start saving your cash for a plane ticket and accommodations.
- (C) Decide it's too far from the local 7/11 and rent *Slumdog Millionaire* instead.

3. It's time to pack. The first thing you do is:

- (A) Buy all-new luggage and an all-new wardrobe, then handstitch your name into everything.
- (B) Lay out your trusted suitcase and your favorite clothes (after consulting "Big Trip, Big Bag, Big Decisions on" pp. 144-45 for tips, of course).
- (C) Go to the kitchen and grab a garbage bag and some duct tape. Instant luggage!

4. You're at the airport. After boarding the plane and locating your seat, you:

- (A) Disinfect the cushions with an alcohol-based spray and put on your surgical mask.
- (B) Sit down quietly, power off your electronics in anticipation of takeoff, and apply some hand sanitizer before you break into the free snack bags.
- (C) Plop yourself down, taking up as much room as possible, not sharing the armrest. You still reek of the McDonald's Double Quarter Pounder you ate at the airport, but who cares?

5. In the middle of the trip you need to use the restroom. Unfortunately, you've requested a window seat, which means you need to squeeze past the person sitting next to you, who is sleeping. You accomplish this by:

- (A) Holding it until the person next to you gets up to use the bathroom herself.
- (B) Politely waking the person when you can't wait any longer, and excusing yourself.
- (C) Either climbing over the person next to you, or using the airsickness bag as a makeshift porta potty.

6. After checking into your hotel room, you realize the room hasn't been cleaned, or isn't exactly what you expected. In response, you:

- (A) Race out of the room, scream at the manager (calling him a "worthless sack of incompetence"), and then cry.
- (B) Put your things in a corner, go to the front desk, explain the situation, and walk around the city for an hour while the room is cleaned.
- (C) Don't notice. It's certainly cleaner than your own house.

7. It's your first day in a new city. What to do?

- (A) Wake up at the crack of dawn and hit as many tourist hot spots as possible, racing through them so fast you can't enjoy a single one.
- (B) Wake up early, have breakfast, consult your guidebook, and figure out which museum you want to see first.
- (C) Sleep until whenever and check out whatever landmarks are visible from your window. Then go to the hotel bar for happy hour.

8. When it's time to check out of the hotel, the people behind the reception desk:

- (A) Are happy to see you go. In fact, as you climb into a taxi, you think you can hear them cheering.
- (B) Thank you for staying with them, and ask you to fill out a feedback card.
- (C) Are still wearing the gas masks they put on when they had to clean your room.

QUIZ KEY

Count up all your answers and see which of the three letters you had the most of. If you are:

Mostly A's. Anal Annie: Despite what you may have heard, there *is* such a thing as being over-prepared and worrying too much. Even on academic trips it's okay to let your hair down once in a while. You don't have to completely abandon your stringent sense of How Things Should Be Done—but remember, the whole point is to try something new and *different*.

Mostly B's. Traveling Tina: That get-up-and-go initative, coupled with your willingness to try new things (and take small inconveniences in stride), are two of the best qualities to take with you on any trip. Keep doing what you do best: rolling with the punches and enjoying all that life (and the world) has to offer.

Mostly C's. Sloppy Sally: I've said it before and I'll say it again: Travel isn't for everyone. While seeing the world and experiencing new cultures are wonderful in theory, some people are better off renting movies that feature far-off lands and sticking to the comforts of home. You fall into the second category, so we'll let you stay homebound. It's better to confine your laziness (and general bad attitude) to as small a geographical area as possible.

Q&A:

A Lady Goes Abroad

The best part about creating this book has been the responses it's caused among the young women I've met at my book signings, over e-mail, and even on the street. There are some smart girls out there, and they've had some fabulous questions. I liked some of them so much I wanted to include them here.

Q: *What's your favorite place in the world?*

A: Call me a mama's boy because I love coming home. I've seen some amazing places in my travels, but I feel most relaxed back home in Missouri. (This is a picture of me with all my childhood neighbors at a book signing I did in St. Louis.) However, I will say that anywhere with sunshine and a beach runs a close second.

Q: *Did you go on your high school spring break?*

A: Ha! Yes, I did, and it was in Puerto Vallarta, Mexico. I was rather well behaved, although I can't say the same for some of my girlfriends, like the ones who ate worms in their tequila shots, entered wet T-shirt contests, and made out with each other to entertain the locals. (Not very classy, let me assure you.) Sure, they had fun, but if I ever need anything from them, I've got good blackmail pictures! There's a good tip: If you have a wild night on the town, do your best to avoid incriminating evidence! (And, for your amusement, here's my senior class portrait from high school. Don't laugh too hard!)

Q: *What's the most important thing to pack?*

A: When I leave for a trip, I make sure I have my passport, computer, iPod, camera, phone, and chargers for all of them. Everything else (even clean underwear) can be purchased abroad, although you'll probably pay a premium for it!

Q: *What's the best vacation you've ever been on?*

A: I don't think I can say just one, but I could probably round up a top three: First, a trip around India that I took with a friend will always be one of my favorites. We backpacked, took local trains with third-class tickets, and experienced the real India. Second, after I graduated high school, I toured around Europe alone and found out more about myself than I ever would have spending that summer at home. And finally, I once had a gig to cover a music festival in Rio de Janeiro: Mariah Carey, Grace Jones, and P. Diddy on the beach? It was a once-in-a-lifetime experience! Working in fashion has afforded me lots of fabulous trips, like the time I saw Mary J Blige perform at the private residence of the US Ambassador to France in Paris. Sure, fashion is a tough industry, but there certainly are some perks.

Q: *What's the dumbest thing you've ever done on vacation?*

A: There's something about being far from home that temporarily relieves us of our good sense, and I have more stories than I'd care to remember when it comes to stupid decisions. Getting in a fight with a friend in East St. Louis, Illinois, storming out of the car, and claiming I was going to walk home comes to mind. So does the time a friend and I got into a stranger's car in the desert of Morocco looking for a rave. (We ended up paying him to turn around when we couldn't see the end of the sandy road.) Once, I let a girlfriend go home with a DJ she had just met, which I've always regretted. I can't stress it enough: Travel should be fun but not dangerous.

Q: *Do you research a place before you go there, or do you go to be surprised?*

A: Research, absolutely! When I was younger, my mother used to buy me a guidebook for the country where I was going so I would know a little bit about the history of the foreign land and some convenient phrases. (Believe me, you want to know how to say, "Where's the toilet?" no matter where you go.) Now, I spend some quality time on the Internet, so I know some places of interest and tidbits. I'm sure some people think it's dorky, but what's the point of going to a new place and not retaining any of the information?

A Lady Makes Friends

━━━━━━━━━━

"The only way to have a friend is to be one."

RALPH WALDO EMERSON

YOU GIRLS ARE EVIL. Evil, I say! I've seen it my whole life: In high school, when y'all would fight over the same sweater at the mall and then over the same cheesy football players with acne problems; in New York, where socialites fight each other to have their pictures taken; on the West Coast, where L.A. girls fight over press and movie roles. Heart disease might be the number one killer of women (that's according to the American Heart Association), but girl-on-girl crime has to be the number one assassin of a lady's self-esteem.

But enough moaning. Instead of sitting here and lamenting how difficult it might be for a forthright and intelligent girl to form lasting relationships with members of her own sex, let's have a look at frenemies and backstabbers more closely; this way you'll be able to detect the early warning signs of inner trampness and steer clear. In addition, we should discuss some general friendship rules, including some Do's and Don'ts, so you can be sure that you're not slipping into Mean Girl territory.

As difficult as it might sometimes seem, forging true, meaningful relationships is possible in modern times. I've found a few good girls and boys as I've navigated this world, and chances are you will too. The trick is to do your part to seek out, cultivate, and preserve these relationships. A real lady is never lacking for friends.

Frenemies, Fair-Weather Friends,

I n my day, I've seen enough girl-on-girl crime—*Mean Girls*-type drama, when girls are randomly mean to each other because of insecurity, jealousy, or purely for entertainment—to write a whole series of made-for-TV movies on the topic. (Full disclosure: As a young man, I was a total mean girl.)

Girls stealing their friend's sweaters; girls stealing their friend's boyfriends; girls calling a friend fat behind her back. It's by no means a new problem. (If you want to know the true meaning of the word *backstabber*, look up the ancient Greek story of Electra and her mom, Clytemnestra.) And let's be honest: XX-chromosome-encoded meanness is not a phenomenon that's going to disappear anytime soon. As long as y'all are hormonal, you're going to have your bitchy days. I'm not blaming you for that, but something should be said for trying to avoid sustained bitchiness levels.

There are a few things a young girl can do to sidestep the drama ('cause there's no avoiding it altogether—the sooner you know this, the sooner you can be prepared). Apart from trying to keep your own man-and-sweater-stealing bouts to a minimum, be on the lookout for the type of girl who is friends with you only when it's beneficial to her: a fair-weather friend, who can often turn into a full-blown frenemy. [If you're not sure you can tell the difference, see "Are Your Friends BFFs or Backstabbers?," pp. 170-71.]

When I first got my driver's license, my parents always told me a good driver was a cautious one. Same thing applies here. With the exception of your ab-

A Lady knows how to give a compliment—and mean it. She also knows how to receive a compliment gracefully.

solutely bestest friend, don't say anything to a girl you wouldn't want mass e-mailed to your entire social circle. Be wary of girls who obviously want something besides your quality time, whether it's help with algebra homework or free rein at a new club where your boyfriend DJs.

When it comes to gossip, be careful about the rumors you spread and in what social quarters you spread them. Ideally, you'll learn to keep your mouth shut. And don't forget that if a girl is willing to bad-mouth other people behind their backs, chances are she's willing to bad-mouth you too.

While it's all fun and games to talk about the type of people you want to steer clear of, just make sure *you're* not the person others are avoiding. Don't say something about someone else that you wouldn't say to their face. (This isn't carte blanche to say mean things to people's faces, however. I used to be that guy—I would tell a girl she had an eggplant-shaped body to her face just as soon as I would say it behind her back—but then, I didn't have that many friends back then.)

Though at times this rule is nearly impossible to follow, it's completely accurate: If you don't have something nice to say, don't say anything at all. (Well, if you don't have any-

and Backstabbing Bitches

"True friends stab
you in the front."

OSCAR WILDE

thing nice to say, you can say it to me—but in general, it's in your best interest to keep it to yourself and your bestest of friends.)

You've probably heard the expression "Kill them with kindness." And you've probably laughed at it. To be honest, I used to think that only wussies—and spineless girls incapable of sticking up for themselves—would follow such silly advice. (Although I think some important person in the Bible said something about turning the other cheek. . . .) It wasn't until recently that I realized just how effective this tactic can be at deadening the drama. Here's the thing: Nine times out of ten, a girl is mean to you because she is either jealous or wants attention. That one other time is because she's (1) evil, (2) a sociopath, or (3) just so wrapped up in her own world she's unaware of her own level of spoiled bitchdom. Unfortunately, we all know at least one girl like that.

When a girl spreads a rumor that you're fat, or that you had your stomach stapled, or that you have bad breath, or that you're a slut, it can be difficult, nearly impossible, to ignore. But generally speaking, she is looking to provoke you and looking for you to respond, and doing so will only make things worse (just like scratching an itch only brings relief for a second—afterward, the itch gets worse). I have a friend in New York City who is the picture of elegance—the expensive clothes and real diamonds and blowouts, the whole package. She described this situation with

"We all went through a bitch phase that makes us cringe when we remember it. We tried being good; we tried being bad; we made other girls feel like shit before we knew what it felt like."

CHLOË SEVIGNY

"Always forgive your enemies; nothing annoys them so much."

OSCAR WILDE

"It's the friends you can call up at four a.m. that matter."

MARLENE DIETRICH

the most perfect, if somewhat surprising, analogy: "Shit doesn't really stink until you start poking it." And then it reeks. So don't let an evil girl trick you into poking her shit.

Here's the tricky thing: Ideally, you want to make sure you're on the good sides of the meanest girls in town. Mind you, there's a difference between staying on their good side and being their best friend. This social dance is a bitch—actually, they're a bitch—but that's life. You have to keep your friends close, and your frenemies closer.

Apart from the fact that ignoring drama and being nice to people who are unkind to you is an unexpectedly efficient way of dispatching a rival, I truly believe in something I would like to call Estrogen Karma. It's like karma—the ancient Indian belief that actions are cyclical and that what you put out in the world will come back to you— but specific to emotionally unstable ladies. If a girl spreads a rumor that a friend's boyfriend is unfaithful, chances are later in life she will marry a philandering husband, who will leave her for a secretary, a hooker, or a friend. Or, even worse (for her—though infinitely more entertaining for the rest of us), a man. If a girl tells everyone that another girl is fat, she will never lose her pregnancy weight. I firmly believe in this idea, because I've seen it happen. I've seen perfectly beautiful young women turn into hideous beasts as they've grown into evil, manipulating bitches.

So it's a simple equation: If you want to be pretty when you grow up, be nice now.

IF ____ HAPPENS	A GOOD FRIEND	A BAD FRIEND
You've put on a skirt and it's just a little bit too small	Politely suggests you wear those black pants that are so flattering on you	Calls you fat; or tells you to wear it so that she looks skinny next to you
You've lost a lot of weight	Compliments you on how great you look, but doesn't mention the weight loss specifically	Asks if your secret was bulimia, anorexia, or chemotherapy (and she's not kidding)
You have new heels that are hard to walk in	Walks arm in arm with you until you get your footing	Parks on a cobblestone street and calls you Frankenstein
If you have a particularly bad experience at the salon getting highlights	Tells you they look great	Asks where you got them done—so she knows to never, ever go there
You've been fired	Says she's heard you left your job	Says she's heard you got the axe
You've just started a diet and you've gone to dinner together	Gets a salad and asks if you want to go splitsies on an entrée	Orders mozzarella sticks for a starter and then a cheeseburger for a main course
You've had an onion and your breath is a little funky	Discreetly passes you a breath mint	Announces to a large crowd that your new nickname is Fire Breath
You're late to meet up with her	Waits, no problem	Is gone when you arrive
Your culinary experiments have gone awry	Says nothing and eats whatever she can salvage from the burnt chicken	Has already ordered a pizza by the time you get out of the kitchen

Are Your Friends BFFs or Backstabbers?

It has been said that if you have one real friend in life, you've had more than your share. However, you'll certainly meet more than just that one friend, including people who seem like buddies—and turn out to be anything but. Take this quiz and find out whether your friends are BFFs or fair-weather frenemies.

1. A boy has just dumped you, leaving you completely broken-hearted, depressed, and listening to really angry '80s rock alone in your bedroom. Your friend:

- **A** Sends you a generalized text saying that she hopes you're feeling better. You later discover she started dating your ex when you were busy sobbing to Metallica's "Enter Sandman."
- **B** Tells you your ex was a total jerk (even if he wasn't) and lifts your spirits by making you laugh.
- **C** Writes your ex hate mail and offers to spend every waking minute with you until you find a new boyfriend.

2. You're invited to a black-tie party, and your friend has a dress you think might look great for the occasion. It turns out the dress is a tad small. Your friend:

- **A** Gives you the dress anyway, then either makes you feel bad for not being able to fit it or makes snide comments about how much better it looks on her.
- **B** Admits that it's not the best dress for you, and either loans you a wrap to help conceal the unflattering spots or offers to help you find something else to wear.
- **C** Offers to go to every store in town to find the exact same dress in the next size up.

3. You're throwing a party, and you absentmindedly—completely by mistake—forget to include one of your friends on the evite. In response, she:

- **A** Tells everyone you're a slut, refuses to accept your apology and belated invitation, and then throws a competing party on the same date as yours.
- **B** Accepts the explanation you offer for the oversight, then happily comes to the party— with homemade artichoke dip!
- **C** Is just soooo happy to be invited, and is the first person to arrive and the last person to leave.

4. There's a rumor going around that you had an inappropriate relationship with a teacher/your boss, which is completely false. Your friend:

- **A** Tells you she hasn't heard it, even though *everyone* has heard it. You later find out she's the one who started it.
- **B** Sticks up for you when you're not around and changes the topic when you are.
- **C** Offers to assassinate anyone who says even one bad thing about you.

5. You're trying to live a healthier life, going to the gym and dieting. In response, your friend:

(A) Tells you it's embarrassing to sweat and eats chocolate cake and candy bars whenever you're around.

(B) Verbally encourages you and tries to eat healthily when you're around—even though she's a candy junkie.

(C) Buys you workout clothes for your birthday, joins your gym, and completely gives up carbs because once, in passing, you mentioned the Atkins diet.

6. It's raining, and your friend has two umbrellas. She:

(A) Opens one and keeps the other one hidden in her bag—what if the first one breaks?

(B) Gives you one of her umbrellas, then jumps with you in all of the good puddles.

(C) Insists you wait inside while she schleps through the rain to find you a taxi.

7. You're throwing a party, and at the last minute, your friend says she can't come. Her reason?

(A) She had a better party to go to—or was going out on a date with your ex.

(B) Her sister has unexpectedly come into town for one night only and insists on having family bonding time.

(C) Impossible. Your BFF would skip her grandma's funeral to spend a night with you at your party.

8. It's your birthday party, and your friend:

(A) Shows up late, dressed to the nines and proceeds to take the attention off you whenever possible. For example: When you're cutting the cake, she's asking your boyfriend to tighten her bra strap.

(B) Is on time, in a good mood, and has bought you a top you had on hold at your favorite store.

(C) Planned the party, had a sleepover with you the night before, schlepped you to the venue, is writing down who got you what, won't leave your side, drives you home, and gives you her present: a giant mural she painted of your face.

QUIZ KEY

Count up all your answers and see which of the three letters you had the most of. If you are:

Mostly A's. Your friend is a Backstabbing Bitch. But don't completely write her off. Sometimes a young frenemy can turn into a real friend—when she grows up and realizes how mean she is. The trick here is to keep this particular lady at a careful distance. (Keep your friends close, and your frenemies closer.)

Mostly B's. Your friend is a Loyal Lady. A good friend is hard to come by, so don't take her for granted. Make sure she knows you really appreciate her.

Mostly C's: Your friend is Crazy Glue: Just because a friend isn't mean to you, doesn't mean she can't be annoying as hell—and even a bad influence. Girls who try too hard to be your friends either don't understand that friendship should be reciprocal (fooling you into thinking it's okay to be some sort of queen bee), or will demand something from you in the future. Lesson? Be suspicious of girls bearing gifts. **SIDE NOTE**: *However, a person who fulfills the Crazy Glue criteria can often make a pretty good GBF. (Turn the page.)*

The GBF: A Lady's Secret Weapon

Never underestimate the importance of a Gay Best Friend

Often he's a hairdresser. Or a really great person to shop with. Maybe he does your makeup for you, or gives you endless advice about the silliest things, like shoes and boys. Perhaps he's the perfect roommate, a live-in stylist, or someone who vocalizes all the catty, screwed-up things you think of but would never say out loud. Who am I describing? Why, a girl's Gay Best Friend, or GBF, of course.

(For the record, I am completely aware that these are all stereotypes and generalizations. I have many gay friends, and, yes, some of them have bad taste and, no, not all of them work in fashion. I know some gays who hate Madonna and work in banks. But these types, no matter how sweet, don't always make for the best GBF—unless you're looking for financial advice.)

Every girl needs a GBF, just like she needs a pair of sunglasses and jeans that make her look ten pounds lighter. But there are a few guidelines to follow if you want to ensure that the GBFship continues to function smoothly. Two things a girl should know right off the bat: First, this should be a mutually beneficial relationship. It may seem that the girl is getting the majority of the perks here—the free fashion and relationship advice, the biting wit, the self-esteem boosters (these are just some of the services I offer to my stable of ladies)—but this is no Queen-and-Servant GBF dynamic. The gays need their love too; they need to be defended and coddled and spoiled. Friendship is always a two-way street. When that golden rule goes out the window, the GBF relationship often goes sour—and, trust me, you do not want

> *A lady* seeks the support and counsel of trusted friends.

> "We have been friends together in sunshine and in shade."
>
> CAROLINE ELIZABETH SARAH (SHERIDAN) NORTON

to piss off a gay who knows all your secrets.

The second rule to bear in mind: This sort of union cannot be forced. There's no formula for finding the perfect boyfriend or husband. Similarly, when it's time to decide on a homosexual male to spend your life with, it needs to happen organically. I was very young when *My Best Friend's Wedding*, a movie in which Rupert Everett plays Julia Roberts' wise and wisecracking GBF, came out (ha! Get it? When it came out? Never mind). Suddenly every woman in America was desperately trying to latch on to the first well-dressed, well-groomed homosexual man she saw. I know for a fact that many of those forced relationships ended in tears.

A word to the wise: A red flag when it comes to the GBF is how he gets along with a boyfriend or potential love interest. If your crush gets along with your GBF, at least you know he's progressive and mature—only the simplest, smallest-minded person would judge someone else based on his or her sexual preference. And if your GBF likes the guy you're thinking of dating, chances are he's good for you. But you will have to balance spending time with both of these men, which can be difficult. Be aware that you need to service them both. You do not want to see two grown men catfighting for your attention.

And if you really have to make the choice, be honest with yourself. Sure, love and boyfriends and relationships are important—but gays are forever.

FAMOUS GBF'S IN HISTORY

While the term Gay Best Friend is a relatively new one, beautiful women seeking moral and comedic support from same-sex-oriented male friends isn't exactly a new phenomenon.

Socrates and **Plato** thought that perfect love existed between a man and a boy—and I bet there was a special water maid they liked to dress up in different versions of the toga. **Alexander the Great** probably complimented a few women as he conquered the entire known world, perhaps even dispatching fashion advice to the willing; and you just know that **Leonardo da Vinci** told more than one young female the right way to swish her satin skirt. **Oscar Wilde**, the literary legend who went to prison for his alternative lifestyle, was perhaps the wittiest female foil, and gave tips to anyone who would listen (and often to those who wouldn't).

Examples from the twentieth century include bisexual French poet **Jean Cocteau**, a close friend of Coco Chanel's; designer **Halston**, who helped Liza Minelli pick the spectacular Upper East Side apartment I myself have been to; and **Elton John**, who counted Princess Diana as a confidant. **Truman Capote** had an entire stable of swans, as he called them, and **Andy Warhol** immortalized his favorite ladies in his portraits.

Nowadays, actresses and ladies-who-lunch often put their gays to work, which explains why so many of today's GBFs are hair and makeup artists, or personal stylists. It's like the fashion icon and Oscar-nominated actress Chloë Sevigny once told me about a hairstylist she considered one of her nearest and dearest: "I trust this guy with my hair, which is kind of a big deal. So he had better be my best friend."

Online Friendship Etiquette

The pen is mightier than the sword, though both can be used to stab a friend in the back

"You look so fat in this picture." Those seven words, conveyed via e-mail or text message, can be interpreted a variety of different ways. Maybe you intended sarcasm—maybe you sent this to a willowy friend to imply she looked so skinny, the idea of even deeming her chubby being absurd. But if your friend is a Sensitive Sally, she might read those words on a computer screen or the tiny display of a cell phone, and believe you are actually accusing her of looking plump. Cue downward depression spiral!

The point I'm making is that while the whole world goes viral, and friends and family are all available at the punch of a few keys on a mobile phone, we can't forget the importance of face-to-face communication. The Internet has of course redefined how to flirt with someone. [See "Online Flirtation," pp. 190-91.] But it has also had a significant impact on how we communicate with our friends.

I have to pay extra special attention when composing an e-mail or text—especially since half of my friends are ridiculously image conscious, and the ones who aren't typically speak English as a second language and take things literally. (To be honest, I haven't totally mastered this: I still routinely upset my friends with insensitive

:-(

"An injured friend is the bitterest of foes."

THOMAS JEFFERSON

"A man never discloses his own character so clearly as when he describes another's."

JEAN PAUL RICHTER

"We cherish our friends not for their ability to amuse us, but for ours to amuse them."

EVELYN WAUGH

e-mails and accidentally give them psychological complexes when I don't carefully think through a text message.)

Be cautious, and be aware. Choose your words wisely; think about what you're saying as you type it and the other ways it can be interpreted. I've actually lost friends or had to beg and beg for forgiveness when I've e-mailed something in jest, and the recipient has most definitely not seen the humor.

If you have something important to say, or if you're going to say something you're worried a friend might misunderstand, pick up the phone or wait until you see him or her in person.

This type of rationale does not only apply to the people sending potentially hurtful e-mails: If you're a recipient of an e-mail that you think may—or may not—be offensive, take it with a grain of salt. If the correspondence is from a good friend, try not to be oversensitive; if you can't let the issue go, pick up the phone and explain your feelings. Give your friend an opportunity to tell her side of the story.

And if your friend did mean it—if she intended to tell you via text message that your boyfriend is hideous or that your mother doesn't love you or that you're fat—at least now you know you need a new friend.

The Big, Bad Bloggers

Nowadays a girl's reputation can be ruined with a few strokes on a keyboard. But be careful; so can yours

It's going to happen at least once in your life: You are going to get very mad at a friend whom you love dearly. Maybe she leaks a secret of yours, or flirts with your ex, or wears your shirt without telling you first. Don't feel guilty just because you feel like throttling her—girls have been hurting girls' feelings since the beginning of time (I'm sure Eve was pissed at her first girlfriend at least once, probably for thinking she saw her flirting with Adam).

Things get dangerous, however, when you are tempted to exact revenge. Maybe, for example, you send a mass e-mail about your friend's recent pregnancy scare or call the paper to claim that she passed out in the bathroom of a strip club the night before.

Modern technology intensifies the risks and dangers of getting into arguments with friends. In previous generations, you might make up a rumor that a rogue girlfriend had a crush on the gym teacher or had really bad dandruff—and this rumor would go around your little social circle, create a few giggles, and then be forgotten. In time, both girls would be friends again. But with the aid of the Internet and social networking sites, when you

> "One of the most time-consuming things is to have an enemy."
>
> E.B. WHITE

> "It takes twenty years to build a reputation and five minutes to ruin it."
>
> WARREN BUFFETT

> "We can travel halfway around the world while the truth is putting on its shoes."
>
> MARK TWAIN

> "Tact is the ability to describe others as they see themselves."
>
> ABRAHAM LINCOLN

start a rumor or decide to ruin someone's life now, um, you can actually do it.

With a few clicks on the keyboard you can tell everyone that your former bestie has gonorrhea or just tried to seduce the married father of one of her friends. While technology is efficient in this respect—the meanest e-mails have a way of spreading faster than the nastiest colds—they can also be more damaging than even the most virulent flu.

Good gossip on the Internet has a life of its own; truly vile e-mails have a habit of being forwarded and forwarded (I know this from experience—receiving them, forwarding them, and having nasty e-mails of mine make the rounds once or twice), and if your friends have blogs or online messaging posts, whole new audiences can weigh in on your drama. Before you know it, a rumor can snowball out of control.

Here's the thing: Chances are if you were good friends with someone at some point in your life, you will want to be friends with her again. Maybe not best friends, but friends nonetheless. Feuds pass and hatchets are buried all the time. So before you tell a gossip website that you just saw your

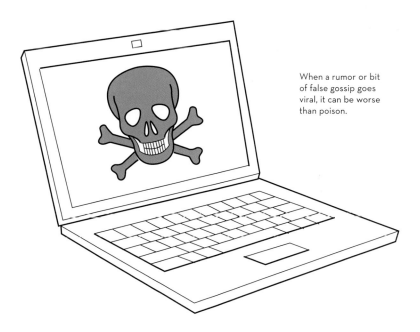

When a rumor or bit of false gossip goes viral, it can be worse than poison.

frenemy on all fours at a seedy West Village S&M club—before you e-mail someone's mother pretending to be Planned Parenthood with "exciting" news— think about the long-term consequences of your actions.

(Also, just FYI: There is no such thing as an anonymous tip or a protected source. Even if you think you are leaving an untraceable comment or an anonymous tip, you're probably not. I know people who found this out the hard way. Internet karma is a bitch.)

There's one thing I've learned recently about the Internet: The stuff that you want to go

A Lady
does not
spread rumors
online.

away the most never does. The stuff that is most cringe-worthy when you Google yourself will most likely be there for all time. So before you put someone else through that, ask yourself whether you really think he or she deserves it.

And if the answer is yes, you'll have to ask yourself another question: How will that person retaliate? 'Cause once the Internet is involved—once an audience of millions is prepared to chime in—you're playing a dangerous game, and just because you took the first swing, doesn't mean you're going to come out ahead.

Nobody Likes a Meanie

The real test of a person's character is when she meets someone—whom she thinks is no one—for the first time

It's important to be mindful of the feelings of your friends. But a true lady is equally sensitive to the feelings of strangers.

I have a friend who is a very successful male model in London. Before he hit the big time, however, he made ends meet by working as a part-time waiter, which has provided him with an endless supply of good-time gossip. On one memorable occasion, he took a catering gig at a charity function. One of the members of the English royal family made a brief appearance. While he served her several— and I mean several, as she went home quite sloppy—glasses of champagne, she never once made eye contact with him. While that was slightly rude (the conventions that dictated that a royal never make eye contact with the help have long been obsolete), as the fete went on, her behavior became more and more unruly. She snapped her fingers, snipped at him, and was generally abusive, all for her own personal amusement. At a charity event, don't forget.

His response to this gross display of arrogance? For the second half of this grumpy royal's attendance, her champagne was given an additional ingredient: his mucus. Yep, the (very distantly) possible heir to the English throne was downing sneezers that night. And I can't say she didn't deserve it.

(When I told this tale to a friend, she told me this was a junior-varsity story; she had once been to the country home of a sophisticated family who would punish an unruly or classless guest by using his or her soup bowl as a urinal. But I won't horrify you with the details of this "pee soup" here.)

This tale of the mucus-and-champagne cocktail has always reminded me of something my mother told me just before I moved to New York City: Be careful of the toes you step on today— they may be connected to the ass you'll need to kiss tomorrow.

I'm sure you've seen someone abuse a waiter, or a taxi driver, or a bathroom attendant. I always wonder whether these bouts of sporadic rudeness are actually windows into someone's true personality. They say that you can judge a man's character by the way he treats someone who can do nothing for him, and I think that is completely true (and applies to ladies as well). Only a complete jerk would get some gratification from being rude to a busboy—and ladies shouldn't keep company with insecure jerks. Also, a lady knows that those in

> "Be nice to nerds. Chances are you'll end up working for one."
>
> CHARLES SYKES

A Lady knows when to say, "Excuse me." And she says it.

A Lady knows to be herself. Unless she's an asshole.

the service industry—whether doormen or flight attendants—not only keep modern society running, they also perform a difficult job and deserve respect. Look, waiting on people is a hard job; and let's be honest, a lady needs help from hairdressers, waiters, and cooks, more than from anyone else!

This is not to say that everyone need be a spineless, complimenting lemming. But there's a fine line between being assertive and being a diva.

Let me clarify. Everyone knows the successful bitch. The diva type, who asks for what she wants and gets it. People gravitate to her because of her honesty, because she says what's on her mind. Sure, there are a few girls like that in the world, and more power to them. But it gets ugly when young people without that God-given ability to be a good bitch attempt to emulate their tell-it-like-it-is style, and wind up coming off as the Wicked Witch of the West Side.

Chances are you have met, or will meet, a mean girl who is popular at school, in the office, or in your social circle. Who knows why being evil works for her? It's one of those great mysteries of life, like why some people can eat whatever they want and never gain a pound, while others blimp up when they even smell a doughnut. Remember: Chances are it won't work for you.

There's a big difference between not accepting bullshit, between standing up for what you believe and living your life with integrity—and just being a mean girl because you see other people doing it. If you are the successful nice bitch, congratulations. And if you're wondering right now if you're the nice bitch or not, let me clear it up for you: You're not. So be nice.

Never Be Rude . . .

It can be tempting to let your temper flare, but in some situations it's critical to keep cool

I once did a story on the Venezuelan, New York City–based fashion designer and society icon Carolina Herrera. This was only a few years ago, but she looked the same as she did when Andy Warhol did her portrait decades earlier: chic, sophisticated, and in control. Mrs. Herrera is a nice woman—though she never accepts or receives anything but the best—and she once told me that there are a few people she would never, ever be rude to: airplane pilots and people who work in the restaurants she frequents. She explained that she is powerless with them. If a pilot wanted to give her the scariest ride of her life, or a server a bad case of indigestion, they could. So even if a waiter is a snippy, rude skank, she will smile, nod, and ask for her dressing on the side.

This makes complete sense to me. That's why, using the same rationale, even if I find myself in a situation during which I cannot take the aforementioned advice and be a nice person—when the urge to be an asshole overtakes me, I am never, ever rude to the following people: policemen and customs officials (especially if they're short; you can assume they'll have a Napoleon complex); anyone who works in government offices, most notably the Department of Motor Vehicles;

"Don't reserve your best behavior for special occasions. You can't have two sets of manners, two social codes—one for those you admire and want to impress, another for those whom you consider unimportant. You must be the same to all people."

LILLIAN EICHLER WATSON

or the girl who makes my nonfat venti chai latte every morning at Starbucks.

Here's why: Some policemen go into the force because they're power hungry, and some people work for the government or in a coffee house because they can't get a job elsewhere. So they're in a perma state of pissed off.

And while it might be tempting to tell that barista to pull her big lip over her face and swallow, hold back. 'Cause the second you let loose is the second that government official puts you on some list for permanent jury duty—or, even worse, when the barista gives you 2 percent milk when you ask for skim. Jerk!

... Unless You Absolutely Must

And then there are times when it's absolutely okay to get nasty

I'm suddenly anxious that I sound like some sort of tree-hugging hippie. Just because I think that a lady should practice random acts of niceness, or just because I think that a lady shouldn't be mean to strangers (or friends), doesn't mean that there aren't times to step up to the plate and let the bitch inside out of its cage. I do not believe that a girl should be a walking doormat for mistreatment.

Quite the contrary. A lady knows when and how to stand up for herself. Perhaps a man has tried to take advantage

of her; perhaps a classmate abuses her generosity; perhaps a former friend is belittling or degrading her. In such cases, fine. Let it out. Yes, be rude. Be a bitch. Do not be nice to someone who is attempting to manipulate or take advantage of you. A better recourse might be to walk away from the situation and move on, sure (no good comes from dealing with terrible people). But in case that tactic doesn't work, never

settle for second best. Never settle for being underappreciated or abused.

Breaking out the bitch is a last resort, however, so be certain you have no other options before you do. Anyone who is cruel for her own entertainment is not only rude, she's completely simpleminded. If the only recreational activity you enjoy is being mean to other people, you have a problem.

Buy a book, go to a museum, see a movie. There's more to life than being an asshole.

A Lady tips. Always.

A Lady is nice to waitresses, busboys, and doormen. She knows to respect the service industry.

A Lady does not snap at waiters. In fact, the only time she snaps is when she's musically inclined— and in that case, she better have rhythm.

"No one can make you feel inferior without your consent."

ELEANOR ROOSEVELT

"Don't be too afraid of making an enemy—sometimes courage and honesty require it."

LUCIA VAN DER POST

The Educated Insult

I f you've decided to temporarily sidestep your lady duties, or if you do find yourself in one of those previously mentioned situations when turning the insult meter up to high is necessary, please remember: A lady chooses her words—even the four-letter ones—carefully. I cannot tell you the number of times I've heard women get into an argument that is essentially the world's most boring linguistic tennis match, where "bitch" and "slut" are the only shots volleyed back and forth. Whenever I overhear those exchanges, all I can think is how much I'd like to get these two tramps thesauruses for their birthdays.

Insults are like parties: Only the really creative ones are memorable. If you need to insult someone, come up with something original. It will hurt way more if it's specific. For example, if your victim is a frizzy-haired girl who jumped on the boho trend of flowing dresses and fur gilets, then the term *slut* won't work. Try something a bit more original: perhaps "Chihuahua-faced tramp who looks like she's shoved one of her anorexic arms in a light socket before falling into a pit of dead raccoons."

Whatever you do, don't just call someone a slut. That's far too simple. (Unless the girl you're insulting really is a slut. But even then, there are ways to innovate. Try suggesting that she "start getting paid for it, since everyone gets free handouts anyway," or imply that she's like a birthday cake— 'cause everyone gets a piece.)

The fact is anyone can rattle off the b-word or the c-word. In fact, due in part to a bunch of silly twentysomething Hollywood rich girls and spoiled starlets who have popularized

A lady is careful with her words, even the nasty ones.

the terms, words like *bitch* and *slut* have become forms of endearment in modern culture. (Which, to me, is just weird. Because if a girl can offer her salutations to a group of her friends with a "See ya, sluts," or enter a room with a "What's up,

bitches?" what's to say a group of guys can't do the same? If you girls are going around calling each other bitches, you can't very well expect a guy not to, right?)

Besides, by using big words— after you've done your research and are 100 percent confident you know how to use them correctly—you'll not only have the pleasure of insulting the person who has upset you, but also of looking really, really intelligent. There's nothing more gratifying than leaving foes not only insulted, but confused and scratching their heads, trying to figure out just how insulted they were.

Believe me when I say there's nothing better than really hitting the haters where it hurts. Just make sure they deserve it.

"He is not only dull himself; he is the cause of dullness in others."

SAMUEL JOHNSON

"His mother should have thrown him away and kept the stork."

MAE WEST

"He has the attention span of a lightning bolt."

ROBERT REDFORD

"He has van Gogh's ear for music."

BILLY WILDER

"The trouble with her is that she lacks the power of conversation but not the power of speech."

GEORGE BERNARD SHAW

"She not only kept her lovely figure, she's added so much to it."

BOB FOSSE

"She was a large woman who seemed not so much dressed as upholstered."

JAMES MATTHEW BARRIE

"Her only flair is in her nostrils."

PAULINE KAEL

"She was so ugly she could make a mule back away from an oat bin."

WILL ROGERS

"That girl is so fat, she puts mayonnaise on an aspirin."

JOAN RIVERS

"I never forget a face, but in your case I'll be glad to make an exception."

GROUCHO MARX

"That woman speaks eight languages and can't say no in any of them."

DOROTHY PARKER

"He's a nice guy, but he played too much football with his helmet off."

LYNDON BAINES JOHNSON

How to Accept an Apology

It was a moment country music fans, hip hop followers, and those of us who value tween blonde singers above all else won't forget. In 2009, on live television, Kanye West bum-rushed the graceful and angelic Taylor Swift on stage at the MTV Music Awards, ripped the microphone from her hand, and announced that Beyoncé Knowles should have won Swift's award.

In the days that followed, it seemed there would be no apology big enough to warrant forgiving West. Even President Obama called the rapper a "jackass."

But why I find this story even more thrilling is how Swift handled the fallout. Instead of playing up to the legions of writers and bloggers who thought Kanye was pop's biggest bully, Swift accepted his apology and blew off the incident shortly thereafter. She made some jokes, released a few statements, and moved on to bigger things, like writing more catchy tween songs and cashing even more checks. Her behavior proves an important point: Gracefully accepting an apology is an admirable skill. Nothing positive comes from holding grudges.

Of course, if your best friend steals your boyfriend and sends you a text message with an apology the next day, I'm not suggesting the three of you go for brunch and act like nothing happened. Chances are, however, if she was truly a best friend, she'll miss you and realize it wasn't worth it. I can't emphasize this enough: Accept an apology when you're ready. While it's not always easy (I can attest to that!), fight off that grudge and leave the space in your heart for a sincere apology.

Though you may feel validated receiving an apology (there's a sick pleasure in having someone apologize to you, right? Or is that just me?), a grudge begets more grudges. I've been mad at someone so long I forget what I'm mad about, and I've spent twice as much energy avoiding them as I would expend just to say hi. Don't lose an entire

A Lady accepts an apology, even if she doesn't want to. There's nothing ladylike about a grudge.

friendship over something trivial. And don't start a lifelong feud when it's not deserved.

I once got into a big tiff with a friend because she felt snubbed that she wasn't invited to a party I organized for someone she didn't know. I missed her wedding, I wasn't at her baby's first birthday party, and—to make a long story short—I missed out on huge moments in her life because we were both stubborn.

It's one of my biggest regrets. Ask yourself if whatever your friend did is really worth giving her or him up for good. Often, the answer is no.

Accepting an apology isn't easy, and I know that. I've had some people do me wrong, and have wished them bodily harm and professional failure. Once, it was revealed that some random person was saying really cruel and awful things about me on the Internet, sending nasty stories to gossip sites, and leaving really brutal comments on other blogs, and I wanted that guy to get hit by a truck. But at the end of the day, the bigger person moves on. Be the bigger person.

While we're on the topic of accepting an apology, let's briefly touch on the topic of accepting a compliment, which is just as important. There's only one polite response to accepting a compliment—and that's saying thank you (and maybe offering one in return). To deny someone's compliment is insecure, and to bask in the glory is worse. I sometimes say thank you and add, "You're making me blush." And then you can change the subject.

How to Say You're Sorry

Though we would all prefer to be on the receiving end of an apology, chances are you'll end up needing to apologize once or twice in your life. And if you're reading this and thinking you rarely have to apologize, chances are you should be doing it a lot more. (Quit being so stubborn!)

First, never put off an apology. The longer you wait, the bigger your gesture will need to be. Really, there's no reason to hesitate: If you even think for a second that you owe someone an apology, then you probably do. Barring extenuating circumstances (like apologizing every single day, which is annoying), over-apologizing won't get you into as much trouble as never saying the words "I'm sorry."

Someone once explained to me that a true apology means that you've acknowledged that your actions have upset the other person, but more importantly, your admission of guilt will result in a change in behavior. So if you're saying sorry just to get someone off your back, yet you actually do not regret your actions, don't bother. Doing the same thing twice hurts twice as much, and people will stop taking your apologies seriously if you don't mean them.

Now that we've resolved to say those two important words—"I'm sorry," which are very different from "My bad," by the way—let's talk about how to do it. In person is always best, but when that's not an option, an impassioned written plea will work. (Snail mail will show extra thought, but if timing is an issue, e-mail will do the trick.)

A Lady makes an apology, not an excuse.

A Lady never uses a lie in an apology. That's a recipe for disaster!

There's no need to get into the details with an apology—just get to the point, which is the apology itself. Don't offer a long list of excuses. Instead, say that you've made a mistake and regret it and hope that the recipient will forgive you. In person, this requires turning and looking at someone head-on, having both shoulders facing their direction, and offering a from-the-heart apology with eye contact.

In text, that means sending an e-mail that is brief but poignant, explaining your desire to rectify the situation. Especially in an e-mail, don't write a novel: This person is already mad at you, so don't waste their time on top of it! After that it's a waiting game. A good friend will come back (even if the friendship has changed), and a bad friend won't.

A good "I'm sorry" can feel amazing, and maybe there will be some crying, soul searching, re-bonding with a person, and friendship growth. Renewing a relationship, moving on, having closure and a sense of pride in your behavior are all rewarding emotions. It's sad to say, but there have been times when I've wished I'd apologized much sooner and hadn't missed out on time together. Don't let the same thing happen to you, or else then you'll be really sorry.

Q&A:
A Lady Makes Friends

The best part about creating this book has been the responses it's caused among the young women I've met at my book signings, over e-mail, and even on the street. There are some smart girls out there, and they've had some fabulous questions. I liked some of them so much I wanted to include them here.

Q: *Do you still have friends from Missouri?*

A: I most certainly do! In fact, I have two girl-friends called Maria and Maja who have been my best friends for as far back as I can remember. (Maria was my first kiss, in kindergarten.) Here's a picture of the three of us at our high school graduation. We can go long stretches of time without talking, but as soon as we see each other it's like we've never left. When I moved to New York I definitely found myself rolling with a whole new crew, but childhood friends are like family. You have to cherish them.

Q: *Are your friends in New York divas?*

A: I will absolutely be the first to admit that I have some high-maintenance friends. But typically, they're such good friends, or so freakin' funny or totally loyal, it's worth putting up with a few diva fits. And let's not forget that there are divas all over the world: Pushy women with big personalities exist, even in small towns!

Q: *Is there a good place to meet a friend?*

A: I have made great friends in some truly random places: at flea markets on New York's Sixth Avenue and in the checkout line at an organic food market—and that's just a sampling. I'm always up for a funny conversation or learning something new about a stranger, and that positive attitude can be contagious. That said, places not to make friends include prison, court, police stations, the free clinic, and the gutter.

Q: *When do you know a friend is a bad person?*

A: To be honest, I've always thought that the way people treat waiters or concierges or busboys is a true testament to their characters. If I ever see someone I care about be rude to a member of the service industry, I cringe. And then I say something about it.

Q: *Who makes the first move in a friendship?*

A: I never thought about it like that, but yes, I guess making new friends (especially in a new place, like a new city or a new school) can be like meeting a boy or going on a date. I guess I've always been the first person to make a move, but my suggestion is never to hesitate to ask people for their e-mail addresses or if they want to meet up sometime. The worst thing they can do is say no, and then that's because they're probably rude jackasses you don't want to spend time with anyway. (So there!) But to be clear: similar to dating, you don't want to stalk, harass, or obsess over friends, no matter how nice they are or even if they have the same shoe size as you and fabulous high-heel collections.

HOW ARE YOU, TOOTS?

Q: *Is there ever such a thing as too many friends?*

A: I'm not sure if the answer to that question is a simple yes, but I know what you mean: People who overextend themselves when it comes to friends can run the risk of not making enough time for themselves, and that can show up in their diets or their attitudes. There's not a specific number of friends that qualifies as "too many," but if you feel like you're shortchanging someone— or yourself—think about the people who really matter in your life.

Q: *Have you ever been really disappointed in a friend?*

A: I've been blessed when it comes to friends. When I was promoting the first edition of this book, my friend Lauren opened up her home for the festivities (that's us on the top right). But when someone asks about crazy nice things that someone has done for me, I first think of my friend Dasha. Once, for my birthday, she sent me a singing mariachi band. Not the most practical gift, but as you can see from my facial expression, not one I'll soon forget.

Q: *What's the nicest thing that a friend has done for you?*

A: I've been blessed when it comes to friends. When I was promoting the first edition of this book, my friend Lauren opened up her home for the festivities (that's us on the top right). But when someone asks about crazy nice things that someone has done for me, I first think of my friend Dasha. Once, for my birthday, she sent me a singing mariachi band. Not the most practical gift, but as you can see from my facial expression, not one I'll soon forget.

A Lady
Looks for Love

"Every woman should have four pets in her life.
A mink in her closet, a jaguar in her garage,
a tiger in her bed, and a jackass who pays for everything."

MAE WEST

NOT TO SOUND TOO MUCH LIKE AN OLD SOUTHERN NANNY (as I'm prone to do), but I have to say: It is difficult for a young lady to find a good man nowadays.

Generations ago, girls had debuts and cotillions; they had chaperones and dances, society gatherings and church fund-raisers. Namely, there were a bunch of places that respectable ladies could go to meet respectable guys. And then they'd live happily ever after and go to the sock hop and drink a single milk shake from two straws and blah blah blah—who knows, it was the '50s. Before that, it wasn't uncommon for parents to make quasi-arranged marriages (which might not sound so bad when you're at home on Friday night, cruising online personals).

The problem is that today people don't know where to look for love (spoiler alert: The answer is not Hotbodies.com). Apart from school, college, or work, it's difficult to know where to go to meet a good guy. A bar? A house party? A sporting event? A chat room? In place of responsible chaperones and fancy balls, we have the Internet and webcams, which unleash a whole other set of romantic demons.

Modern technology has provided people with dozens of new ways to flirt with, trick, annoy, or dump each other. With cell phones, text messaging, e-mail, online social sites, Skype, video networking, blogging and—for those retro types—the telephone, getting dumped in person is almost unheard of anymore.

The truth is there's no formula (or Rules) for meeting and keeping a mate. Still, there are some big-picture facts that should be helpful to keep in mind: Don't play games and pretend to be someone you're not. When it comes to dating, like attracts like. A girl who acts like a nice lady will attract a nice gentleman, whereas a tramp will probably attract a douche bag. Read on for more thoughts on the modern plight of love.

Online Flirtation

The Internet has changed the way we flirt, and more technology has brought additional temptations to tramp it up

The Internet has changed the game; it provides a hundred new ways to connect and a thousand new temptations to tramp. (I've always been scared of dating when it comes to the Internet—the fact that a giant server logs every conversation, and, for you kinky girls out there, every picture, is terrifying.)

Imagine this: A stranger compliments a profile picture of you. Maybe this mystery suitor compliments your smile, or your braces, or the color of your eyes, or the way your sundress offsets your skin tone. (Hey, I've read worse.) And you decide you should write him back, or send him some more pictures.

This is all fine and innocent. Hell, it's fun. It's a thrill!

Here's where it gets weird: It's three in the morning and you're in the shower, setting the self-timer on your mom's digital camera so you can take a picture of yourself decked out in a (now-translucent) wet T-shirt and send it to this person whom you've never even met in the flesh.

Unfortunately, this predicament is increasingly common. It's like when that girl from *High School Musical*—one of the most amazing franchises in Disney history, by the way—made headlines for all the wrong reasons (hint: It involved an untrimmed pubic area, total

nudity, and photographic evidence). Surely she was mortified. (The picture was kind of sweet, actually—with candles lit and stuff, like she wanted to be romantic and intimate—but probably not with the millions of horny teens who ended up downloading the picture.)

The rules of dating have changed dramatically: In generations past a girl might get a haircut to get a guy's attention. Now, instead of trying out a new lipstick color, a girl can send pics of her nipple to anyone with a WiFi connection.

Think about it: Wouldn't a nice text message that says, "You're so cute," or even, "I

If this visual is too familiar, stop what you're doing and send a nice e-mail to anyone to whom you've sent that picture. And make a mental note to never, ever piss that person off.

want to make out" get the point across just as much as a poorly executed one-woman wet-T-shirt contest?

Take this advice to heart, girls: If the day comes when you want to show your private parts to a gentleman, you'll be much happier that you didn't give him a grainy, pixilated preview on his laptop.

A question to ask yourself before hitting "send": Is this

picture, video, or communication something you wouldn't mind having your girlfriends see? Would you be happy if the recipients' friends saw it? What about friends of friends of friends? Or complete strangers and maybe even your grandmother? If the answer is no to any of these, then you should abort mission.

Further, you should ask yourself if what you're doing is part of some romantic tale you will want to tell your children one day. In the narrative of your longest relationship, do you want the first few chapters to involve webcams and porno pictures?

This tale of nudie e-mails and file sharing is part of a larger issue. Beyond the fact that no one wants a picture of her yoo-hoo making the rounds on the Internet, the simple fact is this: Being intimate with someone is something to do in person, when you can actually touch each other. It shouldn't involve a visit to an Internet café full of tourists, or a login and a password.

Besides the fact that there's no guarantee that the Tommy you met in a chat room is in fact a nineteen-year-old Lacrosse player studying art history (we've all heard stories about Tommy really being Otis, a fifty-five-year-old construction worker with some sick fetishes, so I don't need to bore anybody with a lecture about online sex safety), there's also the plain and simple fact that tech wizards around the world still haven't come up with anything that beats the pleasure of human touch. Not only can it be dangerous to flirt with someone you

DOS AND DON'TS OF ONLINE FLIRTATION

⊙ **DO** Say what hobbies you enjoy.

⊙ **DO** Send pictures of your beautiful face.

⊙ **DO** Retouch your photos slightly to give yourself a brighter smile.

⊙ **DO** Post a well-chosen group of pictures that shows off the variety of your interests.

⊙ **DO** Show yourself as a smiling, happy young person.

⊙ **DO** Reveal certain basic facts about your life, like where you went to school or your scholastic interests.

⊙ **DO** Respond to as many messages as you can.

⊗ **DON'T** Give out your number, address, or any personal info.

⊗ **DON'T** Send pictures of bare breasts or reproductive organs.

⊗ **DON'T** Lie about your age.

⊗ **DON'T** Post hundreds of pictures of yourself, or you run the risk of looking vain.

⊗ **DON'T** Show yourself as a drunken skank.

⊗ **DON'T** Repeal your whole life story, like when you had your first kiss at recess, what you got on your history test, or which teachers you think are the hottest.

⊗ **DON'T** spread yourself thin by being an Internet tramp. Invest yourself in one or two online friendships or you'll forever be chasing social sites.

can't actually see and touch, seeing and making physical contact with someone are part of the joy and excitement of flirting.

Listen, someday when you (hopefully) have a soul mate, you'll miss flirting. You'll miss the excitement and your heart's pitter-patter and the butterflies in your stomach—so don't waste it on a webcam. Save it for when you meet and get to know someone special. Your body (or mind!) really is a temple, so don't just let any idiot with an Internet connection traipse through it.

Say It, Don't Sext It

T ext messages provide new ways to flirt—and, of course, new ways to inadvertently reveal your inner tramp. So let's discuss some basic text etiquette.

First of all, never send bad news via text. (An extension and clarification of this rule: It is not okay to break up with someone in a text message.) [For more on breakups, see "To Dump and Be Dumped," pp. 210-11.] Be sure not to text a novel. Anything over 160 characters, according to Verizon, should be written in e-mail form. And perhaps most important, if it's late at night or if you're inebriated in any way (maybe you've been drinking, or maybe you've just had your wisdom teeth removed and you're still under some sort of chemical sedation), do not come within texting distance of your phone. Many a tear has been spilled over TUI, or Texting Under the Influence.

Never, ever try to express genuine human emotion with abbreviated text language—and be warned if a suitor does it to you. If a guy were to text you, "u r so hott n i think i will b n luv wit u 4 eva," would your heart really skip a beat? Or would you wonder how you had fallen in love with someone who had apparently never graduated the second grade? We are not in ancient Egypt, so there is no excuse to rely on some weird hi-eroglyphic form of communication to express yourself. Telling someone you love him or her is not the easiest thing to do in life, and expressing the sentiment requires time, patience, courage—and whole words. One way not to share such a sentiment: "I luv u 4 eva n eva. U r da purdiest grl n da world. C u fri."

> "The problem with most men is they're assholes. The problem with most women is they put up with those assholes."
>
> CHER

Older generations moan how texting and e-mailing are destroying the English language, and I think that's a bit of an exaggeration. But relying solely on the written word can produce major problems. [For more information on e-mail misunderstandings, see "Online Friendship Etiquette," pp. 174-75.) A lady should expect—no, demand—that she be treated and spoken to a certain way. I mean, really, if a guy will love you forever and ever, can he not take the moment to actually spell out the words on his touch pad or keyboard? If he's scrimping on letters—literally—early in a relationship, what is he going to scrimp on later? If he really thinks that love is spelled L-U-V, won't his complete and abject idiocy get in the way of your enduring love?

I have to confess: I've used my share of abbreviations. On occasion, I may have thrown an LOL or BTW into a text message. But these occasions are few and far between, and they've never included serious, romantic, or professional correspondences. A lady knows how to spell and insists that her friends and boyfriends do too.

And once again, I feel I should repeat: Actual human interaction is a critical part of the social ritual. No matter how fancy our mobile communication devices get in the future—and regardless of whether you can send voice notes or pictures or videos in real time—there will never be a replacement for connecting with people face-to-face.

TOP 5 HORRIFYING TEXT MESSAGES FRIENDS HAVE FORWARDED ME

1. I wanna hav babies w u sexy bitch
2. [sent at two a.m.] Wanna cum ova and watch TV??? Nothin funny promise
3. Sorry to here ur gma died. Sux
4. My fav song is 'when I think about u I touch myself' Wanna kno y?
5. Baaaabe, I didn't know she was ur friend. I was thinking of u the whole time. I love u so much

Are You Single or Desperate?

Dating, romance, falling in love—these are dances of the heart and soul. And unfortunately, there's no manual to teach you all the steps. However, I've seen my fair share of young ladies attempt to flirt—and come across as totally desperate. Answer the questions below to find out what kind of vibe you're giving off.

1. A boy you like has just sent you a text message. Your response?

(A) Ignore it. You're worth a phone call, damn it!

(B) Wait until you're done with dinner/soccer practice/homework/a meeting, and then respond with a similarly flirtatious text.

(C) Call him back. If he doesn't answer, send a text. If he doesn't answer that immediately, drive to his house and look through the windows.

2. You bump into your secret crush in the street. Sadly, he doesn't see you, so you:

(A) Keep on walking. Is he effing blind or something?

(B) Shout out, and if he hears you, stop for a little chat.

(C) Jump into a taxi and demand to be taken back up the street, so you can again walk by your crush and give him the chance to notice you. Repeat this until you attract his attention, or until you run out of cab fare.

3. Your flame asks if you are free for coffee one night next week. You:

(A) Tell him to screw himself. Coffee? He can at least take you on a real date.

(B) Ask for his number and find a night that is convenient for both of you.

(C) Give him your phone number, e-mail address, bank PIN, and mailing address, and say that you'll make whatever night he chooses work, offering to change all previous plans, including religious pilgrimages and family vacations.

4. A good-looking guy compliments your perfume on the subway/in the street. You respond by:

(A) Telling him to shut up and die. Ugh. Why are all guys such pervs?

(B) Thanking him for the compliment.

(C) Asking if he wants to make out.

5. You meet a gorgeous vegetarian while picking up food at the supermarket. Your cart is full of bacon and sausages. You:

(A) Tell him you love the smell of pork chops in the morning, and call him a wussy.

(B) Strike up a conversation about why he quit eating meat, adding that you admire his willpower and saying you've actually had some great tofu.

(C) Throw the meat into an old woman's bag and start chugging soy milk.

6. A guy asks you out on the same night as a family funeral, so you:

(A) Invite him to the funeral. If he can't handle a few tears, that's his problem.
(B) Explain the situation, say you need to be with your family for a few days, and suggest he ask you out again in a few weeks.
(C) Go out with him—people die all the time, so surely someone else in your family will bite it soon.

7. How often do you have a new crush?

(A) Never. You don't like boys. Boys like you.
(B) Not too often—but when you like a boy, you really like him.
(C) Every hour. On the hour. Basically whenever you see a person of the opposite sex.

8. Once you like a boy and want to know more about him, you:

(A) Rely on your first impression to make a (usually negative) snap judgment.
(B) Ask around, and gain an understanding of his likes and dislikes from mutual friends.
(C) Google him. Talk to his friends. Make up a fake online persona just so you can befriend him online and dissect each comment and photo on his profile.

9. When you go on a first date with someone, you usually talk about:

(A) Whatever.
(B) Current events, the kind of music you like—casual getting-to-know-you topics.
(C) Hereditary disorders that run in your family and what his mother is like—you need to know whether you can have babies together right off the bat.

10. You need a date for the prom/a family wedding/a work party, but no one has asked yet, so you:

(A) Go alone and get drunk by yourself.
(B) Go ahead and ask someone who also doesn't have a date. Maybe he was just too shy to approach you!
(C) Beg someone to go with you, offering him cash, limo, a new suit, drugs, hookers—whatever it takes.

QUIZ KEY

Count up all your answers and see which of the three letters you had the most of. If you are:

Mostly A's. You're playing so hard to get, you're going to wind up getting nothing. There's a fine line between keeping your cool and coming off as stuck-up or a bitch. If you like someone, don't be afraid to let him know it. No matter what you've heard, if you keep playing this tough-girl mentality you will end up losing the love match.

Mostly B's. When you like someone, it's a good idea to seem interested but not obsessed, and you do a great job of walking the line. Keep it up and happy dating!

Mostly C's. Why buy the cow when you're just giving away the milk for free? When a guy thinks he can have whatever he wants, he won't offer what you want him to give. Be careful not to make yourself too readily available—physically, emotionally, or otherwise—to anybody, even your newest number one crush.

The Good, the Bad, and the Gay!

Nobody said finding a boyfriend was easy—and it's not!— but this guide should at least help weed out the potential boyfriends from the boy friends and the bad boys

N ow, I'll be the first to say, as a rule, stereotypes and generalities are a bad thing. But, c'mon, aren't they fun? So let's talk about three types of men most girls will encounter: the bad boy, the good boy, and the gay boy. Maybe you already know all about these types. Maybe you've encountered them before; maybe you fell in love with a bad boy, rebuffed a good boy, and are best friends with a gay boy. (I just hope for your sake you didn't fall in love with the gay boy. That can get tricky.) For the rest of you, or for a refresher, let's look at these three breeds.

First, let me add a disclaimer: This is not a scientific, fool-proof process. While appearance can help you classify a boy into one of these three categories, some of the worst types of boys can dress amazingly well, and some of the best boys just don't know how to clean themselves up. And, hey, surely there are some gay boys out there who don't wear Daisy Dukes.

Furthermore, not every bad boy stays a bad boy for his entire life. We've all heard about bad boys turning into good boys—and gay boys, for that matter—but let's not forget that for every empire-building-billionaire college dropout (Bill Gates and Brad Pitt), you have bad boys who just don't seem to make it (Kevin Federline and the guy who tormented me in high school and now works at a gas station in Illinois). Not every good boy stays a good boy either: I've met my fair share of college-graduate drug addicts. Also, not every guy with perfect eyebrows and an expensive wardrobe is automatically same-sex oriented—with the rise of the metrosexual, those types of external clues can often be misleading.

So while we can't automatically assume, it's not a bad exercise to acknowledge—strictly by appearance—some of the identifying traits of the good, the bad, and the gay.

Generally speaking, it's best to steer clear of men who sport anything visible that has been cut off—whether pants (a), sleeves, or body parts. Witness another bad sign: The remaining shreds of fabric are either worn-out and disgusting or ridiculously baggy (b), a general sign of laziness. If he can't bother to buy clothes that have been hemmed and fit correctly, what do you think his idea of romance is? (Answer: ESPN and a six-pack of Coors Light.) And why is his underwear showing (c)? It's bad enough when a girl shows off her lingerie. Other questionable style choices include those combat boots (d)—presumably, he won't be in combat on his way to history class. Speaking of class, would it kill him to own a bag (e)? And let's not even get into the vices here, like smoking (f) and drinking (g). If he can't get through the day without being wasted and sedated, surely he'll have a hard time getting through a relationship.

BAD BOY

FIG. 1

FIG. 2

The modern good boy doesn't have to dress up all the time—jeans, as long as they aren't distractingly baggy, worn below the crotch, or covered in holes, are completely fine on a young man—but it's nice to see this guy actually owns a suit (a) and a nice pair of slacks (b). Notice how he's actually smiling (c). Surely a sense of humor is an attractive quality in a man. He has a bag (d), which shows that he is at the very least trying to be organized; and he apparently knows how to tie a tie (e), which could be some indication of professional ambition (or at the very least, good hand-eye coordination). Take note of the general fit of the clothes: The sleeves (f) allow just a tiny bit of the shirt to show, a classic fit; the waist of both pairs of pants (g) are actually on his waist, and the crotch (h) is actually on the crotch. Last, it's nice to see he's not afraid of color (i) and clothes without holes in them.

GOOD BOY

FIG. 3   FIG. 4

Some general rules of thumb when it comes to the sartorial decisions of the opposite sex: If he shows more leg than you do (a), if he has more accessories than you do (b), if his pants are tighter than yours (c), and if his sweaters are tighter and smaller than yours (d)—he might be a better boy friend than boyfriend. This can be tricky territory: The modern male reads magazines and knows it's okay to spend money on his appearance. But there is such a thing as too much flamboyance in collars (e), accessories, and color coordination (f). Not that there's anything wrong with being flamboyant, color-coordinated, or gay, for that matter. In fact, every smart girl has a good gay in her life. [See "The GBF: A Lady's Secret Weapon," pp. 172-73.] But it's absolute torture to fall in love with one. And oh, finally, if he can incorporate more exotic skins (g), furs (h), leathers (i), and animal prints (j) into a wardrobe than you can, not only is he gay—he's probably an *amazing* person to go shopping with.

GAY BOY

FIG. 5

FIG. 6

A Lady Falls in Love

Be wary of the
Relationship Chameleon!

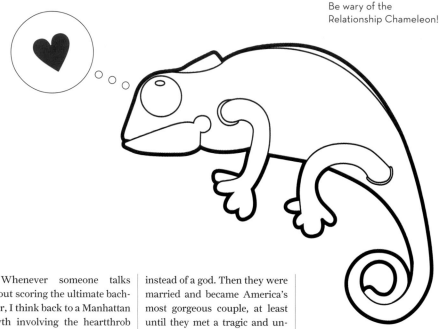

Whenever someone talks about scoring the ultimate bachelor, I think back to a Manhattan myth involving the heartthrob John F. Kennedy Jr. and Carolyn Bessette. (If you are unaware of the sorts of heart-flutters the twenty-something John-John inspired in girls around the world, I suggest you hit the Google machine immediately.) Legend has it that whenever he would call Carolyn at work, her assistant said she was unavailable. Every time. Even if she was sitting across from her assistant. Carolyn wanted New York's most sought-after man to see what it was like to chase something too.

She wasn't exactly playing a game. Allegedly, she'd return his calls when she had a chance—but unlike most girls who would drop their own baby if JFK Jr. called, she kept him at bay, treating him like a normal guy

instead of a god. Then they were married and became America's most gorgeous couple, at least until they met a tragic and untimely end in the Atlantic Ocean.

I like this tale of their flirtation because it reinforces that, while a modern lady doesn't need to employ a series of tactics to get herself a man (Carolyn didn't say she was going on vacation, she wouldn't wait three days to call him back, and so forth), she does have to cultivate her own life. For the most part, judging by how many of my girlfriends have scored their better halves, games don't work on a man. There have been entire books—and movies—devoted to ways to deceive and devour some man-prey. But an honest and forthright girl will attract an honest and forthright man. (And likewise, a girl who plays games gets a guy who likes games.)

Some of the theories out there are pretty amusing: how many dates one must have before it's appropriate to kiss (or more), how many days a girl is supposed to wait to call someone back. What if he was calling to extend an impromptu invite to a concert that night? Why not answer?

While I agree that you don't want to call a new significant other every second of the day, I think it's a good thing to be attentive on the phone and on e-mail. But being attentive isn't the same thing as being desperate—Carolyn Bessette wasn't, but she had the calmness of

A FEW THOUGHTS ON WHAT TO WEAR ON A DATE

There's nothing more nerve-wracking for a girl than putting together an outfit to wear to meet a boy. The questions are endless: What makes me look thin? What makes my butt look perky? What's a good color on me? What will make him tremble with desire when he lays his eyes on me?

Since I've played consultant to more than one girlfriend when she's faced this vital decision, I consider myself sort of an expert. Let me tell you what I tell them: You want to mildly seduce a boy, flirt with him, and make him want more of you on a first date. You don't want to hit him over the head with your sexuality—and I mean that figuratively and literally. (Make sure all your goodies are firmly strapped in.)

Sure, it's fine to show a bit of décolletage, but you don't want to do anything near X-rated. Or even R, to be honest. Keep it PG-13 on the first date. That means no side-boob, no under-boob, no under-butt visuals, and no crack shots. Tight is fine, but not so tight you can make out an appendix scar. (Refer to the first chapter of this book for more on the difference between looking slutty and sexy.)

Yes, a good guy should like what he sees on the first date—and hopefully you will too—but that's not the only thing you want to focus on. Wear something that showcases your best features but doesn't overshadow a good personality. Let's face it: Girls who dress like strippers on first dates are more likely to become a mistress or the crazy girlfriend a man meets before he finds his soul mate. Be the wife, not the mistress. (The mistress never gets anything. Trust me!)

mind and the grace to keep her wits about her. Remember that—and if you don't have that calm grace, fake it! It's like that old saying: Fake it till you make it. Or in this case, fake it till you make out.

Another thing to do when you're single is a good sweep of your online profile. Are there pictures of you kissing someone else, and have you put "getting blackout drunk" on your list of hobbies? Sure, these may attract a little attention from a member of the opposite sex, but probably not the kind that you want.

Finally, let me offer this disclaimer: When meeting a person of the opposite sex, don't be what a girlfriend of mine calls a Relationship Chameleon, which is a person who changes her entire life for a significant other—i.e., the former hamburger queen who goes vegan for the cute tree-hugging hippie, or the girl who starts smoking weed because she has a soft spot for the really hot pot head. It never turns out well. I'm reminded of a quote my friend always used to tell me: "It's all right to let yourself go, but just make sure you can get yourself back again." If the guy of your dreams falls for a person whom you've merely been impersonating, it's only going to spell heartbreak for you both.

Dating for Dummies

Finding love can be difficult—even for those people you think have everything

I have a friend who is considered by those who would know one of the coolest girls in New York City. She's one of those downtown, dark-haired girls who are too cool to smile in pictures and always looks like she's just stepped out of a magazine. Given her coolness quotient, you can imagine my shock and horror when, on a plane to Barcelona together, I looked over and saw that she was reading *Men Are from Mars, Women Are from Venus*, a relationship guide that teaches women how to communicate with members of my gender. This was actually good news to me and should be to you too. See? Even this girl was having troubles with her handsome actor boyfriend. So trust, if she can't figure out boy issues, it's fine if you are having trouble with them too.

The good news is that by counseling so many girls through fights, breakups, make-ups and broken engagements, I've learned a few tricks of the trade. Perhaps the biggest is to chill out.

Genetically speaking, boys and girls have different personality traits and respond to situations differently. It's typically the girl who takes the more emotional route; a boy might ignore a problem unless he can generate a concrete solution for it. Generally speaking

(note: Making generalizations is tricky, so take even these tidbits of advice with a grain of salt), women prefer to talk things out and men prefer to act things out. To put it even more bluntly: Women like to talk and talk, and boys don't. But don't be offended by this behavior. Sure, encourage as much conversation as you can, but don't take it personally if he's not willing to discuss your relationship for hours on end.

> "Common sense is not so common."
>
> VOLTAIRE

There's no way around relationship games. Even if you tell yourself that you don't play games when it comes to romance, and even if you find a guy who says the same, there will come a time when you find yourself performing some curious communication dance: Do you answer the phone when he calls? Do you e-mail him back on the same day or respond to a text as soon as you get it?

The answer to all these questions is the same: Do whatever you want to. (Unless what you want to do is send him flowers

every hour on the hour.) [See "Are You Single or Desperate?," pp. 194-95.]

Confidence is key. Don't be afraid to be the first person to call, and don't be afraid to call him twice if he hasn't called you back. But there is a difference between confidence and aggression: Men are not conquests (unless you're into some kinky dominatrix stuff—which is a whole different book, you tramp). Most men agree that confidence is sexy; and the ones that won't are probably into passive, subservient chicks and mail-order brides—and you don't want to be with a guy like that anyway.

A guy will let you know if he likes you. Even if he's shy or introverted or has a hard time expressing himself, even the most socially backward young man will find some way to let you know that he thinks you're special. (And let's be honest: If a guy can't do something as simple as show that he has a crush on you, do you really want to be with the wimp?)

If it's clear, however, that he's not into you, do your best to move on and forget about him. Yes, I know that's easier said than done, but be confident in the knowledge that you will find someone who will care for you the same way you cared for that jerk.

Be kind. Respond to calls and e-mails, especially if you really like someone. Also, try to speak on the phone or in person as much as possible—much can be lost or miscommunicated in e-mails and texts, so try to limit online chats and text messages if you can, especially in the beginning of a relationship when feelings are raw and people might misunderstand or over-exaggerate the importance of these types of communications. Unless you really know someone and his personality, online communication should just be for making plans. [For more on online miscommunication between friends, see "Online Friendship Etiquette," pp. 174-75.]

Know that you're not going to change a man. I find it interesting that most girls will acknowledge the fact that they wouldn't change themselves for anyone, and yet they believe they can control or change a man. And if a man is trying to control you, ask yourself why you'd be with someone who doesn't like the person you are.

Also, trust your instincts. While there are exceptions to any rule, it's typically clear within the first few moments of meeting someone whether you're attracted to him or not. But also keep in mind this little tidbit: Studies show that men are more likely to fall in love at first sight, whereas women need to know someone in order to fall in love. Don't be disappointed if life isn't like a romance novel.

Life, love, and relationships are hard work. And as with any job, it might take some effort—and a few failed attempts—before you find the right one.

SOME DATINGS DOS AND DON'TS

A Lady knows it's okay to screen calls. Sure. She also never calls from a blocked number—if she's worried a person won't answer, she doesn't call.

A Lady knows to carry money for a taxi, but she chooses whether or not to pay for her arrival with a date or to split it. If she elects him to pay, or if she's stingy, or if she doesn't have cab fare home, she at least pretends as though she's going to pay as a courtesy.

A Lady can certainly judge a man by what he looks like and what he's wearing—but she knows what he says is more important. If only by a little bit.

A Lady offers to make dinner reservations.

A Lady is a flirt at the right time.

A Lady doesn't worry about getting lipstick on a guy when she kisses him on the cheek; look: a good reason to touch someone's face.

A Lady always thanks someone for flowers, even if she's not fond of them or the person who sent them. Two exceptions to this rule: If a stalker is involved, or if she's deeply allergic to flowers.

A Lady doesn't give fake numbers. She either gives an office number or makes an excuse to leave before numbers are exchanged.

A Lady only ignores creepy text messages.

A Lady is proud of her Daddy complex if she has one and is into older men. But she had better not be a gold digger.

A Lady can be kissed on the hand, but she must act like it's ridiculous. Because it is.

A Lady isn't afraid of arriving before a date, and she waits at the bar before being seated.

A Lady believes in love. And doesn't settle for less.

Lady vs. Tramp: In Relationships

Good men are hard to find. But remember: Anyone who wants to see your Christmas presents before December isn't worth it!

I can't say it will definitely happen to you, but chances are that at some point in life, someone may ask you to make a sex tape. Or maybe take some naked Polaroids. Maybe you're not even old enough to be having sex, or maybe you're not old enough to really know what sex is—but that doesn't mean someone won't ask you to sit down for a game of strip poker.

My advice is simple: Don't do anything that you're not comfortable with. Despite the success of a few morally questionable young people who have found fame and fortune after allowing themselves to be taped while they had sexual intercourse with a sort of boyfriend—which says a lot about our culture, no?—sex tapes are not sexy. They're the hallmarks of sluts, skanks, tramps, and big lapses in judgment. [See "Lady vs. Tramp: In Fashion," pp. 4-7.]

Purely from an aesthetic perspective (and we all know that the aesthetic perspective is the most important perspective of all), a sex tape is a bad idea. That's just common sense: An amateur photographer with a crappy webcam and some black lights taped to his ceiling will certainly do your body no justice—even if you have a supermodel figure. It's very hard

to find a flattering angle from which to film a sex tape, and if someone is taking a nude picture of you, he's most likely (a) not worried about finding your "good side" and (b) focusing on a very specific part of your anatomy—meaning the rest of the junk in the picture is often blurry and poorly posed.

> "Don't compromise yourself. You're all you've got."
>
> **JANIS JOPLIN**

> "Love is a fire. But whether it is going to warm your heart or burn down your house, you can never tell."
>
> **JOAN CRAWFORD**

So I guess I could adjust the sex tape rule: If Steven Spielberg wants to shoot you naked, go ahead and do it. Otherwise, be prepared for a true horror film, my friends.

Sure, there are some exceptions. My friend Lou Doillon, the model/actress/French style

icon daughter of the '70s muse Jane Birkin, shocked some people when she did a nude photo shoot for a French men's magazine, but the pictures are beautiful and tasteful. So let's say someone is requesting that you get naked. Feel free to ask yourself, "Am I Lou Doillon? Am I posing for a classy French publication or a magazine revered for its artistic integrity? Or am I posing for some sticky Polaroids that will be passed around a frat party?" More often than not, an amateur attempt at an artistic sex tape will end in tears. And a bunch of embarrassment.

While we're on the topic of psychologically damaging or reputation-ruining images, let's go ahead and discuss the evil of the Internet and the Google machine. I'm sure you've heard this, but it's not uncommon for a potential employer or college-admissions officer to pop an applicant's name into a search engine in order to unearth biographical information that might not have found its way onto the application.

For example, a college application might state that you speak three languages and worked three summers as a volunteer in the organ transplant office of a local hospital—but it may neglect to mention the

Unfortunately, pictures like these (and worse!) aren't uncommon. And in all honesty, they aren't that sexy.

trip you took to South Beach for Mardi Gras, when you thought it would be funny to hang beads from the nipple rings you got during a moment of adolescent rebellion. Photo evidence is, however, featured on your best friend's blog—so you better hope that the college-admissions officer thinks nipple rings are the hallmark of a scholar.

We've all heard about beauty-pageant queens who lose their crowns because some sordid pics turn up—and several model girlfriends of mine have lost giant campaigns and contracts because they have a reputation, and the pictures to prove the reputation, for making decisions unbecoming of a role model. (Even if your boss isn't looking for a role model, he or she isn't looking for someone to embarrass the company or agency either.)

The Internet, in combination with digital pictures and sex tapes, make for a scary and explosive situation: a network where mistakes can not only be immediately broadcast, but broadcast to literally millions of people, making them nearly impossible to control or erase.

I've learned one thing from the Internet: The bad stuff never goes away. If you take those lewd pictures, or make an ill-advised nudie tape, they will eventually end up in the wrong hands. Hell hath no fury like a boyfriend spurned, especially if he just happens to have a home video of you rolling around in nothing but athletic socks.

HAIR COLOR
Subtle, sweet, and natural—
hopefully, like the girl.

In a Relationship

The line between dressing for
a first date and dressing for an
audition at the local strip club has
become blurred in recent years.
How much skin is too much? How
tight is too tight? When do I flash
a smile and when do I flash an
orgasm face? To help clarify which
is sweet and which is stripper,
here are some tips.

FACIAL EXPRESSION
She looks attentive,
interested and eager to tal

MAKEUP
The makeup is playful,
because this is a date, but not
overly elaborate. (It's not a
date in a clown car.)

EXPOSURE
Bare arms and her
toned legs seen from
under the knee: shows
enough skin, but not
too much.

LADY

POSE
Her stance says
flirty and delicate,
as opposed to
cheap and easy.

THAT'S YES CLASSY!

GROOMING
Clean nails, styled hair,
moisturized skin—and
she probably smells
nice. It's a good step
to appease senses like
touch and feel from the
beginning.

FIT
While the dress is no
doubt conservative in its
length—even her knees
are covered—it is very
tight. A classy girl picks
one: tight or short. You
can't have both.

SHOES
High heels aren't
slutty (unless they're
clear and wrapped
around a stripper pole).
Just make sure you can
walk in them.

ATTITUDE
The look to give a guy, unless you're a stripper working for tips, should not be a provocative one. This look here shouldn't come for free.

BAD ROOTS
If she can't keep up on her hair appointments, what other body parts hasn't she maintained?

MAKEUP
Darkened lids and big red lips: It's hard to know if she's wearing too much makeup or if she's trying to cover up black eyes and open mouth sores.

CHEST
Exposed, stuck out, and sparkling in the sunlight with all this attention-drawing bling—it makes you wonder if there's anything in her chest besides silicone.

TRAMP NO STAMP

S

TRAMP

FABRIC
If your swimsuit and your dress are made from the same fabric, it's a serious problem.

SKIRT LENGTH
It's simple: Crotch shots are embarrassing. And gross. Not sexy.

POSE
If her legs were any further apart, she could give an anatomy lesson on childbirth.

LEGS
Yes, they're good, but what's the point of wearing a dress if it's the same length as a top?

The Future Politician's Argument

W hen I was young, my mother had a very specific way of controlling me. She discouraged all of my questionable behaviors—from failing a biology test to driving drunk—with the same rationale: If someone found out about *fill in the blank*, it could ruin your whole life. In eighth grade, she told me that I could never run for President of the United States if I wore a Grateful Dead T-shirt in my yearbook photo. (So I totally did.)

Despite that moment of yearbook-photo rebellion, this angle was actually a very effective deterrent. When I moved to New York City I found that many of my friends, especially the bad girls from good families, had been reared with a similar mind-set: Were an incriminating photo or video of them to go public, they would never get into a good school or become First Lady or the princess of some minor principality in Europe.

This politically minded thinking applies very well to the relationship arena. The idea that a good boy promises you a good future is a sound one. Even if you don't plan on becoming the President or the First Lady, it's never too soon to think about how your actions—and perhaps, most importantly, who you date—will affect the rest of your life.

I'm not suggesting you need to find someone rich and good-looking, with a house in the Hamptons, in order to have a happy life (though, believe me, those don't hurt). But you do need someone honest, forthright, hardworking, and respectful. Someone who won't embarrass you; someone who won't release a sex tape after you break up.

Now that I have friends who are actually in politics or related to successful politicians, I can say that following this dictum

A lady knows that a good boy promises a good future.

is not a bad way to live your life. Sure, I get that sometimes the bad boy seems really attractive, especially if you've had a very controlled childhood. (It's always the boarding-school girls who go wildest after graduation.) But you need to be careful of the company you keep and be mindful of what your boyfriend says about you, literally and figuratively.

This political vantage doesn't only relate to the behavior of the guys you meet and date, however. It's important to think about your own habits and attitudes in this context. (A lady can be a political asset, don't forget.) And it's never too early to think about how your decisions—even the ones you are making now—could affect the way a handsome Prince Charming, or even an average Mr. Right, will think of you.

Every politician has heard the example about John F. Kennedy's choice of women: He was attracted to Marilyn Monroe but knew he had to marry a Jackie Bouvier. Personally, I think both women were fabulous, but the old adage holds true. Look at it this way: The scandalous blonde OD'd tragically, and the well-groomed and manicured brunette became a style icon and the embodiment of sophistication.

While it's helpful to think about this in the political context, it's not only politicians who are looking for clean-living, well-groomed ladies. If there are a bunch of pictures of you on the Internet, smoking weed from a bong made out of a teddy bear shaped honeypot, chances are, a future husband on the fast track to success won't say to himself, "I can see that woman as the future president of my children's PTA."

This reminds me of a friend I have in New York City. She was raised by a good family and went to two Ivy League schools for her bachelor's and then her master's degrees. From the outside she looks the picture of elegance. So you wouldn't guess that she spent her early twenties as a chain-smoking, club-crawling, player-dating party animal. The main reason? Because she cleaned up her tracks. Whenever someone took her picture, she ditched the cigs; and she never got wasted in places where it would be gossip fodder. She did the next best thing to being a good girl: She was a smart bad girl. [For more on the bad habits that may upset a young girl's chances at political success, see the chapter *A Lady Faces Temptation*.]

Fortunately, there's good news for bad girls looking to shape up their image: It's never too late. Consider Mette-Marit, the Crown Princess of Norway. She'd already had a child—and, reportedly, a whole adolescence of indiscretion—before she cleaned up her act, met a prince, made a public apology for her wild youth on national TV, and became the future queen of a country. Now she has a tiara. (But just be aware that not every nation is as nice, or forgiving, as Norway.)

Everyone has skeletons. Everyone! But it's best to find someone who has them stuffed in the back of a (hopefully really big) walk-in closet!

"It is useless to hold a person to anything he says while he's in love, drunk, or running for office."

SHIRLEY MACLAINE

"Look for a sweet person. Forget rich."

ESTÉE LAUDER

"The devil hath power to assume pleasing shape."

SHAKESPEARE, *HAMLET*

To Dump and Be Dumped

Taking the end of a relationship in stride can be difficult

No matter how easy it seems in movies or romance novels, finding Mr. Right isn't simple. I hate to break it to you, but that quiet guy in math class probably isn't secretly a prince who will love you for you and make you a princess, nor is a really hot transfer student about to join your Spanish class. Now that I think about it, *Pretty Woman*, the movie about a hooker with a heart of gold who meets a lonely workaholic, is probably the most realistic romantic comedy I've ever seen.

Don't let me discourage you, though. (You never know: Maybe you will fall in love with your high school sweetheart and live happily ever after—and if it happens, good for you!) Part of dating and part of being young is the thrill of finding a boyfriend, of waiting for him to call, of flirting. But after all that fun comes something that can be tough: Unless you marry, eventually, you will break up.

First let's talk about the appropriate ways a woman can let a man down. There are a few general rules. The first is this: Never break up with someone on an invention (like via text message, e-mail, or the phone). The second important rule is to never, ever gloat or gossip about the guy behind his back once you cut him loose. Yes, this can be difficult, especially if you have a new boyfriend lined up or if your ex was a jerk and you've only recently gotten the courage to kick him to the curb.

Even the toughest (or dumbest) jock has feelings, so it's important to be assertive but kind when delivering bad news. Don't tell his friends to do it for you, don't tell your friends you're going to do it if you're not

> "After all, computers crash, people die, relationships fall apart. The best we can do is breathe and reboot."
>
> SARAH JESSICA PARKER
> AS CARRIE BRADSHAW
> IN *SEX AND THE CITY*

> "Your heart just breaks, that's all. But you can't judge, or point fingers. You just have to be lucky enough to find someone who appreciates you."
>
> AUDREY HEPBURN

ready to (it's always rough to get bad news—even premature bad news—from someone else, and that applies to any situation), and don't do something cruel just for the sake of it—like start dating his best friend. There are other ways to get back at boys besides being mean.

I know it sounds corny, but the best revenge really is living well: being successful, looking good, and living happily ever after. Yes, it can be hard to be nice, especially if you feel that someone hasn't been nice to you, but a lady knows that how she treats the people close to her—even a detested ex-boyfriend—is a real measure of her character. (This goes for boys too: If they're not nice to their girlfriends, they're probably just not nice.) This is where the Golden Rule applies: Dump unto others as you would have others dump unto you.

The flip side of the break-up equation is a little trickier. What happens when a girl is dumped? When her heart is broken by the evil race known as mankind? Does she handle it maturely, keep her emotions under control, and move on? Or does she act like a freak and stalk him and get a voodoo doll in the hopes that he'll be sterile when he grows up?

There really isn't a "trick" to being dumped. There's no cure or curse or secret ritual you can do to expunge a lost love from your mind. The only advice to remember is to remain calm—especially in front of others—and retain some common sense.

Take solace in knowing that it's better to end a doomed relationship sooner rather than later. And keep in mind that anyone who dumps you isn't the guy for you—which means the relationship was doomed. Everyone—dare I say, even the tramps of the world!—deserves a person who would never even think of breaking things off.

There are a bunch of other mantras you've probably heard—that there are other fish in the sea, that you're better off without him, that your babies would have been hideous—and they may or may not help. But the way I like to see it is that being dumped is a rite of passage, and that only through pain can you truly grow.

It's like this: Everything happens for a reason, and if he's not into you, don't push it. It's pain-ful (and painfully embarrassing) to lust after someone who doesn't like you back, and the sooner you can move on, the better. If you're kicked to the curb, accept it. Yes, yes, yes, I know rejection is hard to stomach and a broken heart is the worst feeling in the entire world. But a lady can—and does—stomach it.

Here's a little story that might help the heartbroken: A good friend of mine—a beautiful friend, the envy of many of her peers, with perfect blonde hair and long legs—had a string of successful, monied, sought-after bachelor boyfriends. Then, randomly, she fell for a salt-of-the-earth surfer who lived in a shack, cared more about his surfboard than he did her, and was immune to her manipulations and material gifts. She was devastated when he dumped her, especially since up until then she had ditched boys left and right, leaving a trail of tears, love letters, and broken hearts behind her.

The serial dumper was dumped. She was a wreck. It took her a bit of time to get over that failed relationship, but when she finally did, she met someone (rich, handsome, successful), got married, and was finally happy. She always said that the only reason she found someone to share her heart with was because she had had hers shattered. She honestly believes, and will still tell you to this day, that you won't know true love until you've had your heart broken and need someone to help you put it back together.

See? A broken heart can be a good thing.

Tissues and ice cream help with an emotional hangover, but don't overdo it. It's hard to find someone new if your nose is rubbed raw and you can't fit into your jeans.

THE GET-OVER-HIM PLAYLIST

"This Love" —— **PANTERA**
"I Will Survive" —— **GLORIA GAYNOR**
"Before He Cheats" —— **CARRIE UNDERWOOD**
"You Keep Me Hanging On" —— **THE SUPREMES**
"You Oughta Know" —— **ALANIS MORISSETTE**

"Cry Me a River" —— **JUSTIN TIMBERLAKE**
"So What" —— **PINK**
"Survivor" —— **DESTINY'S CHILD**
"Fighter" —— **CHRISTINA AGUILERA**
"Achy Breaky Art" —— **BILLY RAY CYRUS**

A Few Words on Online Relationships

This will be quick and blunt: Don't mess around when it comes to the Internet, particularly when it comes to romantic interactions

People lie online, and people will manipulate you, especially when they don't have to interact with you face-to-face. We've all heard the horror stories about young girls meeting predators and perverts on the Internet, and it's not my place to tell you not to date someone you meet online (I have a few friends who have met their husbands and wives online). But take the warning to heart.

Here's a good anecdote: My friend says that she looks at meeting people online—on a dating site or one of the many social networking sites out there—the same way she does buying things on eBay. If a Chanel handbag is for sale at a ridiculously low price, you can be damn close to positive that there's something wrong with it. Same thing with guys—if they're too good to be true, they probably are. Maybe the Chanel bag is a fake; maybe the guy is a fake. Maybe the Chanel bag has a stain or a hole; maybe the guy has intimacy or mommy issues. Maybe the bag is really old, and really beat up; maybe the guy is old enough to be your father, looks nothing like his online profile, and has a dungeon in his basement where he wants to tie you up and dress you in Little Bo Peep costumes.

Just be cautious. You wouldn't spend your life savings on a Chanel handbag that might or might not be real, so don't invest all your emotional savings on a person who might or might not be real either.

I'm not trying to insinuate that a possible new boyfriend is as important as a Chanel bag—the bag is definitely much, much more important—but be smart when it comes to online relationships. A lady is a smart shopper, whether she's on the hunt for a new clutch or a new man.

"We cannot get grace from gadgets. In the bakelite house of the future, the dishes may not break, but the heart can. Even a man with ten shower baths may find life flay, stale, and unprofitable."

J.B. PRIESTLEY

A lady doesn't substitute inventions for face-to-face touch and communication.

A lady doesn't believe everything she reads online.

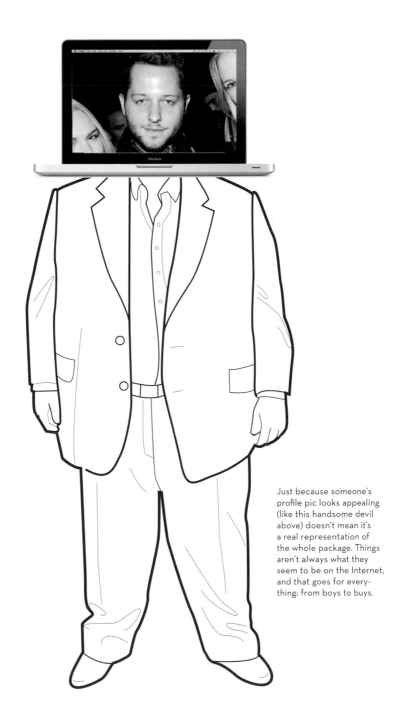

Just because someone's profile pic looks appealing (like this handsome devil above) doesn't mean it's a real representation of the whole package. Things aren't always what they seem to be on the Internet, and that goes for everything: from boys to buys.

His and Hers Ideas of Monogamy

Unfortunately for you, someone you're dating might have a different idea of exclusivity than you do

A Lady doesn't cheat—on cards, tests, or boyfriends.

When I moved to New York City and was still a freshman in college, I took some classes at the health center to become what we called a Sexual Health Advocate, or SHA. I can't remember if I did it to make friends, or to be a role model student and actually disseminate important information about safe-sex practices, but some of the training still sticks to this day.

One of the very first things we learned was the importance of creating a personal definition of monogamy. What is exclusivity? For each person and each relationship, there is a different set of rules, and it's important to define these rules from the start. Will it break your heart if your honey goes on a date with someone

else? Or kisses someone else? Will you absolutely lose your mind if your boyfriend of three weeks asks some other hussy to prom, or you see him trolling around the mall with a rival lady friend?

Get that off your chest now. While this won't safeguard you from having your feelings hurt—being honest isn't the same thing as being exclusive, remember—it's good to have this discussion early on in the relationship. A lady is always honest about what she wants, and she does her best to respect what her significant other wants too. Otherwise, why bother with a boyfriend at all?

One Is Not the Loneliest Number

Sometimes being single and sexy is more fun than being bored and with boyfriend

This may seem obvious, but it's something that bears repeating: It's okay to be single. It's okay to go to the movies alone or go shopping alone or eat at a restaurant alone. To be completely honest, I often crave me-time. After spending the majority of my days with so many high-maintenance people, taking a few moments for myself is probably what keeps me sane. It's like Karl Lagerfeld told me once: Being alone is a luxury.

Not only are people who need constant attention—specifically, constant attention and reassurance from members of the opposite sex—irritating as hell, they're unhealthy.

Early on in my career, I had the good fortune of interviewing Diane von Furstenberg, the legendary designer and icon of beauty. She told me that the first and most important lesson she learned was that she had to be her own best friend. She also told me that although she did not always know what she wanted to do, she always knew who she wanted to be. Today, she is that woman.

It's a cliché, and I probably sound like your mother or some sort of motivational speaker here, but you need to love yourself. If you can't stand to be alone with yourself, how can you expect anyone else to?

SONGS FOR THE LONELY PLAYLIST

Song	Artist
"Womanizer"	BRITNEY SPEARS
"Single Ladies"	BEYONCÉ
"I Need a Man"	GRACE JONES
"Don't Speak"	NO DOUBT
"Erase/Rewind"	THE CARDIGANS
"Grow Up and Blow Away"	METRIC
"Brand New Love"	UFFIE
"Single Women"	DOLLY PARTON
"When You Were Mine"	CYNDI LAUPER
"She's Lost Control"	JOY DIVISION
"I Will Survive"	GLORIA GAYNOR
"Leave Me Alone"	THE VERONICAS
"Destroy Everything You Touch"	LADYTRON
"I'm Every Woman"	CHAKA KHAN
"Talk to Me"	PEACHES
"Single"	NATASHA BEDINGFIELD
"Independent Women"	DESTINY'S CHILD
"Dancing Barefoot"	PATTI SMITH
"Since U Been Gone"	KELLY CLARKSON
"You Think You're a Man"	THE VASELINES
"Fucking Boyfriend"	THE BIRD AND THE BEE
"Brand New Lover"	DEAD OR ALIVE
"Date with the Night"	YEAH YEAH YEAHS
"New Attitude"	PATTI LABELLE

Q&A:
A Lady Looks For Love

The best part about creating this book has been the responses it's caused among the young women I've met at my book signings, over e-mail, and even on the street. There are some smart girls out there, and they've had some fabulous questions. I liked some of them so much I wanted to include them here.

Q: *Have you ever been dumped?*

A: Of course, and I think having your heart broken is an important life experience. Everyone should have it happen to them at least once! My friend once told me you have to have your heart broken to know how it fits back together again. But one bit of advice: if possible, try staying friends with your exes. Not only because there must have been some redeeming qualities about them, but also because they know all your secrets! (Especially if they have incriminating pictures

Q: *Do you believe in love at first sight?*

A: Only in a song! I wish I could say yes, but I've found that true love takes time, trust, and confidence. But don't listen to me: I want to believe in the romance too!

Q: *What happens when your friends all hate the guy you're seeing?*

A: That's simple: Listen to them! I'm not saying that if your friend doesn't like your significant other you need to dump him on the spot, erase him from your life and cell phone. However, I will encourage you to at least calmly (that's the key word) listen to your friend's point of view. You can listen or not, but at least give your friend a chance to warn you. And remember: boyfriends come and go, but best friends last forever. It's cheesy, but it's true.

Q: *How do you prevent your heart from being broken?*

A: You can't! And you shouldn't. You can learn just as much about yourself falling out of love as you do falling in love.

Q: *What's the best place to meet a guy?*

A: I know people who have spent hours researching good places to meet men and who harass their committed or married friends to set them up with someone. (It's rather silly and rather annoying, respectively.) Yes, there are some spots that work: A party at someone's house will yield better results than a bar or a nightclub, and if you have a cute puppy, it's always a good idea to stop in at a dog park. But ultimately, it's about living your life and letting go of the frantic desire to shove someone into it. Be natural and keep your eyes open. Just don't look desperate—that's a surefire way to keep them away, no matter where you are!

Q: *Can you see more than one person at the same time?*

A: As long as you're open and honest about your relationships—and not sleeping with an entire sports team or office carpool—I think it's fine to test the waters with more than one person. (It only gets dicey when someone has ulterior motives and tries to play the field in order to make another person jealous.) But there are a lot of fish in the sea, so feel free to cast your line! One caveat, however, is that you can't lead people on, and if you start seeing someone more exclusively, be up-front and honest with the others. Treat everyone's emotions with respect. I truly believe in relationship karma, which is basically that what you put out in the world is what you'll get back. For example, if you cheat on someone, you'll definitely be cheated on.

Q: *Do you set up your friends? Or is that a terrible idea?*

A: Yes, I have set up my friends, and so far it's been smooth sailing. They've been in love, and if (or when) they've broken up, they have been mature enough to not ask their mutual friends to pick sides. That's not always the case, and in those instances it's sad and immature for someone to ask you not to speak to the ex. (For the record, I never take sides. I'm like Switzerland when it comes to dating!) But you have to respect the situation: Don't gossip about the other one, and don't try to be middleman between the two. It's simple: Stay neutral and stay friends.

Q: *What's the worst place to meet a guy?*

A: I like to think it's easy to meet someone anywhere, from the dry cleaner to the bank. But if I think about it, maybe don't try to pick up guys at your therapist's office, a gun shop, a strip club, or an Alcoholics Anonymous meeting.

A Lady
Stays
Healthy

"Since you were born, what has your body done for you? Since you were born, what have you done for your body?"

ZEN PROVERB

WAIT! BEFORE YOU SKIP THIS CHAPTER, allow me to clarify. This isn't the place for pep talks or nursery rhymes that will make you think your insides are happy thoughts and pink clouds and rainbows. This chapter is more about general internal health: not just what you put in your body, but also what you've got in your head.

I'm a firm believer that the best-looking people in the world aren't just the ones who can skip dessert and spend a few hours on the treadmill. (In fact, I've met quite a few young women who skip lots of meals to keep a lean shape, and they're not at all attractive. It's a concept I call Skinny Fat, which we will talk about later in this chapter.) No, what truly makes a girl gorgeous is the entire package: She needs a healthy body and a healthy mind. A truly classy lady is a well-rounded one.

Let's break it down: Even if you are gorgeous and stylish and well mannered (as you should be by now if you've read this book from the beginning), but you're all messed up in the head, you won't actually be considered attractive. We all know people like this: a beautiful, talented actress whom nobody wants around because she's mentally insane, or a well-mannered, sweet girl whom no one can hang out with because she doesn't make any sense.

In this chapter, I want to talk about those general health issues. Like why it's important to exercise (even if, like me, you hate to do it) and to eat healthy (even if, like me, you think it's nearly impossible to do). While it's true that our culture has grown to accept that we all don't have to be waif-skinny to be considered fashionable, let's not ever think that it's attractive to completely ignore our health. And I mean mental and physical health. So yes, while I love French fries and mozzarella sticks more than I probably should, I still know how nice an apple tastes once in a while.

Sweating Can Be Sexy

When I started college in New York, my exercise regime took a nosedive. Big time. I went from playing three sports in high school and being Missouri's Scholar Athlete to late nights with college books gorging on French fries. You would have thought that walking around the city and going to downtown dance clubs would have been enough cardio (after all, we did drive in Missouri), but it wasn't as much exercise as I needed, and my body suffered for it.

It's an interesting paradox: Not until we get older and slower do we realize how much our bodies relied on fast metabolisms, and by the time they start to slow down, we miss that childhood energy. (And don't think you're too young to be reading this! Most people's metabolisms start to slow in the teenage years.)

So, let's work on working out. And let me say from the beginning that staying in shape shouldn't have to be a pain.

I'm definitely not one of those people who think that running a marathon is a lovely way to spend an afternoon. But spending part of your day maintaining a healthy figure is important—and not just so you can fit into your skinny jeans. Being on a yo-yo diet, and putting that sort of physical toll on your body of weight gain and then starvation, isn't healthy at all, even if Janet Jackson has made a whole sideline career going up and down on the scale.

A Lady isn't afraid to sweat (in the appropriate fitness venue, in the appropriate fitness attire).

A Lady dresses up for the gym, but not too much.

A Lady knows that the gym is a place to work out and work hard. Not cruise for boys.

A Lady tries to make fitness a regular part of her life. Not a part-time hobby.

My advice? Work in visits to the gym, runs around the block, or laps in the pool five times a week, and really put that commitment into your schedule like you would a class or a meeting. Stick to it.

If you're just getting into your gym routine, remember to mix things up so it seems interesting. Believe me, even with the TV on, running for hours on a treadmill is the world's most mind-numbing experience.

Why not try a spin class (which I like for the good music) or yoga (which, when I lived in Missouri, I thought was an Asian food dish) or even a hip-hop dance class (my personal favorite because it allows me to fool myself into thinking I've fulfilled my childhood goal of being in a boy band)?

Another good tip? Spend some time on an iPod playlist: there are certain songs (like the Red Hot Chili Peppers' "Higher Ground," Michael Jackson's

"Smooth Criminal" and, of course, Beyoncé's "Single Ladies") that get me amped up even at the end of the day. And oh, don't be afraid of lifting weights. Remember, a real lady likes to sweat.

While gyms can be expensive, there are other ways around big membership fees: Take advantage of trials, join a community gym or try the YMCA, ask your family to sponsor your membership, or just go running outside to enjoy the natural beauty that surrounds us (and can't be found at the gym anyway).

I once wrote an article entitled "Strong Is the New Beautiful," and it's something that I really endorse today. Even though I work in fashion, where thin seems to always be in, I can tell you that the best models aren't emaciated and unhealthy. The models that the fashion industry is drawn to today work out and have muscle tone. I've seen Gisele in the flesh—and she could pull a powerful punch if she ever needed to. No one wants to see a skeleton walk down a runway.

Still, one word of caution: If you find yourself able to bench press a refrigerator, or your boyfriend for that matter, maybe it's time to put down the weights and pick up a book.

Workout Chic

What you have on at the gym can be just as important as what you do at the gym. Make sure you're dressed appropriately—and inspiringly—when you work out.

Going back generations, the entire idea of a gymnasium where you pay money to run on machines that don't take you anywhere and bicycles that don't move no matter how hard you pedal would be a confusing phenomenon. But as we've seen gyms become commonplace, a whole new section of a woman's wardrobe has developed: What constitutes classy workout clothes?

Living in New York has provided me with all sorts of visuals when it comes to exercise attire. I've seen girls, probably believing they look very sexy, wear strapless flesh-colored Spandex to run down the Hudson River, and I've gone to gyms where young women pose on machines in outfits that show more cleavage than clavicle. These women are workout tramps, and I'm not entirely sure if they're there to work on their bodies or on a new husband.

When I first started going to the gym, I was unenthusiastic about my attire. I was wearing workout shorts my parents had bought me when I was in elementary school (no joke), any old T-shirt I found on the floor and beat-up tennis shoes. It took me a while to realize this wasn't doing me any favors in the gym, and wasn't really providing much motivation to hit the StairMaster. What you wear to work out doesn't only affect the way you look; it also affects the way you work out.

This is the unsung truth of any successful exercise regime: The gear impacts the performance. If you spend some time and money putting a fabulous workout look together, chances are you'll be keen to wear it and sweat through it. Have a look around the gym: The person goofing off and playing with the TV remotes is probably dressed like a schlub, but the girl with the toned abs and perky boobs is probably decked out in well-made, well-fitting workout clothes.

There are a few things to remember when you're getting dressed to work out. How practical are my clothes? If they're baggy, will they slow me down? Are they made from good, breathable fabrics? Are the fabrics itchy? Are the clothes too tight in places that would become a nuisance? (One rule of thumb: wearing spandex and heavily elasticized clothing is a privilege for people who go to the gym often, not a right for anyone. Have the sense to know what is sensible style.)

Only after these questions about the actual usefulness of a garment have been answered should you start thinking about the extras: what color looks good on me? Which shorts make my butt look smaller and my breasts look bigger?

Please note, however, that there are some questions you never want to find yourself asking in a sports shop: Does this bra come with more padding and a cleavage support system? Do those shorts come in a thong

DO

-supportive, chic workout attire

-comfortable sports shoes

-inspiring playlist

NOT

-stripper clothes

-drag queen makeup

-distracting communication devices

shape? Does that top come in clear? (Some of you may think those questions are satirical, but I've actually heard them all. And worse.)

Gym clothes aren't always cheap, and I'm not suggesting that you go out and spend an entire paycheck on brand new looks to sweat in. Just make sure you get the basics, and make sure that you like them and like to put them on. For most of us, going to the gym is hard enough. But looking cute makes it that much easier.

And, oh, when it comes to makeup, just don't do it. Please,

I beg you, skip the false eyelashes, acrylic nails, or any other sorts of decorative or cosmetic indulgences. Not only do I say this because it's ridiculous and a waste of perfectly good lip gloss, but also because I've seen more than one girl start to sweat with a face full of makeup and hop of the treadmill looking like a crazy clown lady.

The gym has certainly become a more social place, and you will no doubt bump into friends, ex-boyfriends, and future ex-boyfriends when you work out. So there is pressure to look good. But don't be

distracted by boys when you should be working on yourself.

While it's perfectly fine to strike up a conversation with someone at the gym, bear in mind it's a place to work out, first and foremost. No one wants to see Cupid shooting arrows by the free weights. If you believe you've stumbled upon romantic gold at the machine next to you, great! Say hi and swap e-mail addresses, if you're really feeling it. But please choose a more romantic place to meet up in an hour or so. And just remember to take a shower first!

SMILE
But not too much! It's okay to make friends at the gym, but be sure you're not acting like it's a singles bar. It's a spin class—not happy hour!

PONYTAIL
A sleek, tight, high ponytail. Keep your hair out of your face (with the aid of a chic headband, if need be) so you're not distracted or, worse, have sweat dripping down your face.

MAKEUP
Sure, a little lip gloss can't hurt at the gym, but what you want to avoid is a face full of pancake makeup. You want your skin to be able to breathe too!

At the Gym

Working out is an important part of the modern woman's lifestyle: Let's keep our minds and our bodies healthy, ladies. But getting dressed for working out can be a tricky style conundrum: How sexy is too sexy at the gym? And how much is too much skin on a treadmill? Check out this illustration to see the difference between looking sexy and looking slutty while working out.

LADY

HIT ME!
Boxing and kickboxing can be exhilarating for a girl—who doesn't like to hit somebody? Don't be afraid to experiment with fitness: try a spin class or Pilates. Don't get bored at the gym.

THAT'S YES CLASSY!

BAG IT UP
Stay organized at the gym. Having a separate gym bag is a great way to do that. Stock it with everything you need—fresh clothes, athletic socks, a lock—so that you have no excuse not to work out!

FIT
Clothes at the gym should be sporty and allow movement, which often means tight. But there's a difference between gym tight and club tight, and you want to make sure your gym clothes couldn't double at a strip club.

HYDRATED
Stay hydrated, and nature's hydration system (water) is alwa~ a good bet. Trust me, it ain't cute to faint at a gym!

HAIR DON'T
The gym is one place you don't want to whip your hair back and forth.

SKIN
Girls who wear makeup at the gym look more like working girls than workout girls. It's a bad idea for several reasons: it's not good for the skin to sweat with pore-stopping creams on top of them, and if you sweat, your makeup will run down your face, making you look like an insane clown.

POSE
You don't need to be a nun at the gym, but you also don't want to look like the gym's gigolo either. Make friends, but keep the flirting away from the fitness.

COMMUNICATION
Working out is, for most, a solitary moment of self-improvement and reflection. So don't be afraid to leave your phone in your locker.

S**O**

TRAMP NO STAMP

TRAMP

PURSE
Handbags and clutches belong at cocktail parties, not an elliptical machine.

PANTIES
Yes, major athletic brands make very scanty workout gear, and yes, it's important to be comfortable. But a swimsuit is not a gym outfit, and your undies should never show.

SUSTENANCE
Keep your energy up at the gym and be sure to stay hydrated, but avoid gimmicky drinks and snacks that have more calories than protein.

ATTIRE
Be comfortable at the gym, but don't ever confuse pajamas with workout attire. Also, if you find yourself tying a garment, invest in a new article of clothing.

A Few Thoughts on Nutrition

Let's get one thing straight: I was raised in America's Midwest, and I know my away around a buffet better than a bus full of senior citizens at an early bird special. But just because I'm all too familiar with mozzarella sticks and the French fries at the New York restaurant Balthazar (which are twice as good as normal fries because they're fried twice in duck fat) doesn't mean I'm not knowledgeable about the right sorts of things that I should be eating.

That's where healthy eating starts: nutritional awareness, which even those of you with fast metabolisms (curse you!) should have a grasp of.

I'll admit that when it comes to good nutrition, it can be difficult to discern the hoopla from the hooey. When I first moved to New York, I had no idea what the hallmark of a good diet was. In fact, I didn't even know what a carbohydrate was until I was a sophomore in college. But there are a few basic concepts we all should know, which are listed on the following pages.

Losing weight is a billion dollar business. There are, literally, millions upon millions of diet schemes in existence, including books, TV shows, vitamins, suppressants, surgeries, and hypnotists. And sure, I've been tempted to try a couple—who wouldn't want to do a diet that revolves around soup for three weeks? I love soup! But being healthy isn't about fad diets.

I've come to believe in a few nutritional mantras. The first is that what you put in your body directly affects the way you feel; put in junk food and you'll probably feel like junk. Put in a healthy diet of fresh fruits and vegetables, as mind-numbing and trivial as this sounds, and you'll feel healthy.

While I used to think that only hippies and tree huggers insisted on organic food, binging on over-processed foods (even the ones I love, like Gummi Bears and diet sodas) will make you feel sluggish and slow. On the topic of ingredients, let's all agree that the only place that a girl can be a "label whore" is at the supermarket. Make sure you're eating the Prada of peas, and take some time to look at the number of calories and ingredients in the food you're buying.

(One caveat: Just make sure you're not turning into one of those crazy dieters who become obsessed with nutritional labels. You want to be informed of what you're eating, not obsessed by it.)

And lastly, avoid crash dieting. I once had a friend—I won't tell you who it is, because she will hunt me down and murder me—who went on an intense detox plan. On her fifth day into the program, we went to a cocktail party at Barney's and she literally passed out in the middle of the store—and, even worse, when she lost consciousness, she actually lost control of her bladder too, and wet herself. I cannot think of a better reason to avoid crash diets or intense detox programs than passing out and peeing yourself in the middle of a fashion Mecca.

Even if you have a fast metabolism (for now), and even if you seem to be able to eat anything you want and still fit into your skinny jeans (God bless you, you bitch), be smart about what you put in your body. I am not the sort of person to tell someone not to eat something—I would rather jump off a bridge than give up French fries forever. Yet, merely being aware of what you're eating and how it affects your body will ensure that you stay healthy, which should be the most important thing in any classy lady's life.

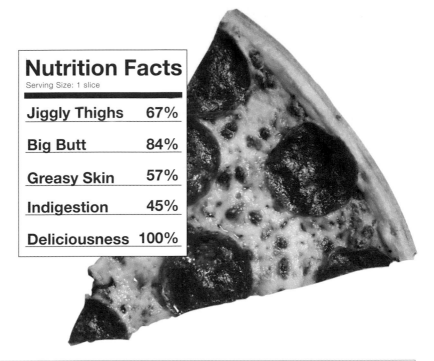

Nutrition Facts

Serving Size: 1 slice

Jiggly Thighs	67%
Big Butt	84%
Greasy Skin	57%
Indigestion	45%
Deliciousness	100%

A Lady understands that working out at teh gym is for self-improvement, not to improve one's network of friends.

A Lady educates herself on what she's eating.

A Lady is aware of what she puts it in her body—but she's not obsessed by it.

"The only way to keep your health is to eat what you don't want, drink what you don't like, and do what you'd rather not."

MARK TWAIN

"Fitness—if it came in a bottle, everybody would have a great body."

CHER

"Physical fitness is not only one of the most important keys to a healthy body, it is the basis of dynamic and creative intellectual activity."

JOHN F. KENNEDY

"Nobody ever drowned in sweat."

JACK "BEAR" ROBERTS

"'How long does getting thin take?' asked Pooh, anxiously."

A.A. MILNE

DIET AND NUTRITIONAL TIPS

Now, I don't profess to know everything about nutrition and dieting. In fact, up until recently, I thought if all I ate was French fries, I could technically be considered a vegan. But, after speaking to nutritionists and a few of my friends who are annoyingly fit and healthy, I've compiled these tips:

⊙ Don't be fooled by diet sodas: Recent studies have shown that diet sodas can actually have a similar effect as sugar sodas (because your body starts to absorb fake sugar the same way it would real sugar).

⊙ Lots of water: Water is nature's flushing mechanism. It not only ensures your skin is looking healthy and beautiful, but also helps the body think it's full—indeed, sometimes hunger cravings are actually thirst.

⊙ Take a few weekends off: Nobody is a saint, and everybody can be expected to want to splurge—especially when they're just adjusting to a new eating regime. If you're struggling to eat healthier, give yourself a free pass over the weekend.

⊙ Avoid bored eating: I find myself doing this all the time. When I don't have something to do with my hands or when I'm at a party and it's boring, you can find me hovering over the cheese plate.

⊙ Skip the buffet: Avoid situations where binging on food is the only option, like all-you-can-eat buffets. (I know the game: The more you eat, the more you feel like you've gotten your money's worth, which is a terrible way to have dinner.)

⊙ Surround yourself with healthy snacks: Be sure to keep cut veggies in your fridge, granola in your purse, and raw almonds at your desk. That way you have plenty of healthy options right at your disposal. Don't even give yourself the opportunity to eat poorly.

⊙ Substitutions: It's hard at first, but subbing vegetables for French fries or other unhealthy sides is a very easy way to cut out unwanted calories and fat.

⊙ Don't stress eat! Especially when I was in college, I would eat and drink as a way to manage stress and work. It's a nasty habit. Instead, reward yourself with activities as you finish projects. Consider going on a walk, taking deep breaths, calling a friend, or meditating.

⊙ Keep it spicy: Peppers and other hot foods or spices are a great way to feel full and also boost your metabolism.

⊙ Eat breakfast: Skipping breakfast is a bad idea: It's a terrible way to start your day, and then you'll want a big lunch earlier on, which defeats the purpose of starving yourself in the morning. Eat something small and full of protein to start the day, like egg whites or oatmeal.

⊙ Portion control: It's not exactly news that portions in America have gotten ridiculously large, but I always feel bad leaving food on the plate. I've had to get over this because cleaning my plate often means buying bigger pants. Don't be afraid to order off the kids menu.

⊙ Replace snacks with green tea: Drinking hot beverages is a great way to curb hunger pangs (unless you're loading your coffee or tea with sugars and creams). Green tea in particular is beneficial as it can help boost metabolism.

⊙ Starvation doesn't work: To totally stop eating is a terrible way to try to lose weight. When you eventually get sick of such a regime (and you will), your body will hold on to the calories you consume for dear life. The same goes for cutting things out completely, like carbs. A healthy diet is a well-rounded one.

⊙ Stay active: At the end of the day, you can cut out all the bad things from your diet and replace them with healthy choices, but the human body craves some activity. Take a walk, buy a bike, join a gym, or do some push-ups in the morning.

⊙ Don't have that bad stuff in your house: This was a hard habit for me to break, mind you, but not buying the ice cream and the other sweets is the best way to avoid the temptation. And then, if you really want to splurge, take a walk to the store for the ice cream and burn it off as you walk home.

The Importance of Sleep

My first job in New York was working at a modeling agency. Any new girl that joined would be given a bunch of information and beauty tips (which would include: always wear heels, always eat green food, and don't have inappropriate relations with the photographers), but the one that I remembered was the importance of sleep. Every single model hopeful was told that the trick to looking good, and the trick to feeling good, was sleep.

Surely you know that sluggish feeling when you haven't gotten a good night's sleep: Your reactions are slower and your brain seems to be working on delay. The human body needs rest to unwind and reenergize for the next day, and the human brain needs to sort out a day's events and recharge itself.

But most importantly, you need a good night's sleep to make sure you don't look like a haggard, insane person. Doctors agree that the human body needs between six and eight hours of uninterrupted sleep— and remember that sleep isn't cumulative: four hours at night and then four hours that afternoon don't equal eight total hours of sleep.

Of course there are moments when getting a full night's sleep isn't possible: if you have a big project or presentation to give at school or at work, or if you're going through a stressful time with your personal or professional life. And then there are those other times when you'll voluntarily choose not to sleep in favor of other extracurricular activities, like dancing or socializing. (No judgment on my part, honey—I've been there!)

Robbing the body of sleep is fine in moderation. But if you find yourself going out to all hours of the night and not getting the proper rest—I should mention here that passing out

> "Sleep is the best meditation."
>
> DALAI LAMA

> "A well-spent day brings happy sleep."
>
> LEONARDO DA VINCI

drunk isn't the same thing as falling asleep—you will look bloated, faded, and worn-down.

Just sleeping isn't the only thing we need to do to give our bodies a rest. If you're a gym bunny, it's important to remember to take a few days off after a few days working out. For one,

your body and the muscles that you're stretching and building need to heal; and for two, you don't want to look like bodybuilding Arnold Schwarzenegger in your bikini, so give yourself some time away from the weights.

It's the same thing with your brain. After exams or a particularly strenuous few weeks at the office, go on a vacation, read a book at home, or take a long walk. Rest is just as important as action—but don't fool yourself into thinking every day is a rest day. That's just being lazy!

If for no other reason, even if you don't care about letting your body recover and your brain relax, remember this: Sleep is important when you want to look good, when you want your skin to be clear and plump, and your eyes to be clear and sparkly. Staying up late or refusing to slow down is bad for your body, and bad for your looks. You don't want bags under your eyes from lack of sleep. In fact, the only bags you should ever want belong at the end of your arm.

⊘ Nap, but be smart about it: I've had some bad days, and there are times when all I want to do is crawl up in bed and be done with it. But during the day, the only smart option is a quick siesta: fifteen minutes is ideal, but no more than thirty or you'll have a hard time falling asleep that evening.

⊘ Try a warm bath: The designer Tom Ford tells me he takes three baths a day, and he doesn't look fatigued at all. (Very handsome, that Mr. Ford.) To get ready for bed, sometimes it's good to do something relaxing, like turning down the lights, lighting some candles, and submerging yourself into the blissful, warm waters.

⊘ Yoga: I know I said before that growing up, I thought yoga was a variety of Asian food, but I know many people who use it, and meditation, to relax before shutting their bodies down.

⊘ Make it smell nice: Studies have proven that some scents, like lavender and chamomile oil, can help soothe the mind and put it to sleep.

⊘ Keep it quiet: Even though I like the sound of New York's streets outside my window, many people can subconsciously be kept awake by other noises. Sound-proofing your walls is probably too pricey, but keeping the windows closed and asking whoever else is home with you to keep the noise down is usually a good way to go.

⊘ Don't eat just before bedtime: When the body digests food, it needs to expend precious energy, which is a process that can keep you awake. So if you're having trouble falling asleep at night, try to eat dinner earlier.

⊘ Keep your heart rate down: While physical exertion during the day can help your body want to sleep at night, don't exercise in the three hours before you want to go to bed. Exercise keeps the body awake and running strong, which is better earlier in the day.

⊘ Don't booze before bed: While wine and other drinks can make you sleepy (indeed, in excess, they can make you black out), it's a really bad idea to rely on them to help you fall asleep. Drunk sleep isn't the same thing as good sleep.

⊘ Pay attention to what you're eating: Some foods are known to aid sleep, like figs, bananas, and anything with a lot of carbs in it. Also, warm milk isn't an old wives' tale: it can actually help you fall asleep. All of these contain tryptophan, which is what the body uses to create melatonin, the body's natural-forming sleep aid.

⊘ Turn everything off: Some people say they need a television on to fall asleep, but that's actually a proven distraction for the mind to turn itself off. Turn off anything that glows or peeps; put your phone on silent, close your computer, and put away all other electronic distractions.

⊘ Read: Even the best book can help me fall asleep.

⊘ Write in a journal: Sometimes the body can't shut itself off because the brain still needs to unwind. Spending a few minutes writing in a journal can help the body wrap up the day.

⊘ Get a schedule going: Just like my dog, who knows his feeding and walking times, the human body likes a good schedule. So start trying to get to bed at the same time every night and wake up at the same time every morning, even on the weekends.

⊘ Drugs are a last resort: This is at the bottom of the list because you should only use drugs if all the other remedies aren't working. In addition to being addictive, sleeping meds can leave you drowsy (and cause you to say ridiculous things to people, which has been my experience) the next day. Melatonin is the body's natural sleeping aid, so it's preferred to harder drugs and prescriptions.

Shrink Love

I grew up in a part of the United States that prides itself on its practicality. And I'm not exaggerating: Literally, Missouri's nickname is the "Show Me" state. So I will admit that when I moved to New York and found all these other young people who were already talking to shrinks about their deepest thoughts, I was a little confounded. The idea of talking about problems as a method of fixing them was rather far-fetched. Is that all you have to do? Talk about it? To a shrink? No pills or exercises or tests? Let's just say in my Show Me state mentality, that wouldn't fly.

It wasn't until I was a little bit older, and after I took some psych classes at university, that I really got into all this mental hocus-pocus. Suddenly, it seemed common sense to want to express yourself and seek professional help on important questions of human behavior. I even started seeing a therapist when my schedule allowed, and I really enjoyed it. (And no, not because I like talking about myself for hours at a time, thank you very much.)

Beyond my own rather infantile experiences with therapists, I can now attest to the success of therapy because I've seen it help so many of my friends. I have friends who have come from some seriously messed up backgrounds, and have needed a professional to talk to, and they've turned out just fine. I've had friends who have battled depression and addiction and things that are even worse, and have found therapy to be enormously beneficial. I'm not saying it has helped everybody every time, but it's a good place to start.

A Lady isn't embarrassed about seeing a therapist, but she doesn't flaunt it either.

That's the true message here: If you ever need someone to talk to, they're there. If you can't afford a shrink, look for a nearby service or a hotline number on the Internet. Be careful while you search though. Looking for someone to talk to on the Internet can provide some pretty freaky results, and then you can find yourself in all sorts of other difficult situations. But know that there's always someone to talk to, and there's always a place to go if you need to speak to someone about something serious.

One thing I do want to point out, however, is that while it's important to keep your brain as fit as the rest of your body, there's no reason to talk about it. Sure, there are some vaguely funny stories about advice that a shrink has given you, but it's generally a bad idea to make therapy sessions regular dinner conversation. No one wants to hear all about you, and what you're doing, and what your doctor thinks what you're saying says about you.

That said, if you think you need to speak to someone, or if you think one of your friends does, there is no shame in talking about it. Addressing life's problems head-on is infinitely more beneficial than self-medicating, or looking for an easy fix. While it's true that we now live in a prescription obsessed culture, the old fashioned way of communication to address issues is still the best. As my parents will tell you, now that I've driven them into therapy, there's no shame even in the Show Me state!

"I love being in therapy. It's just constantly fulfilling for me."

JENNIFER JASON LEIGH

"You don't realize how useful a therapist is until you see one and discover you have more problems than you ever dreamed of."

CLAIRE DANES

"It was either therapy or die."

MICKEY ROURKE

The Importance of a Hangover

For anyone who has ever experienced a very bad hangover, this pronouncement will come as a shock: I think a hangover is a good thing.

I have had some truly awful hangovers in my life: Once, when I went to a friend's wedding in Russia, a country where they serve vodka in large glasses (and I'm not talking shot glasses) with every course of a meal, I woke up the next day with a hangover so bad I actually thought I'd had a stroke in the middle of the night and didn't realize it. It hurt so bad I figured my brain was bleeding, because a hangover couldn't feel that bad.

Turns out it wasn't a stroke, and in time the pain subsided. But, apart from a few aspirin and some caffeine, I would never think of trying to take something else for the pain. In a way, I see it as though I've earned the punishment. I stayed up late, made bad choices, and so I deserve to suffer. (And I'm not only talking to people who drink—I've gone out and been sober, but danced till sunrise and felt awful the next day.) Part of what makes a night so epic is having a painful morning of equally epic proportions!

Hear out my theory: The reason that it's important to suffer the consequences of our actions is because if we didn't understand that poor decisions (and drinking a gallon of vodka) negatively affected our bodies, we probably wouldn't ever make the right decisions. If I never got a hangover, I would go out and be reckless every single night of my life. If I didn't wake up every once in a while (and for the record, it's really not that often) feeling like a truck had just hit me, I wouldn't act responsibly. The hangover is the body's way of telling you to check yourself.

Denying that experience is a cycle that you really don't want to get into: popping pills to stabilize hangovers is not good. In LA and in New York I see this all too often. Gone out too late and feel awful? Take this pill and you'll feel fine. Depressed? Down on your luck? Take a pill. Can't sleep and you're tired? Take a pill.

> "I feel like I have a hangover, without all the happy memories and mystery bruises."
>
> ELLEN DEGENERES

We're looking at a dangerously steep slope with these prescriptions, and it's a little bit frightening to see some of my girlfriends wake up and realize they've gone out every night of the week, or that they haven't been able to sleep in a few months without a pill. So, yes, a hangover sucks. I hate when my head pounds and when I wake up in the morning and I'm constantly dizzy and need someone to help me stand up. (Again, this is a very rare thing for me. I promise!) But I would much rather eat cheeseburgers all day nursing a nasty headache than be tricked into thinking wild nights are best in anything but moderation.

HANGOVER CURES

Just because I've said that hangovers are a good thing (I like to think of them as nature's reminder that it's not good to be bad all the time), it doesn't mean you have to suffer them all day, or all week if it's a real doozy. I'll admit that yes, I've imbibed a few too many spirits occasionally, and have woken up a little worse for wear. But while I respect the hangover, that doesn't mean I don't want to get rid of it. Here are my best tips for getting over that day-after feeling:

⊙ PREVENTION IS THE BEST POLICY. One reason the body feels so awful after a hangover is because it is dehydrated. So, if you're anticipating a wild night on the town, stay hydrated. My tip? Try to work in a glass or two of water between every one alcoholic drink.

⊙ EAT LIGHT THE NEXT MORNING. It's tempting to go straight for the bacon cheeseburger on a heavy morning (comfort food never tasted so good), but you want to stick to something light and easy for the body to digest, like toast or oatmeal.

⊙ SLEEP. Booze makes the body drowsy, which can get you to fall asleep easily. But when your body starts to sober up, it has a restless sleep, which doesn't actually rest the body. So, if you have the luxury of having a day off, go back to bed. The human body is fabulous at self-healing, particularly when it's slumbering.

⊙ DON'T GO BACK TO THE DOG! "The hair of the dog" is an expression that many people have used to explain why they wake up after a night of drinking and order a beer or a Bloody Mary. Nice try. While getting drunk again will ease the hangover, prepare yourself for a double whammy the next morning. There are no shortcuts when it comes to booze, ladies!

⊙ A LIGHT WORKOUT. Reading this may make you ache, even if you don't have a hangover! But getting up, getting out, getting some fresh air, and getting the body moving is one way to get it healing

⊙ JUICE UP! Replacing the vitamins and nutrients that have evacuated the body af-ter a wild night is a great way to start feeling human again. It also increases energy, which can help motivate recovery.

⊙ BANANA MANIA. Potassium depletion is one cause of a hangover, and a banana can help replace that. Sports drinks with potassium can do the same thing, though they often have more calories.

⊙ PICK YOUR POISONS. This is preventative: While you're drinking excessively, look for cleaner alcohols (like vodka and gin) and avoid the more complex drinks (brandy and whiskey). And whatever you do, don't mix everything up. That makes me sick just thinking about it.

⊙ STAY SOBER. Remember, at the end of the day, the best way to get rid of a hangover is: Don't drink so much the night before!

"Our bodies are
our gardens—our wills
are our gardeners."
**WILLIAM
SHAKESPEARE**

"The secret of getting
ahead is getting started."
MARK TWAIN

"Do or do not.
There is no try."
YODA

Skinny Fat Is Worse Than Just Fat

I t wasn't until I moved to New York that I first stumbled upon the concept of "Skinny Fat." In case you don't know, it refers to someone whose actual body may be skinny, but who is living a terrible lifestyle. I'm talking about girls who smoke to stay skinny or only eat raw meat to avoid carbs, never mind they probably have cholesterol high enough to kill a horse.

Ever since my nutrition-obsessed friends introduced me to this concept, I've been absolutely fanatical about it, and how dominant it is in our culture. Think about all the chemicals in diet sodas and other sugar substitutes, and the preservatives in our junk food. I mean, really, how can some of those delicious chocolate cakes taste so good and not have any calories? Something has to be up with that.

The reason I bring it up here is because it can lead to a seriously misguided notion of internal versus external health. Just because you fit into a small size dress doesn't mean you're healthy. Just because all you eat is tater tots and Caesar salads doesn't mean you're actually a vegetarian.

If you're starving yourself, you're damaging your insides permanently. (In middle school, I once read in my health book that anorexia makes all your organs shrink, including your brain, which is something I wish I could un-read. Scary stuff.) And if you're eating the

A Lady takes her health seriously.

wrong foods to keep skinny, you're probably doing equally harmful things to your insides.

Don't get me started on diet pills. Full disclosure: When I was in college and battling a bulge growing from dorm food and more time in the library than in the gym (dangerous combination), I gave those pills a try, and I thought my heart was going to explode. I haven't tried crystal meth, but I can imagine what speed feels like after a few days of those over-the-counter diet pills. Sure, the pills curb appetite, but at what cost? I'm not sure if being skinny is worth looking like a crack head. And what those pills don't say on the bottle is that as soon as you stop taking them, your body goes back to its pre-pill body type.

I'm just as guilty as everyone else when it comes to this concept: I would probably drink gasoline if someone told me it would make me look like Brad Pitt. But at the end of the day, to be truly healthy, we need to be careful about how we're treating our bodies. Diet and exercise are requirements to living a healthy life, and the only way to healthily lose weight is by expending more calories than you take in. If your jeans are getting tighter, you have to eat more green stuff and less fried stuff, and take the stairs a few times instead of the elevator.

Don't get me wrong: I work in the fashion industry, a business that revolves around appearances and is, literally, hung on the skinniest of bodies. I know how important a lean figure is. Hey, I have friends who are afraid to give up smoking because they're scared they'll gain a few pounds. (Sadly, I actually do have friends who if I asked them if they would rather die sooner or gain five pounds, they would start shopping for their tombstones.) But to be truly healthy, fit, and thin, one must respect that being skinny—and I mean truly skinny, not skinny fat—is hard work.

LIST OF WONDER FOODS

I'll admit that my favorite foods are probably the worst for me. (Give me some chicken wings, mozzarella sticks, and a meat lover's pizza any day!) But Mother Nature, in her divine glory, has provided us with some foods that nutritionists agree should be on the top of everyone's list.

Sweet potatoes

Best baked, these vegetables are full of carotenoids, vitamin C, potassium, and fiber.

Greens

This is an obvious food group (think of all those vitamins and goodness) that we should be eating. Broccoli, kale, collards, spinach, turnip greens, mustard greens, and Swiss chard are particularly good bets.

Salmon

All the omega-3 fats you can eat!

Oatmeal

The oat family is great for you, full of fiber, and fills you up.

Quinoa

It took me a while to try this food—I've always said I shouldn't eat food I can't pronounce—but when I did, I liked the taste, and loved what it's made of. A cup of quinoa, which the Inca Indians called the "Mother Grain," has more protein than a quarter-pound hamburger and more calcium than a quart of milk.

Fruits

The fruit family is a good one to get into, but most beloved are blueberries and kiwis, which are powerful antioxidants full of potassium, fiber, and vitamin C.

Dark chocolate

Perhaps Mother Nature didn't want to be etirely cruel when it came to sweets. Dark chocolate isn't nearly as bad for us as milk or white.

The alliums

Onions, garlic, chives, leeks, shallots and scallions. They can give you funky breath, but they can also help prevent cancer.

Watermelon

Watermelon is a heavyweight in the nutrient department. A standard serving (about two cups) has one-third of a day's vitamins A and C and a nice shot of potassium—and for only eighty-five fat-free, salt-free calories! And when they're in season, watermelons are often locally grown, which means they may have a smaller carbon footprint than some other fruits.

Beans

All beans are good beans. They're rich in protein, fiber, iron, magnesium, potassium, and zinc.

A Few Notes On Personal Recognition

It's something that has become very blurry in recent times: Is acknowledgment the same thing as acceptance? Is being well known the same thing as being well liked? The answer, of course, is no.

The idea of fame has become a generational epidemic. I don't say this with judgment, but only from observation. And, in the spirit of being honest, I like recognition as much as the next person. I participate in social media and have put pictures of myself in magazines and on the Internet, so for me to say that self-promotion is a bad thing would be truly hypocritical. But, what I will say is this: Being famous for no reason is not as easy as it looks, nor is it fulfilling in an emotional or financial sense.

As much as it pains me to admit it, there are some entertaining reality shows out there. I love any reality program revolving around truly awful people: Give me a front row seat to a bunch of crazy rich women fighting over the limelight and I'm in heaven. But while that sort of social ridiculousness entertains me, it took me a long time to understand that while these women are becoming more and more famous, they're becoming more and more obsessed with that attention. They crave it, but to their detriment, they're confusing it with power.

Fame and self-promotion have become addictions. I have actually met people who think being on a reality show would solve all their problems. They'll be rich and they'll be popular, and everyone will love them.

Sadly, that's not the case. That sort of fame is misleading, and to be honest, for non-famous names, those shows don't pay much money. I have met stars of reality shows who live in studio apartments in Brooklyn. Pictures in magazines don't pay the bills, sadly.

Also, as Michael Kors, who became a household name after he became a judge on the reality competition *Project Runway*, once explained to me, to be good at something like that is hard work. There's no script, so you have to be your own character. And finally, just because you're on TV doesn't mean that you'll be well liked.

Self-esteem isn't automatically derived from public recognition. Quite the contrary: As soon as you become any sort of public person—from reality TV show contestant to person who has merely posted a picture of yourself on the Internet—you are opening yourself up to criticism. As someone who has read comments about himself made by anonymous people on the Internet, let me tell you this can be soul crushing. ("Derek Assberg" was a pretty low point.)

The reason I feel compelled to put this in a chapter on health is because if we're not careful, the next generation of girls is going to have a distorted idea of fame and success. It is not healthy to crave fame over everything else, or be willing to hook up with someone on TV, or want to put scandalous pictures of yourself on the Internet. That rush is ultimately unfulfilling, and there are better things to do with your time.

Now I'm worried I'm starting to sound like a cranky old person who's afraid of the Internet and progress. Let me assure you that this is not the case: I crave interaction, attention, and communication as much as the next person. I've made friends on the Internet and I enjoy how democratizing industries like fashion have been as global technology has enabled the entire world to play into the conversation. I'm just trying to point out that reality shows, fame, and Facebook friends aren't the most important things in life.

Here's something that someone had to explain to me when I moved to New York: Fame isn't the same thing as power. In fact, many of the world's most powerful people aren't the most famous, and they want to keep it like that. True story: often times the richest people and the most powerful people in the world are pay-ing a bunch of people a lot of money to keep their names out of the paper and their pictures off TV. The truly powerful men and women I've met avoid pa-parazzi (as opposed to calling them) and work hard to keep a low profile. Real, powerful in-fluence won't be found on late night basic cable.

The balance between health and hedonism, which is easy for some and a full-on battle for others, has been an inspirational debate for great thinkers for generations. From taking time to reflect to getting in touch with one's spirit, from the devil to exercise: here is what some of the world's best minds—including Einstein, Jefferson, and Buddha—have to say about maintaining a nourished body, inside and out.

"Just as your car runs smoothly and requires less energy to run faster and farther when the wheels are in alignment, you perform better when your thoughts, feelings, emotions, goals and values are in balance."

BRIAN TRACY

"Take rest; a field that has rested gives a beautiful crop."

OVID

"Just as a candle cannot burn without fire, men cannot live without a spiritual life."

BUDDHA

"The devil has put a penalty on all things we enjoy in life. Either we suffer in health or we suffer in soul or we get fat."

ALBERT EINSTEIN

"Take care of your body. It's the only place you have to live."

JIM ROHN

"Exercise and application produce order in our affairs, health of body, cheerfulness of mind, and these make us precious to our friends."

THOMAS JEFFERSON

Slow and Steady Wins the Race

Perhaps if you've read this far into the chapter, you're seriously considering approaching a healthier lifestyle. That's great, but please heed this warning: Don't try to change everything at once! One of the biggest reasons that most people fail when they attempt diets, new exercise regimes, or healthier initiatives is because they attempt to alter their entire lives overnight. Recent surveys have even suggested that, at most, one should only change 40 percent of one's life—or else one may "implode." That's the word people in the know are using!

When it comes to lifestyle changes, remember this: Start small and gradually adjust. While there are a few people who can flip a switch in their heads and give up carbs, cigarettes, soda, dairy, and anything fried all at the drop of a hat, most of us need a little time to end a lifetime's devotion to unhealthy hobbies.

Like most people, when I was in college I picked up some nasty habits: late-night eating and smoking were just two of them, though I have friends who found solace (and their own addictions) in ramen noodles and microwaved mac 'n' cheese. It wasn't until I was nearing graduation that I realized how bad these habits were for me, and kicking them was no easy task. I managed to tackle them one by-one-with patience and consideration. (Smoking wasn't that hard to kick: I just realized I didn't look as cool as I thought I did with a cigarette

A Lady paces herself.

A Lady sets realistic goals and works hard to meet them.

in my mouth. See "How to Quit Smoking for Shallow People" on p. 254.)

The same goes for you: Start out with one change, then add another once the first becomes habitual. Then repeat.

If you're a soda addict like myself—I could finish a six-pack in an afternoon—the first step can be as easy as drinking water instead of soda at restaurants. (Bonus: you'll save a few dollars, especially if there are no unlimited refills.) Or

if you're a late-night snacker, resolve not to have dinner after eight o'clock, so you're not sleeping on a full stomach. Or if you're addicted to carbs, resolve not to inhale the free rolls a restaurant gives you before your meal. (But be warned: Never-ending breadsticks are a gift that's hard to give up, so you may find yourself avoiding those sorts of restaurants.) The end goal, of course, is to give up soda completely; eat early, well-balanced meals; and eat carbs sparingly.

Once these changes are made, you can build on them: If you've given up soda, your next step could be only eating food that is real. This basically means you won't eat anything with an ingredient you can't pronounce (I still don't know how to say *monosodium glutamate*) or that doesn't come directly from nature (e.g., artificial coloring or xanthan gum). The body can process the nutrients from food better when what you're eating has fewer ingredients (e.g., an ingredients list with five components, not twenty).

This may seem simple, but it can be a powerful change, and it's a great place to start. Before long, you'll develop a craving for the new, simpler foods you're consuming. And when you can make these choices subconsciously (which can take up to a month or so), add another change.

The aim is permanent change —not frustration, which can lead to regressing to your old habits. Failing a diet is maddening, and often when a diet fails, you start eating worse than before you started it. And believe me, you don't want to weigh more after you've done a diet. That's just embarrassing.

The Intervention

I 'm sure it says something about modern culture that novels chronicling the harrowing tales of former drug addicts are on our best-seller lists, and that TV shows that deal with drug and alcohol dependents get top ratings. (Let me be clear: Bill Clegg's *Portrait of an Addict as a Young Man* had me in tears, and I've been known to save certain episodes of HBO's *Intervention* on my DVR. So I'm not passing judgment here.) But while addiction has become entertainment, let's not forget that substance abuse is a disease that many of us struggle with firsthand.

While I have been known to poke fun at some of my friends for going out too much or to satirize someone's drunken behavior, there are times when a friend's antics are no laughing matter. Much of my early career as a journalist revolved around going out and having fun—so I firmly believe there's nothing wrong with a few wild

> "The greatest
> healing therapy
> is friendship
> and love."
>
> HUBERT H. HUMPHREY

nights. But I have had enough friends who have burned out and dropped out, and it's a sad thing to see. We all know tragic tales of teenagers whose lives have ended too soon because of drunk drivers or overdoses.

I think it's important that even while we let loose and live it up with our friends and peers, we're mindful of the difference between a once-in-a-while free-for-all and what can become a dangerous habit. (For a satirical look at addiction, see "Now, the Harder Stuff" on pp. 266-67.) The issue, of course, is knowing when to say something and how to make your point. This can get very complicated: ignoring a problem will only let it worsen, but too much tough love can ultimately push a person out of your life.

Hopefully, you'll be on the side where you're concerned about a friend, as opposed to the one where your friends are concerned about you. (But if you find yourself on the receiving end of an intervention, have the maturity and wherewithal to listen and objectively observe your lifestyle.) There are trained professionals who can deal with these sorts of instances, and a plethora of information exists: from guid-

ance counselors to addiction websites to hotline numbers. If you're seriously worried about someone's behavior, there is someone out there who can advise you on the best way to confront it.

So be assertive yet cautious when you broach this topic. Don't make jokes, don't be preachy, and research what

> "To be tested is
> good. The chal-
> lenged life may be
> the best therapist."
>
> GAIL SHEEHY

you're going to say before you say it. If you see someone falling off the deep end, have the pride and confidence to speak up. In the end, it's better to try to stop a friend before he or she does something stupid. And you will regret it forever if you do it too late.

Health Shouldn't Be a Hobby,

But it shouldn't be an obsession either!

I'm fully aware that this could sound ironic after including an entire chapter on staying healthy, but let me just put it out there: While it's okay to talk about nutrition, exercise and dieting, make sure these aren't the only things you talk about. I have met girls who are so consumed by their weight and the newest diets on the market it seems they have nothing else to talk about. There's nothing less attractive than a girl obsessed with appearances.

You probably know this kind of girl. Someone who sits down at a dinner table and talks about the newest fad diet, the number of calories there were in the Cobb salad she had for lunch, or everyone else's weight—and has little else to add to the conversation. Moderation is important with so many things, and certainly that includes diet talk. Dedication is one thing, but obsession is another.

Sure, there's nothing wrong with saying out loud that you're going to skip dessert because you're watching your weight. In fact, in some cases it's good to tell close friends and family that you're getting serious about your body and consciously watching what you eat. (Two good things come from that: First, telling someone you're on a diet will make you more account-

A Lady knows that devoting time to sleep is as important as devoting time to being active.

A Lady listens to her friends if they're trying to tell her something, even if it's hard to hear.

A Lady looks good when she feels good.

A Lady cares as much about what she puts in her body as what she puts on it. And she doesn't spend disproportionately more about either.

able if you're thinking about going back for a third helping of mac 'n' cheese; and second, perhaps that person won't ask you to join them on their next tasting at the brewery.)

Even your best friends probably want to talk about something besides gastric bypass, even if they're as obsessed with food as you are. While I work in fashion and my life revolves around photography, clothes, lighting, models, and designers, I pride myself on being able to talk about other things going on in the world. The girl who is constantly asking how many calories are in an apple or a stick of gum is annoying, and there's nothing less attractive than a girl who shows up at a dinner and doesn't eat.

At the end of the day, confidence is so much more attractive than an exposed ribcage or six-pack abs. And let's be honest: Good food is such a large part of an active social life, be it work dinners with clients or lunches with friends. Don't let an unhealthy fixation with food affect other parts of your life. (Believe me, the girl who skips the buffet in favor of a box of Tic-Tacs in her handbag and plays with her split ends while everyone else is eating dessert is annoying.) There's no point to looking good if no one wants you around.

QUIZ

Is Your Body a Temple, or a Waste Dump?

Part of growing up is rebelling and getting wild, and we're all bound to deal with effects of late-night eating binges, general laziness, and no doubt a few hangovers. But, to look good and feel good into our golden years, the smart woman knows to start thinking about her well-being sooner than later. Take this quiz to find out just how healthy—or unhealthy—you actually are.

1. What's a typical breakfast for you?

- (A) Depends on what I had for dinner the night before.
- (B) I mix it up between fresh fruit, cereal and oatmeal.
- (C) I take fresh, locally grown organic carrots and make a juice, and then I take all of my probiotics, wellness vitamins and injectables.
- (D) French toast, extra syrup.

2. When you're feeling down, what do you do?

- (A) Eh, getting depressed takes too much energy.
- (B) Turn off the TV, take a deep breath and go on a long walk.
- (C) Call all three of my therapists on their cell phones.
- (D) Two words: jelly beans.

3. When you're having a late night craving you:

- (A) Go the fridge for ice cream. Or maybe a peanut butter and jelly sandwich. Or maybe just a block of cheese. Hell, I'll eat whatever is in there.
- (B) Apple slices are a great way to curb appetite in the evening.
- (C) One does not snack between meals.
- (D) I have a stash of candy bars in my nightstand.

4. If you had to break your diet into food groups, what would they be?

- (A) Delivery and take out.
- (B) I try and eat a well-rounded diet that has lots of fresh veggies and protein, but allow myself dessert once in awhile.
- (C) I never eat anything that has a face, could have had a soul or was ever alive.
- (D) Would chocolate and birthday cake be considered in the same food group?

5. On average, you drink:

- (A) All day.
- (B) Typically on special occasions, and never too much!
- (C) Oh, I don't touch the stuff.
- (D) I only like daiquiris!

6. How far is the nearest gym to your house? And how often do you go?

(A) Wait, is gym really short for James?

(B) I try and stop by the gym on the way home from class, but then again I mix it up: sometimes I go for a jog around the neighborhood.

(C) I have a personal trainer come over to my house every morning at 6:30am on the dot. No exceptions.

(D) It's right next to my favorite cupcake store.

7. What are you looking at when you go grocery shopping?

(A) The word microwavable.

(B) I start in the produce section and work my way around the store, trying to get things with ingredients I can pronounce!

(C) I have a very detailed shopping list that I follow to the letter.

(D) The entire variety of M&M's.

8. Do you believe in therapy?

(A) Nah, but I do love to talk about myself.

(B) If I'm ever upset, I would definitely talk to someone.

(C) Are you kidding? I talk to my shrink more than my mother.

(D) I like going to the doctor when they give me candy afterward.

QUIZ KEY

Count up all your answers and see which of the four letters you had the most of. If you are:

Mostly A's. Lazy Lady: It sounds to me like you're eating hangover food all day and everyday. (Maybe that's because you're hungover?) Now, I'm hardly one to lecture someone about diet and exercise—I know my way around a buffet and I'm not exactly a gym bunny in my own life—but I at least have enough pride in my body and in my health to know that with just a little bit of effort I can feel and look better. Overeating, binge drinking, not exercising, and having a negative attitude about your self worth are all terrible habits to get into—and you should think about breaking them sooner than later! I say this a few times in the book, but it's true: If you feel good you'll look good.

Mostly B's. Healthy Henrietta: Finally, someone who understands how important it is to maintain a little balance with your mind and your body! The modern girl doesn't need far-fetched diets to be healthy, nor does she need to work out every day. What's important is that you make some time for yourself to stay healthy. You're on the right track, and congratulations for keeping your body—and I mean your entire body, both on the inside and the outside—in such fabulous shape.

Mostly C's. Hypochondriac Connie: Take a deep breath, girl. I think you're overthinking things a little too much. While I will agree with you that organic food is better than inorganic, that exercise is an important part of a healthy lifestyle, and that there's nothing wrong with shrinks—I think you might be taking things a little too seriously. You have to live a little, and not everything needs to be perfect. Loosen up and have a little fun. Otherwise, what's the point of being healthy and fit in the first place?

Mostly D's. Sweet-toothed Sally: Let me say this first: I have an unhealthy obsession with Reese's Peanut Butter Cups, and when I was a kid I would easily get into fist fights over them. But as we grow into adults—and most notably, as our metabolisms go down while our responsibilities go up—we need to start being a little bit more strategic with our health habits. You don't have to give up the sweet stuff, but you should be careful that it's not the only thing you're putting in your body. OK, sweetie?

Q&A:
A Lady Stays Healthy

The best part about creating this book has been the responses it's caused among the young women I've met at my book signings, over e-mail, and even on the street. There are some smart girls out there, and they've had some fabulous questions. I liked some of them so much I wanted to include them here.

Q: *Do you work out?*

A: I sure do. I would venture to say that nine out of ten people have to do some sort of diet or exercise to keep their figures. And to the one person who doesn't: I hate you! Either way, it's a good thing to do—even if you're naturally fit, you need to keep your body healthy and your lifestyle active.

Q: *Do you have any alcoholic friends?*

A: In a word, yes, I do have friends who drink too much. Some of them are aware of their addiction and have sought help to get back on their feet. And some of them aren't there yet. From my perspective, it's important to be there for friends no matter what. I know that if I ever have an addiction—be it to booze or otherwise—they would be there for me.

Q: *Do you see a shrink?*

A: With varying regularity, I have seen doctors since I was a little boy. Full disclosure: my parents were worried about me when I was a kid (I would act out and refuse to follow rules), and they sent me to a childhood psychiatrist. I hated it and thought it was a waste of time. But looking back, it was truly a beneficial experience and an important one to my development. (But whatever you do, don't tell my parents I said that.)

Q: *Are all of your skinny friends obsessed with their weight?*

A: Nearly every woman I have ever met is conscious of her appearance, and some form of vanity is a normal human emotion. Sure, girls in the fashion industry are notoriously more obsessed about it, but I would like to think that not all of my friends are obsessively narcissistic. There is truly nothing more boring than a girl who thinks she is only defined by how much she weighs or what she looks like.

Q: *Do you read about yourself on the Internet?*

A: Danger! Danger! Reading about oneself online can be one of the most mentally scarring experiences in the world. Do it only with care, and please bear in mind that anonymous bloggers are notoriously nasty. Be sure to care more about what people who know you think, as opposed to what some random person you'll never meet, who cowardly talks trash online, thinks. Have a sense of humor about it, if you do put your name in the Google machine, and be secure enough to laugh at yourself.

Q: *Can exercise ever be fun?*

A: I'm going to be honest with you: For the most part, I would prefer to sit at home and watch boring morning television than take an 8:30 a.m. spin class. But if I push myself, there is an endorphin rush that comes with exercise, and there is a sense of pride in knowing I don't have to go to specialty stores to buy clothing in my size. It's like Kate Moss famously said: "Nothing tastes as good as skinny feels." The trick, of course, is to stay active and find athletic feats that are enjoyable. Like water skiing, which I have been doing since I was a kid. (And since everyone I've told about my waterskiing prowess laughs in my face, I'm including a picture of me up on skis as proof!) Other things that I've dabbled in while I've lived in the big city: intramural soccer teams, trapeze lessons, and yoga, each with varying degrees of success and enjoyment. I'm definitely not the fittest guy in New York, but I'm proud of the fact that I don't get winded if I ever have to take the stairs.

A Lady
Faces Temptation

━━━━━━━

"I can resist everything except temptation."

OSCAR WILDE

I'M GOING TO BE HONEST HERE, GIRLS: I have been tempted by some of the things listed in this section (even the pole dancing, I will shamefully admit). And chances are, when it comes to cocktails, cigarettes, and even the harder stuff, you also will be tempted at some point in your life. Which is okay. But while I'm going to discourage you from drinking yourself into a hospital or a three-way, let's get something straight here: I'm not a Boy Scout or a guidance counselor or your momma. I'm not going to tell you to be a nun and sit at home in neutral colors, reading the Bible or crocheting socks for homeless children.

The real trick with these temptations is to know what you're dealing with, what your limits are, and when to get out of a potentially dangerous situation. I won't bore you with statistics about teenage drinking (my parents did that—and all it did was make me want a drink), or show you pictures of a teenager's lungs after smoking for a few years (again, when I see those TV commercials with people talking through holes in their throats, it only makes me want to change the channel and light up a Marlboro). But, please, take this to heart: A lady doesn't vomit in her mouth and then swallow it, and only a tramp smells like an ashtray when she leans in to kiss a boy.

All I'm saying is that there are ways to be cool that don't involve alcohol poisoning, illegal activities, dirty needles, and strip clubs. (Wait, did I just describe all my favorite reality TV shows?) I'm not going to sit here and agree with your parents that you don't need to be cool. To be honest, if you want to make it in this world, you *do* need to be cool within your particular social set (maybe you want to be the coolest chess nerd, or coolest jock). There, I said it. Being cool is important. But even if you're out to impress, be responsible and take care of yourself first.

QUIZ How Bad Are You?

According to the Bible, one of the very first human experiences was of temptation. And there's no doubt that being tempted—by the hot surfer you meet on vacation, by those movies that make crackheads look so sexy, by a frozen margarita—is natural and nothing to be ashamed of. What really matters is how you respond when the devil (or the hot surfer) comes a-knocking. Take this quiz to find out how naughty your proclivities are.

1. When you walk into a party, other people usually:

- **A** Don't notice.
- **B** Smile, and make their way over to say hi.
- **C** Cheer, then get out the shot glasses.
- **D** Take off their shirts and fill an inflatable pool full of Jell-O.

2. If you're late to class or an appointment, your boss or teacher thinks:

- **A** *Oh no, something terrible has happened.*
- **B** *She must have had car trouble. She's normally so punctual.*
- **C** *She must be hungover—or drunk—again.*
- **D** *How did this crackhead get a job here/into this school in the first place?*

3. Someone has just offered to share a beer with you. Your response is to:

- **A** Slap him/her across the face. Do you look like a drunk?
- **B** Politely decline until you're settled in and ready to drink responsibly, acknowledging that you can afford your own drinks and don't think it's a good idea to imbibe something you didn't see poured.
- **C** Say, "Hell, yeah!" The more you drink, the cuter the guy offering will be.
- **D** Down his drink, then ask for a bottle of tequila and a straw.

4. You're on vacation, and a cute guy asks if you want to come over and "party" later. You:

- **A** Call him a pervert. Only sluts go to strangers' homes.
- **B** Suggest you'd prefer to meet somewhere public.
- **C** Give him your phone number and tell him to call when he wants you to come over. You don't have anything better to do.
- **D** Go with him right then and there. Saves you the trouble of trying to pick up a guy from the hotel bar later.

5. After a few cocktails you find yourself in front of a tattoo parlor. You:

(A) Cringe at the sight of those people doing such terrible things to their bodies.

(B) Grudgingly admire the carnage but recognize now isn't the time to make a decision about something permanent like a tattoo.

(C) Follow your friends' lead and somehow emerge with a picture of a Disney character tattooed on your ankle.

(D) Lead the charge into the parlor and wake up the next morning with a tat of *The Last Supper* on your forehead, with Jesus in the place of honor on your T-zone.

6. Typically, at a party, when do you leave?

(A) After ten minutes.

(B) When the party is at its best—'cause you want to leave on a high note.

(C) Just before the hostess kicks you out.

(D) When the police come.

7. Medically speaking, you are how familiar with the local free clinic?

(A) You've only read about it in the free flyers you distribute to the needy as part of your volunteer church group.

(B) You've taken a friend there once or twice.

(C) After a few wild nights, you're more familiar with the place than you'd care to be.

(D) When you show up, the nurses give you high fives and all the doctors know you by name (your stripper stage name anyway).

8. How often have you woken up in a strange place you didn't recognize with no idea how you got there?

(A) Absolutely never. Are you kidding? You've slept in your parents' bed every night of your life.

(B) Once. And that was enough to prevent you from ever doing it again.

(C) A few nights a week, which isn't *that* bad.

(D) What? Where are you? And where are your keys? And what time is it? And why in God's name is this book open on your face?

QUIZ KEY

Count up all your answers and see which of the four letters you had the most of. If you are:

Mostly A's. You're a Nun: There is nothing wrong with being a conservative young person. In fact, this world could probably use more serious people. But be careful that you're not depriving yourself of certain typical rites of passage. (Which isn't to say you should go hog wild either. Just remember that being responsible doesn't obligate you to be boring— or worse, judgmental.)

Mostly B's. You're the Perfect Partier: You know that you don't have to be the star of the party (or the drunk of the party, or the crackhead of the party) to have fun at the party. Continue to let the good—and safe—times roll.

Mostly C's. You're a Girl Gone Wild: Take a second to look at the way you lead your life. It's not my place to tell you to slow down— 'cause I've had a few fast nights in my life too—but be careful. If you continue to party so much, you've got a one-way ticket to Disasterville.

Mostly D's. You're a full-on Natural Disaster: Okay, it's time to stay home one or two nights. And it's time to evaluate your behavior (and seriously consider rehab). The party has to end sometime . . . and for once, it's time to end it before your face ends up in the toilet.

Those Seductive Ciggies

L isten, I can't lie: In some cases, it's okay to smoke cigarettes. Maybe you're a saucy rock chick who needs clouds of mystery—literally—to surround you, and the throat damage is vital to your gravelly vocalizations. Hell, maybe you're the next Kate Moss, a supermodel who has made smoking cool since her teens. (Which, by the wrinkles on her face—from smoking, ironically, more likely than age—you can tell were quite a few years ago.)

Chances are, however, you're not Kate Moss. Chances are you're going to start smoking either to look cool, or to be like another person you think is cool. Chances are you saw a movie where the main character, a sexy rebel, smoked; or you saw a picture in a magazine where a beautiful model was smoking; or the girl who is currently dating your long-term crush is a smoker—and you think that by smoking you can get closer to being sexy/rebellious/beautiful/loved.

But, let's be honest, those just aren't good enough reasons.

James Dean was just as cool without a cig as he was with one, and there are other things a lady can do to feel empowered. (Besides, Dean's whole appeal was based on a smoldering squint, casual slouch, too-fast-to-live, too-young-to-die concept—not the fact that he liked Marlboro Reds.) And while some people claim that smoking is a good way to chill out, the nicotine is actually a stimulant. People will always make up reasons to smoke,

> "An unfortunate thing about the world is that the good habits are much easier to give up than the bad ones."
>
> SOMERSET MAUGHAM

> "Habits are at first cobwebs, then cables."
>
> SPANISH PROVERB

> "To cease smoking is the easiest thing I ever did. I ought to know because I've done it a thousand times."
>
> MARK TWAIN

and although I've had my own fair share of smokes in my day—'cause it's cool!—there comes a time in everyone's life when it's just no longer attractive, and by then it's typically a very difficult habit to shake.

Picking up a cigarette at a club or frat party—be it to draw attention to the mouth in an attempt to be sexy, or to do something with your fingers (a BlackBerry does the trick, y'all)—might seem attractive in your teens and early twenties, but eventually it's just gross. I was once told that only teenagers and old women should smoke, and that makes sense to me. 'Cause if you're thirty and still wasting your hard-earned money on cigarettes, there's a problem.

Believe me: There will be a time when instead of looking like a waifish supermodel, you will look like a pathetic, sagging-faced, yellow-toothed, hair-stinking skank who gets passed around the backseat of big-rig trucks. And that's when it's hard to give 'em up. It's just best not to start.

WHAT YOUR CIGARETTES SAY ABOUT YOU

I've discovered that different kinds of people smoke different kinds of cigarettes. So while I still think smoking is a silly thing to do, if you're going stick with the nasty habit you should at least know that your smokes are saying much more about you than that you may have throat cancer. The type of cigs you puff can be an indication of other personality traits, so consult the comical, punny list below to find out what kind of signals your smokes are sending out.

Parliaments: You may be a Russian hooker.
Marlboro Ultra Lights: You're a poser who only smokes to look cool.
Marlboro Lights: You are unoriginal and long to fit in with the crowd.
Marlboro Reds: You just don't give an F about anyone or anything.
American Spirits: You are a tobacco vegan who has convinced herself that smoking isn't that bad for you.
Newports: You are poor.
Virginia Slims: You are not skinny, and you will never be.
Camels: You identify with cool cowboys, but deep down you know you're just another chick from the suburbs of New Jersey.

How to Quit Smoking for Shallow People

T he association between cigs and style has been a historic one: Audrey Hepburn's graceful waftage in *Breakfast at Tiffany's*, James Dean's teenage cool in *Rebel Without a Cause*, Steve McQueen's scruffy and sensual toking while bare-backing a motorcycle. Cigarettes have long been the go-to accessory for angst, carnal frustration, self-abuse, and seduction.

It was this promise of star quality that prompted my own brief love affair with those oh-so-tempting cancer sticks. Smoking was something to do during a conversational lull, a reason to excuse myself from a dinner table; cigarettes were something to focus on in a club when I was waiting for something exciting to happen; cigarettes were something to share with a good-looking fellow partier; and the perfect way to end an indulgent meal. Sure, now I've found better ways to do all these things (and more effective ways to get out of the boring situations). [See "Conversation Enders," p. 71.] But there was a time when cigs were my best friends.

The affair ended abruptly, however. Flipping through a few celebrity glossies, I came to a sad realization: Smoking wasn't cool anymore. Not because it's cancerous or was hurting my body (at the time that didn't bother me—because I was so shallow, I would have happily mixed up Clorox cocktails if someone had told me that drinking bleach would make me look like Brad Pitt in *Legends of the Fall*), but because I noticed that the habit had been picked up by all the wrong people. Wannabes and wankers have replaced the sexy smokers so many of us longed to emulate, taking the habit from rebellious to predictable.

And this is exactly what helps shallow people—like me—quit smoking. The smokers I see now aren't beautiful people who look like they've stepped out of a 1950s cowboy movie: No, they're fat ladies in sweatpants and old men who look like they haven't brushed their teeth in years.

So attention, smokers, follow these simple directions to quit: Find a mirror. Sit or stand in front of it. Light up a ciggie. Now, look at yourself and ask, "Do I look like Kate Moss or do I look like Britney Spears at the height of her mental breakdown, when she wore pink wigs and drove to gas stations without shoes on (ironically, to buy cigs)? Do I look cool smoking, or do I look like I'm trying to look cool smoking?"

For me, it was the latter. Sure, some people can still pull off the art of smoking—tradition-

ally, people who ride motorcycles, horses, or drive big trucks—but for the rest of us, especially those who fell in love with the pre-1990s glamour of the dirty little things, the sad truth is, the moment has passed. And knowing you're uncool, outdated, and looking foolish should be enough to make you kick the habit.

That's right: Forget the patches and the creams and the pills and the hypnotist—techniques that all of my friends have employed in an effort to quit—the simple truth is that if you think you look stupid doing it, chances are you won't do it to begin with.

I honestly think that the surgeon general should pull all of those stupid commercials featuring old men who talk through voice boxes and instead send free packs to unattractive smokers. 'Cause if they gave trashy hookers, fallen celebrities, portly pop stars, and reality-TV skanks an unlimited supply of smokes, most people like me would automatically give up the habit. I don't know about you, but I do not want anything in common with that lot.

FIG. 1: Hipster Cliché

FIG. 2: Granny Get Your Menthols

Chances are, a smoker starts out looking like Figure 1, or at least trying to. But before long, she may more closely resemble an entirely different sort of tobacco user: See figures 2, 3, and 4 on this page.

FIG. 3: Ms. Unhealthy

FIG. 4: Bad Mommy

Cleaning Up a Filthy Mouth

E lizabeth Taylor dominated the silver screen in movies like *Cat on a Hot Tin Roof* and *Who's Afraid of Virginia Woolf?* At the height of her popularity, she was considered to be the most beautiful woman in the world. But here's a little known fact about the icon: She also had one of the foulest mouths in Hollywood and could make even the roughest teamster blush. She got away with it because she was Elizabeth Taylor. And when you have 250 carats of diamonds popping out of your cleavage, you can say whatever you want. (Also, back in those days, there weren't cell-phone recorders that could be used to document and upload to the Internet an f-word-filled tirade.)

The problem now, however, is that we're not all Elizabeth Taylor; we don't all have rotund chests and all the diamonds to cover them. Thus, speaking broadly here, a lady should watch her mouth. There are certain instances when it's okay to cuss—you dropped a curling iron on your foot, you missed the subway by a few seconds, you forgot to call your mom on her birthday—but if you're cursing like a sailor on an afternoon stroll to the supermarket, you have a problem.

Often a foul mouth is symptomatic of an attention craver. Lots of young women think that by using nasty words they can get some unwarranted time in the spotlight, or appear more mature. But listen, ladies, if you're not saying something of substance, dressing it up with a few *fuck*s and *shit*s isn't going to make it any more impressive.

Don't get me wrong: I've met a few badass chicks in my day who could curse a cowboy off the ranch, but in general you want to be entertained by the topic and nature of a woman's conversation, not the fact that she can use *shit* as a verb, noun, and adjective in the same sentence.

> "If you can't be a good example, then you'll just have to be a horrible warning."
>
> CATHERINE AIRD

> "Ultimately all you have left at the end of the day are your name and your reputation. Invest in them wisely, and you and others will simultaneously reap the rewards."
>
> LEONARD A. SCHLESINGER
> HARVARD UNIVERSITY

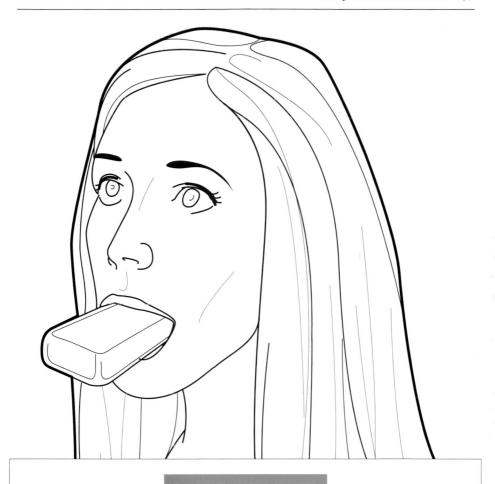

BETTER CURSE WORDS

There are some cases when cursing and using naughty language are appropriate means of expression. It's not very ladylike to scream and cuss, but yes, even the most dignified young person has forgotten their cell phone in the back of a taxi or been aggravated by someone else. A good thing to remember, however, is that you don't have to use the same series of bad words over and over; if you are irritated or disappointed, you don't have to use the f-word to make a point. Below is a list of some of my favorite unconventional cusses. Remember, a lady picks her words wisely, even the naughty ones.

Bollocks: Most popular in England, often yelled in anger or disbelief. It literally means a bull's genitals and is actually fun to say.
Goshdarnit: A nicer way of expressing disbelief, which has the added benefit of not taking the Lord's name in vain.
Panooch and Vayjayjay: Nicer words for the female reproductive organ, the latter of which was promoted by none other than Oprah Winfrey.
Piss off: A milder, less offensive way of asking someone to remove him or herself from your area (physical or metaphoric) without using the f-word.
Twit: A more amusing, less brutal way to describe a stupid person.
Bloody: Yes, people might think you're trying to do a whole Madonna/fake English person thing, but it's nicer on the ears than the vulgarity it often stands in for.
Mofo: This is an abbreviation for a longer, very bad word.
Trollop and Strumpet: Nicer words for explaining that a girl has a less-than-stringent moral code. [For more on how to insult people intelligently, see "The Educated Insult," pp. 182-83.]

Drink Up, But Not Till You Fall Down

P eople have been getting drunk for centuries. In B.C. times, Romans got toasted on local wines. The Middle Ages had a fair share of town drunks, and apparently the biggest writers of the 1920s were bombed when they summed up the excess of America's early twentieth century (ah, love you, F. Scott Fitzgerald). We've all met—or, more likely, are related to—at least one worthless boozehound. Hell, I once read about a horse who chowed down on some fermented apples, drunkenly stumbled into a neighbor's pool, and had to be fished out. So it's not like getting wasted is a new phenomenon.

What is new are the pressures to drink more, earlier in life. Theoretically, if a lady is under the legal drinking age, she should abstain from alcohol completely. But that type of willpower is rare (even I, well-behaved and saintly though I am, had a few drinks in high school and college).

So let's say she drinks. Fine. The important thing is this: A lady must know how to pace herself, when to stop, and when to say no. I have some lightweight girlfriends who drink one glass of water or one Diet Coke for every beer or cocktail, and the others try and milk a single drink for a few hours.

Here's the thing: Being the drunkest girl at a party is not a good look. There is nothing more embarrassing than being that girl. And don't think for a second that such a reputa-

> "Always do sober what you said you'd do drunk. That will teach you to keep your mouth shut."
>
> ERNEST HEMINGWAY

> "Woe to the drunken woman, whose glorious beauty is but a fading flower."
>
> THE PREACHER'S PRIMER OF VIRTUE

> "One reason I don't drink is that I want to know when I am having a good time."
>
> NANCY ASTOR

tion won't spread after you're spotted vomiting in the bushes (ew!) or drooling all over yourself. Between digital cameras, camera phones, and text messaging, people might know that you were a lush idiot before the hangover even wears off.

Furthermore, and I can't say this enough: If a guy goes to a party and sees you slurring your speech and talking to lampposts, he will not think you're sexy. Even if you wore your favorite top and are having a good hair day, if you leave a party with your bra in your hand and little pieces of vomit in your hair, the romance is dead. Depending on the immorality of the guy, he might try to have sex with you, but he will not think you're sexy.

And if you do go there, if you do go to that dark place where it's possible to black out and for-

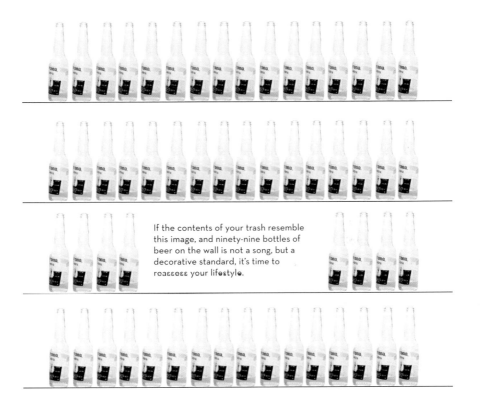

If the contents of your trash resemble this image, and ninety-nine bottles of beer on the wall is not a song, but a decorative standard, it's time to reassess your lifestyle.

get where you are and wake up in a stranger's house—which is one of the dumbest, most dangerous things in the world to do—you'll have no one to blame but yourself. Drinking is a dangerous sport—and if you're an underage drinker, even more dangerous.

For all the shallow ladies after my own heart, something else to think about: Do you know how fattening it is to get drunk? And I'm not talking exclusively about beer, which is loaded with calories. Mixed drinks aren't exactly herbal diet remedies, either. Your White Russian is probably loaded with more fat than a candy bar (and, no, that is not an excuse to drink vodka

straight). Not only will you wake up hungover, no doubt full of regrets about your previous night's behavior, but there's the added fear that you could one day wake up with a beer gut.

I'm not saying a girl needs to sit cross-legged in the corner all night—in fact, I've met that girl, and she's boring—but a modern lady knows how to stick up for herself. If she doesn't feel like drinking, she doesn't have to. And if you don't feel like getting bombed within an inch of your life, you shouldn't either. While I'm not discouraging someone from having an after-dinner cocktail or a few glasses of wine with dinner, I strongly discourage people from finding

themselves voluntarily going on the binge.

A few years ago, I went to a house party with some friends, and an actress who was on a hit TV show was there, drunk as a skunk. By the time I left, she had offended half the party, broken half a dozen glasses and—much to everyone's horror—peed in her pants. Yes, this supposedly put-together young woman had relieved herself in her designer jeans. That alone convinced me never to get sauced in public. I still can't watch reruns of her teen California drama show without the urge to use the restroom.

On the Prowl

It's tricky territory: Who is out looking for a good time, and who has been hired to provide good times? While it's true that going out and drinking socially is supposed to be fun for young women, it's really easy to overdo it. These two visuals help determine what's hot and what's a hot mess when you're out on the town.

HAIR
A messy bun is the perfect combination of ladylike styling and casual fun.

MAKEUP
Eyeliner on the eyes and lipstick on the lips. Fundamental, and not too difficult (if you really think about it).

POSE
Coy, sweet, and smiling: looks like a good time to me!

CLOTHING
A funky Chanel blazer and inexpensive leggings: a good combination of high-low.

THAT'S YES CLASSY!

LADY

BEVERAGE
If you're going to drink, make sure your beverage is tasty—and worth all those calories.

CLEANLINESS
Clothes should be clean, pressed, and unstained—or else they should be in the dirty laundry hamper.

ACCESSORIES
Her Manolos look like they're in good condition, and everything she needs is carried safely in a little red YSL clutch.

CIGARETTES
Smoking is a bad habit, but tucking packs of cigs into the tops of your pantyhose is an even worse habit.

MAKEUP
The second anything starts to streak—be it your eyeliner or you personally—it's time to go home. "Taxi!"

BEVERAGE
Even bottles of beer— especially when mixed with Red Bull—should be consumed one at a time, and in moderation.

STRIPPING
Generally speaking, if you ever find yourself holding an article of clothing that you should be wearing, you need to reevaluate your behavior.

TRAMP

DEMEANOR
Yes, this girl looks like a good time. But, will that handsome guy she has her eye on think so? (With that vomit in her hair, probably not.)

SHOES
Unless you're in a pool, boarding a yacht, or on a white carpet, your shoes should be on your feet.

PURSE
A lady's purse should contain her personal effects, not be on the bottom of a pile of them.

TRAMP NO STAMP

Overindulgence

O kay, so you've ignored all my advice. You've left your good sense at home, and you've drunk your drinks and smoked your smokes and gone out with your friends. And now you're wasted!

Hey, I'm not judging you here. I've been there. More times than I'll ever admit.

But at the very least, take some pointers about what to do once you've reached this point: Never, under any circumstances, vomit in public. Never throw up where anyone besides a loved one—but not a significant other if you want him to be a significant other for very much longer—will see you with messy hair and vomit in the corners of your mouth. If you feel like you're going to do something stupid, just leave. Do not—I repeat, do not—take your seventh tequila shot in the hopes that it will "settle your stomach." Do your best to stand up straight, tell your friends that you're going to the bathroom, and then either find a (trusted) ride home or call a taxi.

A friend of mine, a gorgeous supermodel who drank like a fish, used to pull this disappearing act all the time. She'd be there having fun, and then she'd just disappear. She knew that half of her allure came from looking like a put-together young woman—difficult to achieve if you're drooling down the front of your blouse.

When people are young, and when people are first introduced to drunkenness, they might think it's funny to be a party animal who passes out in

"I like to have a martini, two at the very most. After three I'm under the table; after four I'm under the host."

DOROTHY PARKER

nightclubs and restrooms and on kitchen floors. But it's not. It's not even hygienic. Did you know that herpes can be communicated through toilet seats? Think about that the next time you're tempted to make out with a bottle of vodka and the bathroom floor at the local truck stop.

Other things you want to avoid: making out with a friend's significant other—or making out with anyone if you already have a boyfriend. In fact, it's probably just a good idea to avoid hooking up when you're trashed. (This might be hard. There's something about drunken girls that just says, "Make out with me." Unfortunately, it's a language in which middle-aged truckers named Jimbo seem to be most fluent.) Being drunk is never an excuse for bad behavior. Try telling your boyfriend that one: *Sorry I didn't call, made out with your best friend, lost the ring you gave me, and threw up on the blouse I borrowed from your sister—silly me, I shouldn't have had that tenth Lemon Drop.*

Dancing is something else you should avoid when you're wasted, as is standing on bars or bar stools. Actually, doing anything that requires excessive body movements and/or balance is a bad idea. It might sound strange, but when you're wasted you should act more like a lady than you should when you're sober. Stay put, keep your legs closed, and mind your business. And go home.

DO YOU HAVE A DRINKING PROBLEM?

○ Do you wake up often not knowing where you are?

○ Do you ever complain of pains in your liver?

○ Do you pick beer over food when counting calories?

○ Do you often miss your mouth with your fork/cup while eating/drinking?

○ Do you find yourself buying new pairs of underwear all the time because you can't find the old pairs?

○ Do more bartenders/liquor-store vendors know your name than teachers/work associates?

○ Do you get into fights with inanimate objects, like shoes, walls, couch cushions, or television screens?

○ Do you find things in your pockets—like doorknobs, other people's wallets, hats, stuffed animals, parts of a chandelier—when you come home after an evening out?

○ Do you feel you have to drink when you're out?

○ Do you wake up next to the toilet often?

○ Do you see double?

○ Do you get antsy when people use the word *alcoholic* around you?

○ And lastly, do you think you're a drunk?

If the answer to more than one of these questions is yes, sorry to break it to you, but chances are you may need to slow down and give the bottle a break. Look on the bright side: When you're hanging out at rehab, there's a good chance you'll meet a fallen reality TV star or former famous child actor.

A Bar Behind the Wheel

No matter how cool being casual may seem, driving while inebriated is a bad, bad idea

There are about 2.6 million reasons why someone should not drive drunk—that's the number of estimated crashes per year in the U.S. alone caused by people stupid enough to take the wheel after they've had a few cocktails—but I'm not here to burden you with depressing statistics.

If you drink and drive, what should concern you beyond the very real possibility of imminent death is this: getting caught behind the wheel of a car after you've been drinking. It's humiliating, period. More than anything—more than the points on your license or the additional cost of your insurance or, you know, the possible jail time—it's degrading and selfish and mortifying and disgusting. If you don't have the common sense to get a taxi, or ask a friend to take you home, or suffer the mortification of sleeping on someone's couch (no matter how tough a parent or boyfriend is, the punishment for coming home late is nothing compared to coming home in a police car), you shouldn't have a driver's license.

Need more reasons? Surely you already have the good sense to know drunk-driving is idiotic for safety reasons—but did you know that a DUI can also make

you look really, really ugly? Think about this: No one takes a good mug shot (see opposite page). The lighting is bad, you won't have time for appropriate hair and makeup artists to come and make

A Lady never drives drunk or under the influence of anything else.

~~~~~~~

"It's all right letting yourself go, as long as you can get yourself back."

MICK JAGGER

you look pretty, and there's no re-touching. Believe me, police head-quarters aren't exactly the ideal location for an impromptu photo shoot. (For your own amusement, feel free to Google "worst mug shots." It's kind of fun.)

Then there's the humiliation of having to explain to people that you drove off the road and hit a tree because the local pub was having a two-for-one straw-berry-margarita special, and you just couldn't resist. Heaven forbid you aspire to any high-profile or celebrity-related job. That mug shot of your puffy eyes and mascara-smeared cheeks—because when you were pulled over you suddenly sobered up enough to know that you just screwed up big-time and started sobbing—will follow you around like a bad smell for the rest of your life. [See "The Future Politician's Argument," pp. 208-209.]

And driving drunk won't give you street cred either. Don't think that it comes off as non-chalant—like, *She's so crazy, she got drunk and drove herself home*—because in reality it comes across as sad. As in, *She's a drunken mess who can't even make a basic intelligent decision*. Or worse, *She's a drunken mess who can't even scrounge up ten dollars for a taxi*.

So call a taxi, ladies. Or call a friend. Even bad friends, when faced with the choice of either giving you a ride or letting you drive drunk, should do the right thing. And if they won't, you can make some new friends in Alcoholics Anonymous.

Now, the Harder Stuff

Hopefully, most girls won't be tempted by more than booze, cigs, and some dirty pictures. But never say never

In general, people do drugs for two reasons: one, to look or feel cool and two, to numb some sort of deep-seated pain. While neither is a good excuse—there are other ways to look cool, and there are other ways to deal with internal turmoil—once you start using drugs, you can easily get wrapped up in them. That's when you get hooked and start missing work and selling your TVs or stealing from your grandmother or letting old men do bad things to your bodies to help pay for your fixes. (I know this doesn't happen to everyone who experiments with drugs, but trust me, it happens. Even to people whom you never thought it would.)

Bottom line: Drugs just aren't glamorous. Even if you think the cool people are doing them, and regardless of whether they looked so glamorous in that Johnny Depp movie, believe me, even cool people don't look cool doing drugs. Visualize it—a girl sucking on a giant bong, or huddled over a toilet seat snorting something, or sticking a dirty needle into her inner thigh—and you'll realize drugs really aren't attractive.

That's why I don't understand why so many young girls fall into fast crowds and start doing bad things to their healths, minds, and bodies. Fat men who sleep at truck stops? Sure, I can see them needing to get high. But not young ladies.

Beyond all the bad stuff that drugs do to your body—we've all heard that boring jazz about cancer and increased heart rate and the possibility of, ahem, overdosing and dying—imagine what they do to your social life!

> "Drugs have nothing to do with the creation of music. In fact, they are dumb and self-indulgent. Kind of like sucking your thumb."
>
> COURTNEY LOVE

Amy Winehouse is an icon, and I love her, but have you ever heard anyone say, "I'd really like to go on a date with her?" Absolutely not. A party girl might get attention—but from all the wrong people.

Drugs may make people feel temporarily better; in some cases, the desired effect is to feel nothing at all. But it's a really, really quick fix, and one that leaves even more problems in its wake. When you wake up after a night of drugging, feeling absolutely horrible, and have to apologize to your best friend for throwing up in her potted plants or call your mom and say you're sorry for forgetting her birthday—you'll quickly learn that those moments of feeling good are not worth the days of social and mental repair.

If you want an addiction, try shopping. Both drugs and shopping will leave you in debt, which can ruin your life and credit rating, but at least you'll look cute with a full wardrobe. Drugs don't make anyone look cute.

The effects of crystal meth are shocking—and I'm not talking about the internal damage it inflicts! The scariest thing about this drug is what it does to your face. Here is one example.

A METH WARNING

☞ My home state, Missouri, boasts one of the most prevalent crystal-meth problems in the country. Go Midwest! And while it's easy to ignore the issue—'cause obviously no lady would ever entertain the idea of becoming a crackhead or hoovering enormous amounts of speed fabricated out of cold medicine in basements and bathrooms—the statistics prove it's not just tramps who confront this problem.

Now, there are a bunch of reasons to avoid the stuff. It's really bad for your health, and apparently, specifically with meth, you're addicted the first time you try it (so just one night of experimentation means days of staying awake to steal stuff and trade your flat-screen TV for your next fix). Whatever, it all sounds gross.

But I'll tell you what the most horrifying part of meth addiction is: the before and after pictures. Seriously—go online right now and look up "Faces of Meth" at drugfree.org. You'll see a librarian in the before picture; two months later, she's a hollow-faced streetwalker with no teeth and a dead look behind her eyes. It's shocking: people who have chewed off their fingernails and are losing all their hair, former jocks turned crypt-keepers. These websites post mug shots from every arrest (petty theft, grand theft auto, breaking and entering, etc.), and in each photo, the addicts look worse and worse.

As I've mentioned more than once before, sometimes the most effective treatment is a superficial one. (Which brings up another issue: Instead of boring kids with those D.A.R.E. stats, all public service announcements need to do is distribute these before and after pictures. Much more effective.) So stay sober, stay pretty, and just stay off the bad stuff.

The Allure of the Pole

Unless you're heading up to see Santa Claus in the North, or down to meet penguins in the South, it's in your best interest to steer clear of Poles

Allow me to set the scene: It's the fashion designer Alexander McQueen's birthday party. We're in an underground bar in East London. Everyone who is anyone is there, including the late great stylist Isabella Blow, Yves Saint Laurent's successor Stefano Pilati, and the actress Sienna Miller. (I can't remember if I snuck in, came with someone actually invited, or said I was someone else—regardless, I wasn't invited but I was there, and that's what's important.) In the corner is a pole. Next to that pole is Kate Moss. A devastatingly sexy beat permeates the air as the DJ throws on a sensual track. And—voilà—there's Kate Moss on the pole, grinding and dancing and twirling and working her hair like a pro. It's a moment I will never forget.

Right, so you're probably thinking that after that display, I would encourage anyone to give the pole a go. But you're wrong. After that, my advice to every other person in the world—other than, you know, real-life strippers—is to steer clear of the pole at all costs. 'Cause the time will come when you're tempted to give it a shot. Maybe you're at a strip club, or maybe you're at a basement party, or—worst case scenario, and I've actually seen this happen—you're with some friends on a subway and the poles are calling your name.

The time will come. And if you try it, you will be embarrassed. I repeat: You will regret taking the pole, particularly if your friends have a camera and can record the episode. Kate Moss is a supermodel who, I learned later, had taken professional pole-dancing classes for a fashion story; she later used the moves in a White Stripes video. She had that pole dance down. Chances are, however, you don't. And chances are you're not exactly a Kate Moss doppelgänger either.

So unless you know your way around a pole or you're a supermodel, don't even try it. Don't even think of trying it.

Besides, I'm not really sure how often they clean those poles. Ew.

> "To keep your character intact, you cannot stoop to filthy acts. It makes it easier to stoop the next time."
>
> KATHARINE HEPBURN

Sober Doesn't Suck

W hile I sit here and talk about drinking, smoking, sexing, and drug abuse, I realize that there are probably people reading this book who feel absolutely no desire to do any of those things. And God bless you.

At the risk of sounding like the spokesperson for the D.A.R.E. program, I have to make it clear that there is absolutely nothing wrong with abstaining—from alcohol, from sex, from bad influences in general. Look, even Carrie managed to quit smoking on *Sex and the City*. (And while we're on the topic of that show, allow me to bust another myth: the woman who played Charlotte, Kristin Davis, was sober through most of that show's filming. Which, as she told me at a dinner in L.A. once, is why she found it so funny when fans of the show would send her a Cosmo when they spotted her at a bar or a restaurant.)

The way you see young people in movies and on television isn't always the best or the most realistic representation of life: Contrary to what is portrayed on

"A lady shouldn't do something she's going to feel guilty about later."

THE BAD BEHAVIOR
OF BELLE CANTRELLI,
A NOVEL BY
LORAINE DESPRES

some hit TV shows, most high-schoolers don't hang out in fancy hotel bars, even on New York's Upper East Side, and not every rich kid growing up in L.A. has a substance-abuse problem.

Believe me: A young girl to day has her whole life to drink and smoke and fight the demons of addiction and vices. So don't feel like you're missing out if you're not the first girl to pass around Jell-O shots at a keg party or the first person to spark up a joint at an after-hours rave. In my experience, the sober person in the room can be the most fun—at least she can carry on a conversation without slurring and drooling on herself. And furthermore, sober people can actually remember all the stupid things the drunk people do. (Which is, come to think of it, why I've had to steer clear of the sober girl too.)

Shake Your Groove Thing (Maybe)

Dancing can be many things—fun, intimate, exercise— but it should not be embarrassing

You probably already know if you're a good dancer. Surely, by now, you can tell if people enjoy being around you when you're shaking your groove thing, or if they politely veer away or make an excuse to leave the dance floor as soon as you step foot on it. [See "Conversation Enders," p. 71.] And if you don't know, then— bad news—you're probably not a good dancer. (A few questions to ask yourself, just to be sure: Do people cheer you on or laugh at you? Are you dancing alone or in groups? Do friends ever go out dancing and "forget" to include you? Have you ever been to a dance club in your life? Have you ever been asked to leave one?)

If you are one of the lucky few to have been blessed with a God-given ability to dance, congratulations. Dance away, and be liberal with your gifts. Make sure you take Grandpa for a twirl at family weddings, and why not throw the school nerd a bone and give him a boogie too?

> "The very purpose of existence is to reconcile the glowing opinion we hold of ourselves with the appalling things other people think about us."
>
> QUENTIN CRISP

But to the rest of you, to the girls out there who might be shy or anxious about their dancing ability, don't worry. Take owner-ship of your awful dance moves. You don't have to be a ballerina to have fun listening to music with your friends, and you don't have to be a Fly Girl to have fun dancing at a club.

A friend of mine, a former model (generally models, with their skinny bodies and long limbs, are the worst dancers— like, embarrassingly bad, which is only fair since they are so tall and skinny), once explained bad dancers, and what you can do if you fall into that category, with the following analogy: What do you do if you get a stain on your dress? Do you moan and com-plain about it? Do you just laugh it off and enjoy the rest of the night? Or do you freak out, put on your coat, and race home in tears?

These three scenarios also apply to the bad dancer. So you

BUST A MOVE PLAYLIST

"Holiday"	MADONNA	"Hey Ya"	OUTKAST
"London Bridge"	FERGIE	"Let's Dance"	DAVID BOWIE
"Hypnotize"	NOTORIOUS B.I.G.	"Party All the Time"	EDDIE MURPHY
"Twist and Shout"	THE BEATLES	"I Got a Man"	POSITIVE K
"She Works Hard for the Money"	DONNA SUMMER	"Let's Go Crazy"	PRINCE
"Flashdance . . . What a Feeling"	IRENE CARA	"Crescendolls"	DAFT PUNK
"Freedom"	THE B-52'S	"Word Up"	CAMEO
"Crazy in Love"	BEYONCÉ	"Private Idaho"	THE B-52'S

HOW TO DANCE POORLY

The reason I know how to spot a bad dancer is because I've been one. (But, to my credit, I've cut a few rugs in my day too!) Nonetheless, for your amusement, enjoy these terrible moves I have done in real life that were—luckily for you and very unluckily for me—recorded on film.

The Skirt Flipper

The Baby Catcher

The Skipper

The Voguer

The Sloppy Kisser

The Roof Raiser

have no rhythm. So you look like an electrocuted chicken when you move. You can either (a) sit at your table and complain that you're a bad dancer. Or (b) let go of your inhibitions and hit the dance floor, letting yourself wriggle and writhe to your heart's content. Or, the worst option, (c) as soon as the music starts playing and your friends mosey to the dance floor, you make some excuse—I left my

curling iron on!—and race out of there like a bat out of hell.

The whole point of dancing is to have fun, so go on and enjoy yourself. Mind you, when I'm encouraging bad dancers to hit the floor, I'm talking about people who might not be the most coordinated and are shy about their skills. But if you're one of those jerks who supplements your lack of dance skills by moshing, doing the Worm, do-

ing the Electric Slide or the Macarena when the Electric Slide or Macarena songs are not being played, calm yourself. And stop going to the same clubs I go to.

To the rest of you, though, dance and be merry. (And if you're really bad, just make sure nobody within fifty feet has a camera.)

To Ink, or Not to Ink

Tattoos can be tricky: They can make you look cool, or really, really foolish

This is probably not what mothers and the more conservative readers out there want to hear: I've seen some pretty cool girls with some pretty cool tattoos. But here's the thing: Those girls had thought about their tattoos for a long time and had some sort of connection—be it spiritual or artistic—to this permanent marking of their bodies. Their tattoos meant something. They didn't just wake up one day and say to themselves, "You know what? I think I'm going to get the Japanese sign for *chastity* between my pubic bone and my belly button." (Note: I have Japanese friends, and one of their favorite games is to tell people what these tattoos actually mean. You might think you got "goddess" on your hip-bone, but it could very likely be "toilet seat.")

The thing to remember when it comes to tattoos—or anything permanent, really—is that you shouldn't make a hasty decision, or do anything out of a childish feeling of rebellion. And never, under any circumstance, make such a drastic decision while under the influence. I have a very good friend who descends from a long line of American blue bloods—like, her great-great-great-grandfather founded some town back when America was just a swampland—but while a moody, broody teenager living in New York City and going through a Gothic phase, she got drunk with some friends and got a giant, huge tattoo of a rose just above her tailbone. Problem is, the tattoo is kind of suggestive; to be frank, it looks like a giant flowering vagina. So here is this sophisticated young lady, who has thankfully grown out of this Gothic-rebellion phase, with a giant-flower vagina just above her butt. The poor thing can't even wear backless dresses because she's afraid someone will see it, and she can only go to the beach with her nearest and dearest.

Here's the general rule of thumb when you're thinking about tattoos: You'll have your whole life to look at and admire the thing, so don't rush the decision to get one. And if you decide you absolutely need one,

think very carefully about what you want (Will you still be a Disney fan when you're in your thirties? Will you still like butterflies when you're a saggy ol' grandma?), and where on your body to get it (on your wedding day, do you want to have to wear sleeves 'cause you have the name of an ex-boyfriend on your forearm? Do you intend to permanently avoid backless dresses 'cause you have a dagger on your shoulder blade?). Another good tip is to try it out for a few weeks first: Maybe get the desired marking in henna tattoo ink first, and see how it works with your wardrobe and style. If you can't afford henna, get a Sharpie marker. Writing on yourself in permanent ink will probably piss your parents off, but not as much as a tattoo will.

It's not as simple as saying all tattoos are bad. But it's easy to make bad decisions about them. Listen, you wouldn't shave your head when you're drunk (I hope), and you wouldn't pick your prom dress on a whim— even though hair grows back, and you only wear a prom dress once. Tattoos are forever.

Rest assured: Not all tattoos are tacky. Just be sure to think before you ink.

I think she wanted to "Carpe Diem," or "Seize the Day." Not crap on dimes, which is what I'm gathering from this disastrous misspelling.

It's a shame you can't see the front of this woman's face. Or maybe it's not. She had the face of an angel, and the back of a Hell's Angel.

The "Look at Me!" Era

It's easy nowadays—maybe too easy—to get famous for nothing

Not too long ago, it was said that a lady's name should appear in the newspaper exactly three times in her life: when she is born, when she marries, and when she dies. But the society game has changed, and the days of well-bred young women making appearances exclusively at debutant balls, philanthropic charities, and flower shows are very, very over.

Today, even the most posh and well-educated young women fall victim to the all-too-easy allure of self-promotion. Girls from old-money families do reality shows and show off their breasts in porn videos; recent Yale and Harvard graduates try to "win" the love of perfect strangers on tacky TV shows by competing in ridiculous challenges. (Mind you, I'm not saying these shows are bad, per se. They may be what's wrong with America, but sometimes they make for pretty good television.)

Whether eating bugs in televised challenges or starring in grainy homemade porn videos, a modern girl has ample opportunities to see her mug on television or the computer screen. [See "Lady vs. Tramp: In Relationships," pp. 204-205.]

Now, I'm not going to say it's tacky to make a few appearances on respected websites or in venerable journals or fashion

> "Fame was once seen as a recognition of your accomplishments in the world. Now it just means being recognized."
>
> MICK HUME

> "My advice to those who think they have to take off their clothes to be a star is, once you're boned, what's left to create the illusion? Let 'em wonder. I never believed in givin' them too much of me."
>
> MAE WEST

publications—if I did, I would be a huge hypocrite, as I've been written about once or twice, and my job is to write about successful people. And I'll admit that it's flattering when someone runs your picture in a Best Dressed list or says something nice about you on the Internet.

But today fame is too often confused with power and respectability—a lengthy conversation we don't need to get into here. Just bear in mind, ladies, that the most powerful people in the world—perhaps the most famous—are the ones who typically spend lots of energy and money keeping their names out of the press.

Fame is also confused in our culture with other things, like "notoriety" or "being the punch line of a national joke." Let's get something straight right now: There is a difference between being famous and being infamous. And beneath both headings is the worst one of all: being a press whore.

Press whores—people who desperately seek to promote themselves, constantly crave the spotlight, and most likely think they're the best thing to happen to society since the toilet flush—can be spotted miles away. They'll go to any party, they'll constantly talk about themselves, and they believe any attention is good attention, be it on Page Six or in *Vogue*. But a lady knows that getting good press is like landing the right guy: Often you have to let it come to you. A lady knows that good press opportunities are few and far between. If a story or show sounds too good to be true, it probably is. (I've been burned by this confusion in the past myself, signing on to do things that weren't as plush as they were made out to be.)

Here's the thing: Getting press is addictive. When you're on one website, you want to be on another. When someone takes your picture at a party, you'll miss the flashes if they don't follow you at the next event. It can be exhilarating— that is, until, a bad picture or story runs, which is bound to happen eventually. (Just like any addiction, it has its dizzying highs and abysmal lows. Seeing a close-up of your butt flab posted all over the Internet will make you wish you had

heroin withdrawal to contend with instead.)

Mind you, there are good types of publicity. Jacqueline Kennedy had her picture taken for *Vogue* magazine when she won a writing contest as a young woman, and that tasteful portrait—hair swept off her face and her future trademark pearls

A Lady **never angles to be in a photo.**

encircling her neck—immortalized her youthful beauty and did her credit for the rest of her life. Perhaps someone likes your outfit and runs a picture of it in a magazine, or perhaps you're at an event that raises money for a local charitable organization— these can be optimal opportunities to pat yourself on your back.

But that's the point. The whole secret of making press work for you: Make sure that you at least have something of substance to promote. And, no, the fact that you have a big rack and a penchant for wearing tops cut down to your navel isn't exactly a substantial contribution to society. No one will begrudge a girl her desire for attention if she is saying something besides, "Look at me!"

That's the flip side of desperation: The second you're begging to be the center of attention is typically the same time people look away; or worse, when they start laughing. Remember that once you've put yourself out there, once you've thrown your hat (or two cents, or bra and panties) into the public arena— especially in the era of the Internet—it's hard to gracefully bow out of the fight. (The World Wide Web can be a hateful place, people. Almost anyone can tell you that.)

Leave Them Wanting More

I n the movie *Clueless*—which I consider to be a completely accurate documentary of American high school life—Alicia Silverstone tells Brittany Murphy that she has something no one else in the school has: mystery.

Those are words to live by. Mystery is something you can't buy at the mall, and it's something you can't get back once you've lost it. (Unless you move, I guess. But even then, it's hard to run from your past.)

The point is you don't have to be everywhere all the time. In fact, you shouldn't be everywhere all the time. When I moved to New York City, this was a difficult lesson for me to learn. During college, I often went to three or four fashion parties in a single night (which is not to say I was invited to all of them—I did a lot of party crashing back then).

One Halloween I made it to a total of nine different spots. Bar parties or house parties or awards ceremonies: It didn't matter. If there were free appetizers and an open bar, I was there. (What? Drinks and food were expensive, and I was a student. Don't judge me.) One time I even showed up to my Spanish class in a tuxedo because I was going to a black-tie gala later in the evening. I had missed the majority of the semester (in large part due to too much party crash-

ing) and would have failed if I'd skipped even one more class. So there I was, reading flash cards and adjusting my bow tie and lapel. Talk about pathetic.

The truth of the matter is that I could have done with missing a party or two. Most parties, es-

> "There are moments to indulge and enjoy, but I always know when it's time to go home and wash my knickers."
>
> KATE WINSLET

pecially in a city like New York, are similar and involve the same things: excessive smoking (see p. 252), drinking (see p. 258), and a bunch of other stuff (see pp. 266-67.). The only things I gained from not missing a single party were a drinking problem, a handful of unshakeable hangovers, and the reputation of be-

ing that guy everyone saw everywhere. In retrospect, I would much rather have been the guy regarded as smart, well-educated, and a good conversationalist with a promising career ahead of him. Which is what people say about me now. I think. I hope. But know that it took me a long time and lots of hard work to get here.

Have a look at your date book—are you going out too much? Have you literally accepted every invitation that you've ever received? Would you attend the opening of an envelope? Are you constantly looking for anything to do and anyone to go out with? Are you afraid to be alone, and are you constantly in fear that you'll be left out of something?

It's okay to be missed once in a while. It's okay to want to stay at home and read a book or watch a movie. Stay in a few nights, hang out with old friends or family. Paint. Build model trains. Get a hobby. This took me a while to understand: It's okay to be the life of a party, but you want to make sure that your life is not just parties.

One thing I learned the hard way was that having a full schedule—and going to every party I've ever been invited to—did not mean I was popular.

Extreme Makeover: Vices Edition

D rew Barrymore did it. Angelina Jolie did it. Britney Spears and Courtney Love and Whitney Houston did it. Well, those last three seem to be going back and forth between doing it and not doing it—but my point is that it's completely possible to go from being a train wreck to being a good girl.

Look at the cases of those first two: Barrymore and Jolie. These two fine young beauties came back from a world of vices (Barrymore had a substance abuse problem and was in rehab before she was a teenager; Jolie's adolescent tales were sordid, involving vials of blood around her neck and making out with her brother), and transformed themselves into caring, nurturing, smart women who are now world-famous actresses and, perhaps more importantly, great role models. Joining them is a whole roster of successful young women who rehabilitated themselves, from First Lady Betty Ford to actress Eva Mendes, to former reality show devil Nicole Richie.

Here's why I bring this up: Even if you're a train wreck, even if as you're reading this book you're drunk at a store and thinking about stealing it so you can trade it for a cigarette in the parking lot, there's still hope for you. Even if you drink too much or pole dance to pay for your cell phone bill, you don't have to be destined to an emotionally painful, liver-damaging,

yellow-toothed, overly tattooed existence. Everyone has had a vice. Without fail, everyone still has one. (The person who tells you he or she doesn't have any vices is lying—in fact, dishonesty is a vice in and of itself.)

Abraham Lincoln said, "A man without vices is a man without virtues." So don't lose sleep over your past. After all, part of youth is growing up and learning from your mistakes. Though your mistakes shouldn't be so damaging they're permanent: Don't do something so toxic as a young woman that when you're older you have a seizure every time you hear a bell ring; don't pump your body with so many chemicals that when you have babies later in life they come out with three heads and twelve fingers.

But don't beat yourself up, either. Even if you are a mess, even if you have become the type of girl no one respects, even if you are a tramp—it's never too late to turn yourself around and become a lady. There is such a thing as second chances. (And third and fourth, for that matter.)

Here's the thing: The perfect childhood doesn't exist. Temptation is as old as time; or at least, the history of temptation extends as far back as the moment Eve gave Adam that serpent's apple. But what sets the lady apart from the tramp is the ability to acknowledge she needs to clean up her act—and then, of course, the fact that she actually does clean up her act. Living a better life is an important decision, and one you have to make for yourself (no one else can make this decision for you, and it's crucial to remember that you can't make the decision for someone else, either).

Some of my best friends here in New York have pasts I have a hard time reconciling with the people I'm close to now. But I wouldn't change them—or their pasts—for anything in the world. Their experiences are what made them the people they are today.

And perhaps more importantly, their experiences have provided me with some of the most amusing stories I've ever heard.

"Every saint has a past and every sinner has a future."

OSCAR WILDE

The above quote from Oscar Wilde is one of my favorite that I found while researching this book, and it was the one that people asked me the most about on my book tour. I think the reason is because we humans are eternal optimists, and most of us really hope that even if someone is in a dark place that they will come out of it. I was asked a few times if I could think of an example of this transformation in my own life, and I would talk about teh amazing Nicole Richie.

You see, I didn't know Nicole when she was a young hell raiser—when she and Paris Hilton were playing the parts of spoiled (yet outrageously entertaining) rich girls in their genre-defining reality show *The Simple Life* in Arkansas, I was still one state above, in Missouri, toiling away in high school and driving my Uncle Bob's old Bonneville. The Nicole I met a few years later was much different than the girl who was on that TV show wearing torn-up T-shirts, tiny denim shorts, and hot pink hair extensions. The Nicole I know today is a fabulously put together, fabulously funny fashion entrepreneur who just happens to also be a fabulous mother.

This is why when someone asks if there is a life for tramps—indeed if you are a tramp reading this book right now, wondering if it's even worth it to try to act a little classier and attempt to become a lady—I encourage them to look up to Nicole. She'll be the first to admit that she had her rough patches growing up, but that didn't have any effect on the smart, successful, charismatic woman she is today. A tramp's past won't matter to a lady's future.

Q&A:
A Lady Faces Temptation

The best part about creating this book has been the responses it's caused among the young women I've met at my book signings, over e-mail, and even on the street. There are some smart girls out there, and they've had some fabulous questions. I liked some of them so much I wanted to include them here.

Q: *Can you not drink when you go out? Is that possible?*

A: Yes, of course it's possible. But I'm not going to say it's easy, especially if you're at a cocktail party with a bunch of people who really like their cocktails. A few tips: Drink sparkling water or club soda, because the bubbles at least trick you into thinking it's an exciting drink, and maybe mix in some cranberry. Soda does the trick, and ginger ale sometimes looks like booze if you're afraid of sticking out as the only Sober Sally in the group. Though at the end of the day, you shouldn't be embarrassed if you don't want a drink once in a while, or ever. Sober people are sometimes the most fun—and (this can be good or bad) they'll actually remember everything the next day.

Q: *C'mon, you must cuss once in a while. You live in New York!*

A: I won't shit you. I have been known to have a bad mouth. But I have never used bad words to sound cool, and neither should you.

F.U.

Q: *Is dirty dancing ever classy?*

A: Well, first of all, the movie *Dirty Dancing* is a classic, as well as classy. But this is a good question. Times have changed, and young people are no longer expected to leave wide spaces between their bodies when they boogie down. That said, vulgar groping and slobbery makeout sessions aren't classy, nor are they pleasant to watch. I say contact is good, but crass body writhing is bad. Besides, if you do that on a dance floor, what do you do when you get home? Or if you're already writhing on the dance floor, when you get to your car?

Q: *You must know some people who use drugs.*

A: Drugs are all around us, and I'm not just talking about in New York or in the fashion industry. I grew up in Missouri, which has one of the worst track records for homemade meth crime in the country. So yeah, of course I've seen people on drugs. In a twisted way, I think it's a good thing. Most crackheads look older than they are, can't string together sentences, have poor personal hygiene, and aren't the sort of people you want to spend your afternoons with. In fact, seeing those sorts of people reminds me why drugs are so bad. I've always said if you want to stop drugs, look up the before and after pictures of a meth addict on the Internet. You'll never want to touch the stuff!

Q: *Did you ever smoke?*

A: Yes! I will admit that I was a social smoker, (sorry, Mom!) and I thought I was really, really cool. It wasn't until a few years later, when I was addicted and wasting a bunch of cash, that I realized I really didn't look cool at all. And my breath stank!

Q: *Would you say that attention is addictive?*

A: With the rise of the reality show celebrity and the digital nature of our culture, a whole bunch of new addictions pop up. People who are addicted to attention are just one phenomenon. (As is online porn addiction, which is creepy!) The constant and desperate need for attention and approval is disconcerting: people who want all eyes on them often forget to look within themselves—and even worse, they'll do whatever they can for that attention. Or perhaps you haven't seen some of my favorite shows on Bravo?

Q: *What's the worst tattoo you've ever seen?*

A: I have seen some doozies in my day! Once I saw someone who had a picture of the middle finger tattooed on their sternum. (Classy!) And I've seen people with ridiculous sayings, like "Git 'er done!" on their faces. For the record, I'll never understand the armpit tattoo. But the worst, especially when it comes to tattoos, is when you see someone with something misspelled. My favorites? "I'm awsome" and "Only God can juge me."

A Lady
Is Always
Learning

"All of life is a constant education."

ELEANOR ROOSEVELT

HAVE YOU EVER SAT IN A MATH CLASS or a meeting and asked yourself, "When the hell am I going to need to know this? When will I need to know the major dates of the French and Indian War? Will knowing who was the Vice President in 1903 really come in handy?"

I'll be honest here, and run the risk of pissing off every single teacher I've ever had: Many of the things you learn in high school, college, and even in your professional life are completely and utterly pointless. I have not used the Pythagorean theorem since I graduated, and I don't think I'll be needing it any time soon. (Now watch me get kidnapped and placed, blindfolded, in a triangular room, forced to try to find the exit that bisects the hypotenuse when all I know is the length of the two shorter walls.)

But there are certain basic things a lady should know, things that aren't taught in any traditional education program. When someone says, "That beret-and-scarf combination is so Bonnie and Clyde," what the hell is she talking about? Who's Bonnie? And why does she need so many French accessories? You should know what it means when someone says her boyfriend has less direction than Holden Caulfield, or is dumber than Lenny from *Of Mice and Men*. Every girl should know a wee bit of Shakespeare: bonus if you know a sonnet or two by heart. (Previous generations would commit whole poems to memory and recite them as a way of flirting—but that was before text messages, presumably.)

I've already covered some of this material in previous sections. For example, by now you should already know which fork to pick up during the salad course at dinner. [See pp. 56-57.] But the well-rounded lady knows much more. In fact, a classy lady never stops learning.

And because it needs to be said: If you're really into the Pythagorean theorem, or math in general, chase the dream. Be the hot math-and-science chick, become a really successful engineer and blow your money on pencil skirts and Chanel handbags. But for the rest of you ladies, chuck that math textbook out the window, break out a highlighter, and pay attention. Here are some things you'll actually need—and want—to know.

Quiz **How Smart Are You?**

To a large degree, intelligence is relative. Some people are really book smart, but can't remember to look both ways at an intersection. Some people have great communication skills, but have never gotten through a single issue of the *New York Times*. While it's not my place to judge—I have literary friends and friends who get all their news from trashy gossip websites—it's good to know where you stand on the IQ scale.

1. You have a newspaper in your house because:

  A Your itty-bitty dog isn't potty trained.
  B The former tenant had a subscription, and the papers just keep coming. Plus, sometimes there are pictures!
  C You like to pick up the weekend paper to catch up on current events.
  D Correction: You have *several* papers delivered to the house daily. You read them cover to cover with your morning espresso.

2. If you scroll through the history of your browser, your most visited sites are:

  A EBay and every single department store's website.
  B Thousands and thousands of gossip sites.
  C CNN, *New York Times*, a couple of gossip sites, and JCrew.com.
  D The online sites of papers around the world—in case you missed something in the print editions—as well as various friends' blogs. Most of them live in other countries, serving as peace ambassadors.

3. A friend wants to set you up with a guy who has just spent the past year volunteering in a third-world country. You get ready to meet him by:

  A Buying a new dress.
  B Buying a new dress and new lipstick.
  C Googling the country where he lived so you at least know its basic stats.
  D Nothing. You don't care about the way you look, and you already know all the facts about the country in which he was living, including current population size, last year's GDP, and its most important natural resources.

4. Your high school advisor encourages/encouraged you to:

  A Your what? Who?
  B Go to beauty school.
  C Continue to apply yourself in the hopes that you will get into one of your top five colleges.
  D Stop intimidating your peers with your superior wit and make sure to send a postcard from Yale.

5. When someone uses a word that you're not familiar with, you:

(A) Stare out a window.

(B) Smile blankly and hopefully use context clues to keep up your end of the conversation.

(C) Make a mental note to either ask someone what that word meant later, or jot it down and remember to look it up once you get home.

(D) Impossible. You memorized the dictionary at age five and know every word in the language (and in several other languages as well).

6. Your favorite reading material includes:

(A) Reading? You stopped with those book thingies as soon as the government let you drop out of school.

(B) Magazines and books with bare-chested men on the cover.

(C) Novels—both classics and current fiction and nonfiction—and the occasional magazine. What else is there to read when you're waiting in a doctor's office?

(D) Big books with big words, exclusively.

7. You walk into a room and there's a TV, a book, a magazine, and a window. You:

(A) Stare out the window. Then watch TV.

(B) Read the magazine cover to cover. Twice.

(C) Hope the book is by F. Scott Fitzgerald and start reading.

(D) Put your feet up on the TV and read the book backward, making notes in the margins about how you could make it better, while simultaneously fanning the fresh air from the open window onto yourself with the magazine.

8. When you were little you wanted to be:

(A) A stripper, and you are.

(B) A supermarket cashier, and you are.

(C) A lawyer or doctor, and you are currently studying to be one or the other.

(D) The first female president of the world, and you won't settle for anything less.

QUIZ KEY

Count up all your answers and see which of the four letters you had the most of. If you are:

Mostly A's. You are Special Olympics material. I'll be blunt: The educational system has either failed you, or you have never made any effort to absorb even basic information. And that's a problem. No one wants you to be a doctor, but you should at least be able to have a conversation with one. Or with a plumber, for that matter.

Most B's. Have you ever read a book you didn't buy at the supermarket? Chances are, you're not applying yourself. You have the ability, the capacity, and the opportunity to educate yourself, but due to laziness or lack of enthusiasm, you haven't. But please do. Everyone—from guys to friends—will appreciate you more if you can string together a sentence that doesn't involve a long discourse on hair color.

Mostly C's. You are super smart: It's nice to see someone paid attention in class *and* at recess. There isn't a formula for blending book and street smarts, but you understand that it's important to be able to have both (you don't shy away from letting loose and having fun either). More power to you.

Mostly D's. You are a rocket scientist: What are you doing reading this book? Shouldn't you be brushing up on your Derrida, or performing open-heart surgery, or curing cancer? It's great that you're such a brainiac, but make sure you don't think that reading love stories is the same thing as having one of your own. Don't forget that experience is a kind of wisdom. It's okay to take your nose out of the books once in a while.

Push Your Comfort Zone

I will be completely honest with you: If someone locked me in a room with all three *High School Musical* movies, Madonna's *Immaculate Collection*, the *Hairspray* that stars Zac Efron, the movie *Spice World*, and a few back issues of late-1990s *Vogue* and *Interview*—I could last a year. Maybe even eighteen months.

But here's the thing: Life isn't only about fashion, music videos, and tacky musicals—as much as I would like it to be. Pushing yourself to do something beyond the easy and expected (which is even harder with premium cable and laptops and cell phones) is not only educational, it's invigorating. I'm sure some people will fight me on this, but I truly believe that learning something and acquiring new skills and knowledge—mind you, learning about things that actually interest you, whether art or fashion or American history or the mating rituals of flying squirrels— are enlivening.

The world is a big place; there are thousands of interesting things to do in it. Not only will educating yourself make you a more well-rounded person, but it might even help you discover a new passion. It might even change your life. Maybe you have an undiscovered love of English lit, and reading *Pride and Prejudice* will inspire you to go to Oxford, where you will meet the love of your life. Or maybe you discover you love political science and you become the next Hillary Clinton (but hotter, obviously, with smarter outfits and chicer hair).

Think of it this way: Learning is like exercise for the brain. Sure, it might be hard to get your mental bum off the couch, but you'll feel infinitely better once you do. Read a book that doesn't have to do with celebrity culture. In addition to *Tiger-Beat* and *Entertainment Weekly*, get yourself a subscription to *Newsweek* or the *Economist* and learn what else is going on in the world. Read up on African issues; take a class on Eastern European art history. If you really can't pry yourself away from the TV yet, take small steps. In addition to those fake teen dramas, watch a great documentary film (see pp. 316-18 for some of my favorites) or something on the Discovery Channel about global warming.

My sixth grade algebra teacher told me that learning fractions was like push-ups for the brain after I complained that I would never need to know how to split things into fourths (boy was I wrong: Every time I double-date it's all about quartering, espe-

A Lady doesn't say she's read a book she hasn't read. The same goes for documentaries, independent movies, films, TV shows, plays, or concerts.

A Lady is never worried about possessing intelligence. Being coquettish or dainty for the sake of being dainty are affectations that smart women know are archaic.

Ah, yes, the mental push-ups. You can't do these at the gym, but they're just as important as the ones that work your triceps.

cially since I want to be sure I get my fair share of the apple tart).

I think this concept is really important for young people today. I know a bunch of girls with fat, lazy, stupid brains—which is a major anatomical problem, despite the fact that you can bounce a quarter off their toned bottoms. Beyond the importance of your own mental acuteness, think about your flirtation factor. People with limited views, limited knowledge, and limited goals are about as exciting to talk to and sit with as a box of ramen noodles.

Believe it or not, having something to discuss besides celebrity gossip is appealing. For those of you looking for love: Listen, I can't say that all guys want to date a girl with an opinion and with a grasp of current events—

"The purpose of life, after all, is to live it, to taste experience to the utmost, to reach out eagerly and without fear for newer and richer experiences."

ELEANOR ROOSEVELT

but the type of guy you want to date will want a smart girl. Just so you know, most guys will only be mildly—and temporarily—amused by talking about some starlet's botched boob job or how some teen heartthrob just got arrested in a meth-lab bust.

The days when women were supposed to look pretty and retire to a separate room after dinner while the men got together to smoke cigars and drink brandy went out with the invention of electricity. For most guys, at least the good guys, a smart girl with passions other than the mall is just as sexy as the girl in the corner with the legs that don't stop. But better, because unlike large breasts and full bottoms, in a few decades intelligence won't sag.

Let's Get Political

During the fall of 2008, I joined English supermodel Jacquetta Wheeler in a small town in Pennsylvania, where she had voluntarily moved for two months to help campaign for Barack Obama. This is even more impressive considering that she isn't an American citizen and can't even vote in the States. Never have I been more inspired by a model—and I've seen Gisele in the flesh wearing nothing but a G-string and a smile.

The point is that every sophisticated young woman should be aware of what's happening in the world. But please note the use of the word *aware*. There is a fine but important line between being completely ignorant on the subject of politics, human-rights issues, wars, and genocide—and becoming one of those deranged activists who chains herself to trees or attacks policemen or shouts obscenities at government officials or throws paint on people wearing garments that may or may not be fur. Those people should be sedated. Anyone who thinks it's okay to throw dead animals at someone outside a fashion show needs a long bath and a good book.

Previous generations encouraged young women to either refrain from forming an opinion on current events or just fall in line with their husbands. But a modern lady knows that the days of passive, silent females have passed—or rather, the modern lady knows that those types of women are still around

A Lady is knowledgeable about current events.

A Lady has opinions and lets them be known freely at appropriate times.

"You must learn day by day, year by year, to broaden your horizon. The more things you love, the more you are interested in, the more you enjoy, the more you are indignant about—the more you have left when anything happens."

ETHEL BARRYMORE

but can easily be replaced, including with blow-up dolls.

Every lady should read the paper (or at least glance at it) and know certain facts about this fine nation—like, who the President is, who the Vice President is, and what the major hot-button political issues are. It's not like everyone needs a subscription to every current-event weekly in the world, or every lady should read the World section of the *New York Times* every single day. But if you're that girl who throws away the entire Sunday paper except the Styles section and the magazine, you are running a very dangerous risk of becoming a worthless airhead.

If a lady doesn't stand for something, she'll fall for anything.

Of all the people I thought would convince a few friends and me to campaign for Obama in the fall of 2008, I wasn't counting on it being British supermodel Jacquetta Wheeler (left, with our friend Lyle Maltz).

Sharing the Wealth

There comes a time in a woman's life when she knows that helping others is just as rewarding as helping herself

I will be 100 percent honest here: My first few steps into charitable work were not exactly self-motivated (or even willing) ones. When I was a young boy, my parents would force my brother and me—sometimes despite tears and tantrums—to go to homeless shelters in the inner city of St. Louis and serve hot meals to the underprivileged on both Thanksgiving and Christmas mornings. Some years, we didn't even open Christmas presents until the day *after* Christmas, which was just a little anticlimactic.

Then when I was in middle school, my mother enrolled me in a volunteer program every summer at Barnes-Jewish Hospital. I worked in the vital-organ-transplant department, where I would assist the offices that organize, prioritize, and track heart, lung, liver, and kidney donors and recipients. At first, I thought my mother just wanted me out of the house (and to deprive me of summer fun); then I thought it was her clever ploy to get me service hours early, which would look great on a college application.

Only later did I realize that my parents encouraged me (fine, forced me) to do these things not because I owed it to others, but because I owed it to myself to do something for others. I'll re-

> "If you're going to be passionate about something, be passionate about learning. If you're going to fight for something, fight for those in need. If you're going to question something, question authority. If you're going to lose something, lose your inhibitions. If you're going to gain something, gain respect and confidence. And if you're going to hate something, hate the false idea that you are not capable of your dreams."
>
> DANIEL GOLSTON

peat that: Doing things for other people was, weirdly, something I owed to myself.

At the end of my high school years, when I worked closely with school programs on food drives, fund-raisers, and even some manual labor in rural areas, I realized my volunteer experiences were incredibly beneficial—not only to those who were helped directly by these initiatives but to myself. I'll give you an example: I met a girl at the hospital who needed a lung transplant. She was about my

age, and though it may sound cheesy, seeing how strong she was completely renewed my faith in the human spirit.

In New York City, there are a bunch of great charities that I support. When I first moved here I joined a college group that refurbishes run-down assisted-living quarters for those suffering from AIDS. Later, I started attending, doing my best to publicize and help organize, high-profile events for organizations aimed at young people (like New Yorkers for Children) and for the city's influential museums (like the American Museum of Natural History and the Guggenheim Museum). Every time I do something good for someone else, I get a warm, fuzzy feeling—kind of like being drunk, except without the moral (or literal) hangover.

I sometimes feel that the current generation is depriving itself of this feeling. That's why I'm encouraging you to work on your karma here, and the sooner the better. Remember, not all charitable efforts have to be large-scale ones: You don't need

A Lady has a charitable heart.

to spend hundreds of hours at a homeless shelter or give all your money to the local art museum. Read to underprivileged or sick children for an afternoon a month, or drop off some canned food that you're never going to eat at a local food bank.

Believe me, the feeling of accomplishment and self-worth you will get from giving back is better than any high humans have invented so far. And it's not as hard as you think to get involved. Hey, if you're really desperate and you live in the Midwest, give my mother a call. She'd be more than happy to pick you up on Christmas morning and take you to a local soup kitchen. (And it'd get me off the hook.)

CHARITIES

If someone tells you it's difficult to find a charity to support, he or she is just not looking hard enough. Thanks to the Internet, nearly every charity in the world is only a quick keystroke away. There are all levels of involvement as well, from volunteering a few hours a week to writing a check once a month to helping with fund-raising events. Here are some of the charities I've supported.

⊘ **NEW YORKERS FOR CHILDREN:** This charity helps foster children transition into higher education and the real world when they age out of government-assisted living programs.

⊘ **THE AMERICAN MUSEUM OF NATURAL HISTORY:** This is one of my favorite museums in New York: on the West Side of Central Park and full of fossils, animals, and weird world facts.

⊘ **GOD'S LOVE WE DELIVER:** This charity assists New York City residents living and coping with AIDS by delivering ready-made meals to their homes. The organization started with only a handful of meals per day, but in 2009 I followed Joan Rivers as she delivered the organization's ten-millionth meal!

⊘ **ORPHANAID AFRICA:** After a painful break-up, a dear friend of mine decided to move to Africa and work with orphanages there. During that time she stumbled upon OrphanAid Africa, an organization that has radically changed orphan rules in Ghana.

⊘ **THE CONTEMPORARY ART MUSEUM OF ST. LOUIS:** Though it has had an art museum since 1904, St. Louis got its own museum devoted entirely to contemporary art a century later.

⊘ **DARNA:** I've been to Tangier, a coastal city in Morocco, several times with a friend of mine on summer holidays. It's a lovely town, but the growing number of children living on the streets was startling to the organizers of Darna, which provides boarding, food and, most importantly, education to homeless children so that they can sustain their families.

⊘ **RXART CHARITY:** This New York City-based charity devotes itself to putting art and art programs in children's hospitals in the hopes that through artistic expression and experiencing the arts, the patients can find new ways to heal and grow.

You Are What You Read

Remember this the next time you reach over to your nightstand for something to read before bed: What you read says a lot about you

I have a weird relationship with the tabloids. On the one hand, I love them and can't get enough of them and tear through them with reckless abandon and read every word and absorb every little bit of information about who didn't shave her pits and who had a nip slip at the Cannes Film Festival. Like drugs, once you have a little, you want more and more.

But on the other hand, I know that every time I look at a tabloid magazine, I become just a little more stupid. I know that I'm too smart to be feasting on back issues of *Star*, even at the doctor's office, and that at the end of the day, there are a thousand other things I should be doing with my time. Again, like drugs, even the occasional indulgence leaves me feeling totally guilty.

As a result, for many years I limited my tabloid intake to airports and airplanes, figuring I had my habit under control. But then the artist Jack Pierson told me that he stopped reading tabloids even on airplanes because he could not comfortably fly and dig into an issue of the *National Enquirer* knowing that if that plane went down the very last thing he read, the very last piece of information he absorbed, would be that so-and-so had a tit lift or a fourth baby. This made total sense to me. Sure, dying would suck, but

having your last thoughts be dominated by completely useless information about perfect strangers—and then, obviously, by the all-consuming panic of falling to a fiery death—is an idea too depressing to contemplate. So I went off tabloids completely, cold turkey.

> "Books were my pass to personal freedom. I learned to read at age three, and soon discovered there was a whole world to conquer that went beyond our farm in Mississippi."
>
> OPRAH WINFREY

> "Whatever you find in your mind is what you put there. Put good things there."
>
> MARY FORD

The majority of those stories are superficial drivel made up by publicists and Hollywood agents. Tabloids are full of the same feature stories reworked and republished over and over: people losing weight. People gaining weight. So-and-so's in rehab. So-and-so's out of rehab.

So-and-so's back in rehab.

Half the jazz is complete fiction too. Many of my friends are often featured in the tabloids, and I know that the stories about them aren't true. I've read that a girlfriend of mine spent the night in some actor's L.A. bungalow on an evening when I sat across from her at a restaurant in New York City, talking about the calories in a spicy-tuna sushi roll. Another time I read (no lie) that a certain friend was swinging from a trapeze in a kinky sex den with four leather-clad lesbians—when in reality, the person in question had ordered cheeseburgers and watched *The Notebook* at my house.

Allow me to encourage you to stay away from the tabloids and other such reading materials in excess. If the gossip is good, someone will pass it along. And if it doesn't get to you, chances are the story was so asinine and silly that you're better off reserving that little corner of your brain for something that you can truly use, or something that will move or inspire you—like your PIN number, or a poem, or the lyrics to a great new song, or a boy's e-mail address, or directions to the nearest deli. 'Cause knowing how to get a late-night hero sandwich is infinitely more important than knowing that someone may or may not have had vaginal-rejuvenation surgery.

Tabloids can be a fun read, but bear in mind they should only be supplementary reading material. If you haven't read a book in years—but you know what Brad Pitt had for dinner every night last week and where Reese Witherspoon buys her headbands—you have a problem.

Work Ethic & the Entitlement Generation

A s much as it pains me to say it, recently I've had to admit that I'm part of something my mother resentfully calls the "entitlement generation." That's what geezers like her have named the strictly contemporary wave of youth culture that consists of young people who believe they are entitled to certain material objects. A lot of us grow up believing that when our Founding Fathers asserted that every human being is born with certain unalienable rights, they meant cell phones and new shoes and designer jeans. And while it's true that I would trade a few of my first cousins for a new patent-leather loafer, the idea that we all just deserve the stuff is a disturbing one.

Throughout American history there have been generations of young people who could expect little more than three meals a day and a room to sleep in from their parents. And even that was a stretch for some families. Today, it's like we young folk absolutely expect to have new tennis shoes, fake fingernails, a new cell phone every six months, and a car when we turn sixteen. And it has created wave after wave of vain, materialistic, loud, and obnoxious tramps (as well as a country that is deeply in debt—but you can read about boring econ stuff in the newspapers).

You know who I mean (maybe you are who I mean). Think of all those reality-TV shows: spoiled little Long Island skank number one tells her parents she hates them when they get her a Lexus convertible in the wrong

"I do not believe things happen accidentally; I believe you earn them."

MADELEINE ALBRIGHT

"Work as hard as you can, whatever you do, and try to spread generosity of spirit."

KATHARINE HEPBURN

"God gives every bird his worm, but He does not throw it into the nest."

SWEDISH PROVERB

color for her birthday; or bitchy L.A. girl number two throws a tantrum when her father can't get Justin Timberlake to perform at her bat mitzvah.

Honey, one year all Santa Claus brought me were socks and a couple of DVDs. And I was supposed to be happy about it. And to be honest, I actually was happy about it. (It beat the year all I got was underwear.)

Let's get one thing clear: I am not criticizing luxury goods here. In fact, our entire country and its economy is based on materialism and the pursuit of quality name brands—without Prada, Ralph Lauren, and Louis Vuitton, I would be out of a job. But I think we can all admit that it's scary when a young girl thinks she is entitled to a pink Lexus on her sixteenth birthday for no other reason than the fact that

The first thing I learned as a young man in Missouri: Nothing comes on a silver platter. Figuratively (and literally), I have had to put my workman's gloves on often.

she saw some skank driving one in an issue of *Us Weekly*.

And I'm not saying that a young girl shouldn't long for a Burberry trench coat or a Dior cashmere turtleneck. When I see a young woman who appreciates that kind of quality and elegance, I beam with pride. But that's the whole point: appreciation. A lady should appreciate what she has, what she's been given, and what opportunities she has—be it a trip to Paris or a cute raincoat. She should be grateful.

So remember: Be thankful for what you have. Someone—if

"A man who dares to waste an hour of time has not discovered the value of life."

CHARLES DARWIN

it's not you, then it's your parents or grandparents—had to work really hard for everything you've got.

When the Founding Fathers were drafting up the Constitution of the United States of America, they sought to protect key human rights, like freedom of speech, freedom from religious persecution, and things like that. We're not entitled to Gucci pumps, and we shouldn't be. Besides, trust me, a hot pair of Louboutin wedges look even better when you've truly earned them.

Paying Your Dues

It's important to learn how to do what you want to do before you do it

As more than just your college guidance counselor will tell you, if you want to be successful, you have to pay your dues. I know, I know—this may seem like a dull topic, but hear me out. While it's true that it's nice when people give you things, a lady knows—though it may seem unbelievable—that certain things feel even better when they're earned. You know, like your first big fashion purchase, or a college degree, or a promotion. This applies if you're just starting in the mailroom of a big company or you aspire to be a stage diva on Broadway but must begin as a chorus girl.

In my chosen field—the fashion industry—this meant working as an intern at several magazines. When I was in college, I interned at a bunch of places, to varying degrees of success. Full disclosure: At my first few internships, I was hardly the model assistant. I was always on smoke breaks or making long-distance phone calls on company phones. I always had excuses not to work. But then, maybe that's why I wasn't hired at any of those magazines. My early behavior and spotty employment history are related, for sure. But as I matured, I (somehow) managed to overcome that reputation, actually get work done, and become an assistant who was actually valuable to the office.

Sadly, more often than not, today I find that many young people remind me of my behavior at those early internships. I've met people who come in late or don't show up at all. I've met people who complain when asked to do something, interns who will actually say *no* when the senior editor at a magazine asks for a favor. One time, someone in my office delegated a delivery to an intern. The intern left the office, package in hand, and we never saw or heard from him again.

Not too long ago, the only requirement for getting into college—and landing a job afterward—was a high school diploma. Then it was a high school diploma and some extracurricular activities. Now, to get into a good college and launch a successful career, it's almost expected that you be a recent graduate, speak six languages, have been an intern at eight different places, and have a pilot's license. It can be daunting.

That's why it's more important than ever to take internships—or any job you are lucky enough to get—seriously. My first job after graduation was at American *Vogue*—not a bad place to work, my friends. The reason I was hired was because, having learned from my previous mistakes, I was a dedicated intern. And not only at *Vogue*, but also at other magazines too. When I was in college, I had paid jobs at modeling agencies, one in New York, and two in London; and interned at four magazines, including *W*, *Vogue*, *V*, and *Dazed & Confused*.

I've had friends who have interned at advertising agencies, fashion design houses, lawyers' offices, and big Hollywood studios. Internships are not only a vital way to learn the ropes of an industry in a way that an educational institution cannot teach (I learned more from my year at *Vogue* than I did in the four years I spent at NYU), but they are also a great way to meet other people in the field. But remember this: You have to get over your pride and get to work.

André Leon Talley, someone I consider to be a mentor, the editor at large of *Vogue* and one of the most influential figures in fashion today, once laid it out like this: "When you're in an office, don't be so fabulous that you can't [make copies] when someone asks you to, even if you have a degree after four years and you think you're all that and a bag of chips. In the beginning, you're not."

"The only place where success comes before work is in the dictionary."

AMERICAN PROVERB

"Things may come to those who wait, but only things left by those who hustle."

ABRAHAM LINCOLN

"If you want a place in the sun, you've got to put up with a few blisters."

ABIGAIL VAN BUREN

I'm a great believer in luck, and I find the harder I work, the more I have of it.

THOMAS JEFFERSON

Errands, coffee, psychological abuse: Some of the horrors associated with interning are true. But it's still the best way to learn the ropes of a new career.

The Occasional Professional Mishap Can Turn Out to Be a Personal Triumph

Anna Wintour, the legendary *Vogue* editor, once told a group of fashion industry hopefuls that one of the biggest breaks in her astonishing career was getting axed from a magazine. Her words were amusing and shocking. "I recommend you all get fired," she deadpanned to an open-mouthed seminar audience. "It's a great learning experience."

Indeed, first-time failures seem to be the hallmark of many amazing success stories: JK Rowling, the richest woman in England (yes, her bank account has grown bigger than the Queen's!), was canned from her job as a secretary before she penned the Harry Potter series on napkins at a cafe; Tyra Banks was turned down at six modeling agencies before she found representation as a catwalk hopeful; and even Michael Jordan, the poster boy for pro sports and perhaps the most successful athlete of all time, was kicked off a few teams before making basketball history as a Chicago Bull.

When I was first starting in the fashion industry, I had my fair share of professional hiccups too. I lost jobs and got passed over for promotions and was fired from *Vogue* (ironically, Ms. Wintour's words of wisdom proved true here).

Learning from these sorts of painful experiences is an important part of any career. I probably learned more from getting fired then I did from receiving professional accolades, now that I think about it. (Not that I was this enlightened or happy about being canned at the time.)

It's okay to quit a job, take a break, or suss out other career options. But I wouldn't recommend seeking out an opportunity to follow Wintour's advice on a whim. Don't quit a job because you've had a bad day or because you didn't get the shift that you wanted, and certainly don't ever quit without a backup plan. Wintour was not referring to getting kicked out of school or saying

> "Change is the essence of life. Be willing to sacrifice what you are for what you could become."
>
> TONY ROBBINS

that getting fired for showing up to work with the sour scent of beer on your breath is some badge of honor. One shouldn't be proud of getting canned, but one should learn from it.

Taking risks is important when trying to move forward professionally, but if you're going to pull a Jerry McGuire (which is a reference to the Tom Cruise film where he has a professional epiphany and gets fired for it), make sure you have some money in the bank to pay rent for the next few months. McGuire had a happy ending, but there's no guarantee you will too.

At the end of the day, not having a job is an inconvenience, but it's not the end of the world. Use "funemployment" (what many of my friends call being without a job) to blow off some steam. But then pick yourself up, reprioritize your career goals, and get yourself out there. This is something my grandmother always explained to me when I was a young man: Tough times never last—tough people always do.

SOMETIMES:

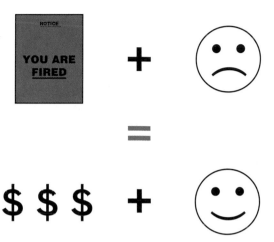

FIRED AND THEN FAMOUS

Think losing your job is the worse thing that could happen to you? Think again. Here's a list of people who needed to get fired before they got famous.

● **WALT DISNEY,** the illustrator whose imagination is now an international empire, was fired because "he lacked imagination and had no good ideas." A few years later he was sketching the characters that have helped define childhood entertainment.

● **THOMAS EDISON,** the genius we should thank every time we flip a switch, was actually told by a teacher he was "too stupid to learn anything." As an adult, he was fired from his first two jobs. But he stuck with it, and those failures ended up producing quite an important invention: the light bulb.

● **OPRAH WINFREY,** who is considered like a god in some circles (and by some circles I mean my circles), overcame quite a few hurdles in her life, including abuse and poverty. She was once fired as a television reporter because she was "unfit for TV." As we all know now, that didn't stop her.

● **MICHAEL BLOOMBERG,** billionaire and New York mayor, was fired from an investment banking firm, which made him reassess his finances and found a company that eventually became the very influential Bloomberg network.

● **ELVIS PRESLEY,** the King of Rock n Roll, was actually told after an early performance, "You ain't goin' nowhere, son. You ought to go back to drivin' a truck." Jimmy Denny, the manager of the Grand Ole Opry, was the one who uttered those words and was no doubt kicking himself when the very same person became one of the best-selling artists of all time.

● **GEORGE FOREMAN,** heavyweight champion of the world, actually lost his first fight: he was fired from his job as a furniture mover. It was the best fight he ever lost, because it sent him into the ring.

Q&A:

A Lady Is Always Learning

The best part about creating this book has been the responses it's caused among the young women I've met at my book signings, over e-mail, and even on the street. There are some smart girls out there, and they've had some fabulous questions. I liked some of them so much I wanted to include them here.

Q: *What was your favorite intern experience?*

A: When I was still in college, I was one of three male interns working at *Vogue* at the same time. The other two were the designer Alexander Wang , with me here at my birthday party, and the stylist Brad Goreski, below with me and the photographer Terry Richardson at a New York Fashion Week party. It was a fun time for all three of us but also one of the most educational. I sometimes think I learned more interning—and later working—at *Vogue* than I did in college!

Q: *Why do you think you were successful?*

A: I'd like to think it's because of my God-given talent, but I'm self-aware enough to recognize it's not always about brains in any business. I worked hard, I stayed late, I asked if people needed more help, I smiled, and I never complained (aloud, anyway).

Q: *You can't really think that school is fun.*

A: I couldn't wait to graduate high school and get to college, and when I was in college I couldn't wait to graduate and start working. But just because those are common sentiments doesn't mean it's a tragedy. At least it wasn't for me. I actually like retaining knowledge, retaining fun facts, and being well versed in things. And it's the ultimate frustration that, now when I'm out of college and have to work, I'm so desperate to go back. In fact, now I really wish I hadn't slept through my entire class on the indigenous history of Papua New Guinea.

Q: *What's your favorite museum?*

A: I feel obliged to say the Metropolitan Museum of Art in New York because it's my local arts center, and the museum's Costume Institute is such an inspiration for my work. But to be honest, even since I was an elementary school student and my family went to France, the Louvre has captured my imagination. (I took this picture from Napoleon's private apartments during a private tour of the former palace-turned-museum.) The gardens, the Mona Lisa, the fact that it's in Paris—the romance! Although, I should say that I can get lost in nearly any museum. I even spent a day in the New York Transit Museum once.

Q: *What do you do to educate yourself now that you're out of school?*

A: The Internet is an addictive little creation that doesn't need to be used exclusively for e-mail and Googling cute boys. It's also an information superhighway where we can learn about almost anything. (FYI: that's what it was created for.) But it's not just my computer that gives me stimulation: I always sign up for a guided tour when I'm in a new city, and I look at guidebooks and websites, and I ask friends for tips and suggestions on where to go. I actually love doing those double-decker bus tours in cities like London, Paris, and even New York when a friend is visiting town.

Q: *What was the best piece of advice you've ever gotten?*

A: Before my Grannie Betty, seen here at my high school graduation, passed away, she called me up after a particularly devastating day at the office to tell me that "Rome wasn't built in a day." It was a good piece of advice: While we live in an instant culture, we have to remember that hard work and dedication pay off, and

Q: *How did you get started in the fashion industry?*

A: When I moved to New York from Missouri, I didn't have a real grasp on fashion. (I thought the Gap was considered high fashion.) But I encountered a vast new world when I moved to the big city, and soon after witnessing the creative choreography between photographer, stylist, model, and all the other bright minds in this world, I knew it was where I wanted to be. I changed my major to journalism, and then I did what I tell everyone who wants to work here to do: find internships, learn the ropes, make friends, and then make yourself indispensable.

Artists to Know

A rt is such a broad topic it seems silly to try to address it in a single chapter (or a single book, for that matter). Art can be anything: the pictures we're familiar with in museums, the graffiti we see in subway tunnels. My point in this section is simply that a knowledge of art—even a vague one—is an imperative characteristic of a chic, well-rounded lady. Every young woman should have at least a general understanding of art history and the current art scene.

My suggestion for finding a passion for—or at least, a pleasure in—art is very simple: Go to a museum, or go to a local gallery, and find what you like. If you're still in school and you have some electives, take studio art or art history, or enroll in a course at a local museum.

(One thing to remember, however, is that as with any matters of taste or opinion, being open-minded is important. Art snobs—the clichéd breed of arrogant, starving, herbal-cigarette-smoking jerks who think their opinions mean more than anyone else's—are annoying.)

Just remember that art is something you won't know if you like until you experience it yourself. Maybe you're a Renaissance girl who likes pretty pictures of pretty ladies. Or maybe you like medieval religious paintings. Hell, maybe there's a kinky little freak under your cardigan set and you can't get enough of Richard Prince's pornography-inspired works or Andres Serrano's pieces made with human urine (though if this is true, you might want to keep your preferences to yourself).

One caveat: Even if you read every single art history book in the library, and trolled every gallery in New York City for the artists currently working, chances are you would still find yourself stumped at a dinner party once or twice in your life when the subject of art came up. The art world is dynamic; there will always be a best new thing, or some random skinny boy working at a shanty studio in Long Island City who wows the art world for a whole week and then disappears into oblivion again. Regardless, there are a few seminal artists with whom every lady should be familiar. Google these guys (and girls), and see if any of them tickle your fancy.

● Francis Bacon (1909–1992): This guy was unafraid to tackle his demons. Much of his work was horrific and tormented. Bacon is the perfect painter when you need a trip to the dark side.

● Jean-Michel Basquiat (1960–1988): In the '80s, when street art first ventured into the mainstream, Basquiat became the center of an artistic maelstrom: He started dating Madonna, worked with Warhol, and was celebrated as the future of art. All of the accolades proved too much, though: He OD'd at the age of 27.

● Caravaggio (1571–1610): Caravaggio was real before being real was cool. In an age when flamboyant ideas and

ideological scenes were big, he painted things as he saw them.

FRANCESCO CLEMENTE
WORKS 1971–1979

● Francesco Clemente (b. 1952): Clemente's style mixes the romantic, the scary, and the expressionistic. Since many of his works are self-portraits, his paintings seem to provide a penetrating look into his soul.

● Salvador Dalí (1904–1989): For Salvador Dalí, nothing was taboo—which outraged some people and enthralled others. (Personally, I think the freak with the funny mustache and wildly imaginative style is fascinating.)

● Leonardo da Vinci (1452–1519): The fact that the original Renaissance man can inspire, nearly 500 years after his death, a *New York Times* bestseller and a blockbuster movie, speaks volumes about the quality of his legacy. *Mona Lisa*, anyone?

● Lucian Freud (b. 1922): Lucian Freud portrays the human body in almost obsessive detail. (Obsessions must run in the family: he's the grandson of the world-famous psychoanalyst.)

● David Hockney (b. 1937): Hockney's works—which have been alternatively described as pop and photographic—are vivid, bright, colorful, and joyful. They are the art world's uppers.

● Edward Hopper (1882–1967): Hopper is one of the few artists my whole family appreciates. My mom likes his landscapes, my dad likes the simplicity of his technique, and I like the individual use of color.

● **Jasper Johns (b. 1930):** Johns was proud to be an American long before it was chic to say so, and I like that this American pop-art aficionado's most famous work centers around the trusty red, white, and blue.

● **Frida Kahlo (1907–1954):** Forceful, incendiary, and sometimes deranged, Kahlo created surrealistic and expressive artwork that mirrored her volatile personal life.

● **Alex Katz (b. 1927):** Katz went to the famed Cooper Union art program and then became a dominant member of the pop movement in the city. His works are bright, full of color, and somehow hopeful and saddening simultaneously.

● **Gustav Klimt (1862–1918):** In his day, Klimt's works were considered pornographic by some and unimaginative by others. But today, his gilded mosaics are hallmarks of one of the most exciting periods in art history: Art Nouveau.

● **Jeff Koons (b. 1955):** A thirty-foot-tall dog made of flowers, a shiny metallic sculpture in the shape of a balloon animal: These are just a few of the loud, irreverent, adventurous works of Jeff Koons.

● **Roy Lichtenstein (1923–1997):** Lichtenstein referenced comic books and cartoons in his works, successfully blurring the distinction between pop and high art, and always puts a smile on my face.

● **Michelangelo (1475–1564):** Best known for his work in the Sistine Chapel in Rome, a must-see destination for millions of people each year, Michelangelo was a quintessential Renaissance man. Not just a brilliant painter, he was a sculptor, architect, poet, and even a military engineer.

● **Claude Monet (1840–1926):** Monet, a famous Impressionist, was immortalized in the movie *Clueless* when a girl is told she resembles the painter's work: Up close it (and she) is a mess of ink splotches and colors, but from afar it's a sweeping, gorgeous landscape. Check out his *Water Lilies* paintings.

Georgia O'Keeffe
Nature and Abstraction

● **Georgia O'Keeffe (1887–1986):** O'Keeffe lived in the desert for much of her life, generating beautiful, precise paintings of sandy landscapes and flowers. Oddly enough, her life and work were a major basis for the first Calvin Klein underwear campaigns.

● **Pablo Picasso (1881–1973):** Typically labeled the greatest artist of the twentieth century, Picasso defined entire artistic movements (like Cubism) and created some of western history's most important works of art.

● **Richard Prince (b. 1949):** Prince didn't really hit the big

time until he was older. But when he did, he *really* hit it. The sales of some of his Nurse paintings broke art-auction records, and he has collaborated with Marc Jacobs on prints for Louis Vuitton.

● **Jackson Pollock (1912–1956):** Pollock used sticks and knives to create a splatter effect on his canvases, pioneering what became known as action painting. His personal life was similarly messy—he died in a car accident at the age of forty-four.

The Rembrandt Book

● **Rembrandt (1606–1669):** Considered the father of the Dutch Golden Age of painting, Rembrandt created paintings that are subtle, poignant, and characterized by their extremely focused use of lighting. Bonus: Like every good artist, he had quite the scandalous personal life.

● **Mark Rothko (1903–1970):** Rothko's work needs to be seen in person, when you can appreciate his paintings' scale and restrained, complex use of color.

● **John Singer Sargent (1856–1925):** Although Sargent was prolific in many artistic genres, my favorite works are his numerous paintings of Edwardian society ladies. He had that whole regal thing *down.*

● **Egon Schiele (1890–1918):** Schiele was one of the most

important Expressionist paint-
ers, and although his body
of work is small, it shows the
promise of genius—cut short
by a deadly bout of influenza.

● **Julian Schnabel (b. 1951):**
Schnabel got labeled an
enfant terrible of the art
world back in the '80s. No one
can argue the importance of
his work, however—and not
just his paintings. Schnabel is
one of film's most celebrated
directors too.

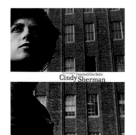

● **Cindy Sherman (b. 1954):**
Sherman has a strong sense
of humor, and in her photographic self-portraits, she is
often playing a different role
or character. Although there

is a comic bent to her work,
it can also be brooding and
reflective.

● **Cy Twombly (b. 1928):** To
look at his work—typically a
labyrinthine, dizzying com-
position of odd shapes and
lines—might make you think
that Twombly was a bit off his
rocker. But the point of his art
was to get people thinking.

● **Vincent van Gogh (1853-
1890):** Van Gogh left behind
an important legacy of colorful and deeply imaginative
post-Impressionistic paintings.
He was also totally crazy: He
cut off his own earlobe and
killed himself in 1890.

● **Andy Warhol (1928-1987):**
Warhol liked famous people.
A lot. His iconic pop-art refer-
ences (and portraits of celebs
like Marilyn Monroe and
Elvis Presley) have continued
to make him a popular and
relevant artist.

● **Andrew Wyeth (1917-
2009):** Wyeth's sweeping
landscapes, which evoke
feelings of both emptiness or
longing, have always been a
favorite of mine.

HISTORIC PHOTOGRAPHERS

My passion for fashion was first ignited by the pictures in high-fashion magazines, like *Vogue* and *Harper's Bazaar*. Even before I moved to New York City and immersed my-self in this industry, I was aware that those images were typically culled from a small handful of talented tastemakers. In a medium like photography, which was completely rebranded when it changed from film to digital imagery (though a few, like Bruce Weber, refuse to make the switch), the players are many, and the truly influential works are re-spected for vastly different reasons. For example, one photographer might be known for making women look ethereally beautiful while another photographer prefers to capture women realistically (which, depending on the subject, can get scary). One might shoot landscapes; others treat bodies as landscapes. Here is a list of people worth spending some time looking up:

Ansel Adams (1902-1984)	**Steven Meisel** (b.1954)
Diane Arbus (1923-1971)	**Helmut Newton** (1920-2004)
Richard Avedon (1923-2004)	**Irving Penn** (b.1917)
David Bailey (b. 1938)	**Man Ray** (1890-1976)
Brassaï (1889-1954)	**Terry Richardson** (b. 1954)
Guy Bourdin (1928-1991)	**Herb Ritts** (1952-2002)
William Eggleston (b.1939)	**Francesco Scavullo** (1921-2004)
Steven Klein (b.1946)	**Alfred Stieglitz** (1864-1946)
Annie Leibovitz (b.1949)	**Mario Testino** (b.1954)
Robert Mapplethorpe (1946-1989)	**Inez van Lamsweerde (b.1963) and Vinoodh Matadin (b.1961)**
Craig McDean (b.1964)	**Bruce Weber** (b.1946)

Fashionable Films to Know

G ood movies are good for different reasons, and what you choose to watch will depend on your mood. For example, if I want a good cry, I'll break out my DVDs of *The Notebook*, *Shawshank Redemption*, or *Sophie's Choice*; if I want a giggle, I'll On Demand *Clueless* or one of those parody films that always seem to be available on long flights. But the real reason I like films is for the fashion (of course), and for the chance to be immersed in a different world or time period. Below, I've listed films I think are not only important for the typical reasons (a good story, good acting, blah blah blah), but also because they are just so gosh darn pretty.

● *Rear Window*, 1954: The reason that Jimmy Stuart spends the majority of this 1950s classic in PJs isn't only because he's in a wheelchair (he plays an injured photographer who spies on his New York City neighbors and is convinced one of them has committed murder)—it's also because the *real* star of the show is the stunning Grace Kelly, who steals every scene with her gorgeous midcentury silhouette.

● *Funny Face*, 1957: This movie stars Audrey Hepburn as a book clerk turned '50s supermodel. She is swept away by a photographer played by Fred Astaire (a character based on famous fashion lensman Richard Avedon) to Paris to shoot for a famed New York-based fashion magazine. (More art imitating life: The editor of the magazine is based on legendary *Vogue* editor Diana Vreeland.) The couture sequences—namely when Hepburn runs down a staircase in a red Givenchy number—have become fashion legend.

● *Breakfast at Tiffany's*, 1961: So many fashion must-haves were born out of this movie, many of them in the first few moments of the film: the Little Black Dress; the black sunglasses; the importance of a well-placed accessory. This film, based on a Truman Capote novella, solidified Audrey Hepburn as a style icon. In it she plays the quintessential New York City girl about town, flitting around aimlessly before falling in love with a writer who lives in her building.

● *The Fifth Element*, 1997: Even before I found out that Jean-Paul Gaultier did the costumes for this legendary sci-fi movie, I was already drawn to the orange bondage look that Milla Jovovich (playing a world-saving superhuman) works in the film. Bonus points go to Chris Tucker, whose tranny talk-show host had some fierce ensembles too.

THE GREAT GATSBY

FEDERICO FELLINI'S LA DOLCE VITA

"REBEL WITHOUT A CAUSE"

GREY GARDENS — THE CRITERION COLLECTION

WILLIAM SHAKESPEARE'S ROMEO+JULIET SPECIAL EDITION

ALL ABOUT EVE

AMERICAN PSYCHO

THE TALENTED MR RIPLEY

THE ROYAL TENENBAUMS THE CRITERION COLLECTION 157

The Philadelphia Story

YVES SAINT LAURENT COLLECTOR'S EDITION

LAGERFELD CONFIDENTIAL

THE FIFTH ELEMENT

PULP FICTION

HELMUT NEWTON Frames From the Edge A film by ADRIAN MABEN

Breakfast at TIFFANY'S

THE WOMEN

aninconvenienttruth A GLOBAL WARNING

THE DUCHESS

UNZIPPED

Streetcar Named Desire

● *The Thomas Crown Affair,* 1968: Steve McQueen was the heartthrob of his day, and Faye Dunaway was the girl everyone wanted to emulate—largely because of this film, in which McQueen plays the role of the perfect thief and Dunaway the lady who tries to pin him for the crime . . . while remaining perfectly coifed and styled at all times.

● The remake of *The Thomas Crown Affair,* 1999: When it comes to remakes, chances are the original is always much, much better than the remake. Luckily, for fashion devotees, when Pierce Brosnan—as the millionaire thrill-seeking art thief—and Rene Russo, as his saucy pursuer, redid this classic, they kept it both modern *and* retro. Thank Michael Kors for the slinky see-through dress Russo sports during the benefit scene.

● *Ciao Manhattan,* 1972: This is the Warhol-directed film that features Edie Sedgwick as the classically doomed starlet, living a fast life that ends in an untimely death. Sedgwick's '60s fashions play a big part in the action too, though the ultimate theme of a beautiful life cut short resonates.

● *The Royal Tenenbaums,* 2001: Wes Anderson is my kind of filmmaker. He pays as much attention to the wardrobes of

his characters—which are always unique, vintage-inspired, and perfectly put-together—as he does to every other aspect of the filmmaking. This movie, which stars Gwyneth Paltrow as a stripe-loving child genius and Anjelica Huston as her sexy, suited-up mother, is a fun and stylish narrative of an odd uptown family.

● *West Side Story,* 1961: Even if you don't like musicals (but you do, so just admit it), this is the perfect combination of camp and '50s fashion.

● *Desperately Seeking Susan,* 1985: There have been major debates over which film best embodies '80s fashion. Some say *Flashdance,* some say all those Molly Ringwald teen dramas. But I prefer this flick, which features Madonna and Rosanna Arquette dueling it out over a case of mistaken identities, fighting over hot motorcycle jackets and hair bleach, and trolling the East Village before it became so gentrified.

● *Hair,* 1979: The movie, based on the classic '60s play, tells the story of a Midwestern boy

who moves to New York City, joins a pack of musically minded hippies, and falls in love with a rich girl called Sheila. Even if you're not into the plot (I was, being Midwestern and moving to N.Y.C. and all), this is one of the best films to feature hippie fashion.

● *Sex and the City,* 2008: Patricia Field, the stylist of the wildly successful TV series of the same name, was under a great deal of fashion pressure when she signed on to do the movie version of the show that tracked the love lives of four women in Manhattan and influenced an entire generation's manner of speech, dress, and dating. But putting Carrie in a Vivienne Westwood dress was fabulous (she even had a bird in her hat), and the rest of the characters turned out equally . . . turned out.

● *The Women,* 1939: The classic version of this film is the only one worth watching. (It was remade in 2008, but the new director completely forgot one of the most important elements of the original film—the decadent clothes.) This is a movie without any men in it. It is shot in classic black and white (apart from a showstopping "fashion show" scene in the middle) and contains quite possibly the best scene ever: Joan Crawford, who plays a man-stealing gold digger, cooing into a phone while neck deep in suds with her hair in rollers. This film perfectly recalls a more glamorous time.

● *Doctor Zhivago*, 1965: The idea of a movie following a poet and a political activist through war-torn Russian countryside during the Bolshevik Revolution doesn't exactly sound like inspiring fashion fare. But Omar Sharif's lady friend, played by Julie Christie, rocks the refugee look to great effect and has inspired countless different uses of fur boots and bonnets, opulent collars and cuffed shirts . . . and military jackets, of course.

● *The Great Gatsby*, 1974: This movie, about a man's infatuation with a woman across the bay and his lifelong pursuit of her affection, is based on three of my favorite things: an F. Scott Fitzgerald novella, the

Roaring '20s, and costumes designed by Ralph Lauren. Throw Mia Farrow and Robert Redford in the mix, and we've got the perfect two hours.

● *American Gigolo*, 1980: Who doesn't love a movie about a handsome male prostitute? Richard Gere, the stud of the '80s, plays lap boy to Lauren Hutton—in one of her first roles as a model turned actress—until he is pegged with a murder charge. This is all about California cool toward the end of the '70s, but more important to fashion history, this was the film that established Giorgio Armani as a Hollywood player.

● *Bonnie and Clyde*, 1967: Laugh if you will, but I always identified with the Faye Dunaway character in this film—she's Bonnie, a bored Missouri housewife, until Warren Beatty's Clyde scoops her away and takes her on a thrilling bank-robbing adventure. When the movie was released, the media focused on the violence of the film. But all the young folks really cared about were Dunaway's hot mod looks,

a style still referenced in collections today.

● *Annie Hall*, 1977: Diane Keaton must really love this film, which follows the relationship of a goofy girl and her neurotic, older boyfriend: It helped define the unique personal style—menswear as womenswear, ties, big hats, lots of jackets—she has been rocking for more than thirty years. This film provides some great lessons for girls looking to learn how to borrow from a man's closet.

● *The Seven Year Itch*, 1955: In this film, Marilyn Monroe plays the role of a regular guy's fantasy. Quite a stretch. This is the movie in which Marilyn infamously works a white dress over a subway grate, exposing her panties—not that the crotch shot is the only memorable moment in the film.

● *Gone with the Wind*, 1939: This story is one most of us know pretty well: A spoiled girl falls in love with a dashing man, who is irritated by her self-centered ways. Sure, the sweeping cinematography is good to look at, but so are all those amazing Confederate-era dresses: Think crinoline petticoats, gloves, and dresses with more fabric and pleats than a Southern mansion's curtains.

● *Bringing Up Baby*, 1938: Legend has it that on the set of this movie, the first on which Katharine Hepburn debuted her now famous look, the studio bigwigs were so upset that she wanted to wear trousers, they stole them from her—so Hepburn spent the day in her underwear until her pants were returned. This movie features good upscale '30s fashions, woven into a plot about a bored rich girl, her pet leopard, and an uptight paleontologist.

● *Sabrina* (the original), 1954: Audrey Hepburn, playing the part of a chauffeur's daughter who returns a sophisticated young lady after two years abroad, is the belle of this ball and swans around in ball gowns that would make a girl cry even today. More important to fashion history, however, is the

fact that it was while filming this movie that Hepburn met Givenchy, forging a fashion partnership that lasted for decades.

● *To Catch a Thief*, 1955: This film revolves around the theft of some of the world's most fantastic jewelry; to prevent these rocks from stealing the show, the always beautiful Grace Kelly, playing an American heiress who agrees to help suspect John (Cary Grant), was outfitted in some of the most elegant and sumptuous looks ever to hit the French Riviera. She shimmies, shimmers, and sashays in one of her most glamorous roles.

● *And God Created Woman*, 1956: The title of the movie makes no mystery of its raison d'être—to create one of the world's most enticing female roles. So the plot (a girl meets two brothers, loves one but marries the other) plays second fiddle to the real star of the show—Brigitte Bardot—who pouts and poses and pioneers some of fashion's most iconic looks, like messy

beach hair, gingham bikinis, and Repetto flats.

● *Belle de Jour*, 1967: This is a straightforward movie about a beautiful wife who, growing bored of her marriage, decides to while her afternoons away working at a brothel in Paris. Makes perfect sense to me! Even better is what Catherine Deneuve, the now-legendary French actress, wears throughout the film, including perfectly fitted coats and shift dresses. Legend has it that the Roger Vivier buckle flats she wears in the film so impressed theatergoers that immediately after the film's release, more than 120,000 pairs flew out of stores.

● *Scarface*, 1983: Cocaine, Cubans, crime, and Michelle Pfeiffer as a mobster's girlfriend—this movie has it all. It's debauched, it's decadent, it's disgusting. But Pfeiffer, playing the part of Tony (Al Pacino)'s abused and underappreciated better half, displays the perfect amount of cracked-out glamour and indifference.

● *Pulp Fiction*, 1994: With all the bullets and blood—and the relatively few scenes that feature the amazing Uma Thurman—it can be hard to appreciate the fashion in this classic Quentin Tarantino film. But when it comes to coolness quotient, the Capri-pant-and-white-oxford-clad Thurman, playing the part of a gangster's wife with a drug problem, gives John Travolta's and Samuel L. Jackson's characters a serious run for their money.

● *Love Story*, 1970: I love a good preppy look, which is why this film, set in ritzy New York City and at two college campuses, is so inspiring. Ryan O'Neal plays a rich jock, and Ali McGraw his poor music-student love interest. Cue comfy knits, letterman's jackets, and adorable hat-and-scarf combos—and we've got a tearjerker on our hands.

● *Dangerous Liaisons*, 1988: Based on the classic work of fiction, this tale of bored aristocrats in eighteenth-century France looking to take advantage of this or that young lady takes place in a golden age of French couture. The first fifteen minutes of this film alone are an eye-opening lesson in what it was like to get dressed during that era. And, honey, it wasn't easy.

● *Chicago*, 2002: Often when a musical is remade for the big screen, many of the production's most important elements—like costumes—are lost. Not so here. When this story about a couple of murdering, vaudeville-bound vixens hit the theaters, Renée Zellweger and Catherine Zeta-Jones rocked it out in 1920s flapper looks and sexy, sheer leggings.

● *Mahogany*, 1975: Unsurprisingly, perhaps, I have a thing for movies that try to portray the inner workings of the fashion industry. This movie is Diana Ross's attempt to do just that. She plays a girl from the ghetto, who becomes a top model and famous fashion designer. But this film's costumes—which Ross helped design—are the real trip, with retro colors, lots of glitter, and more sparkle than you could fit into a disco.

● *The Talented Mr. Ripley*, 1999: With a perfectly stunning cast—Matt Damon, Gwyneth Paltrow, Jude Law, Cate Blanchett, Philip Seymour Hoffman—all sporting that wealthy 1950s American-in-Europe chic, this film is perfectly captivating, even as it gets creepy and weird.

Fictional Characters to Know (in Books You Should Read)

Here's the thing about books: When you're forced to read one, be it by an educational institution or a parent or whomever, it's easy to automatically hate it. And I totally get that. You tell me to do something, and I will automatically want to do the opposite, hate what you told me to do, and hate you for telling me to do it. (Can you say, "authority issues"?)

But a few years ago, I realized that not only had I missed out on some classic works of fiction—I'd missed out on some pretty enjoyable reading too. The reason that some of these books have stuck around as long as they have is because, um, they're actually quite good. What really drove it home for me were the characters: the romantic insecurity of Holden Caulfield in *The Catcher in the Rye*; or the exciting madness of wronged son Hamlet in Shakespeare's eponymous play; the allure of the American Dream and the pain of unrequited love, embodied tragically by the titular character in F. Scott Fitzgerald's *The Great Gatsby*.

So here, in no particular order, is a list of some of my favorite characters. Don't hate me for saying this, but you should really check them out.

● **Alice**, *Alice's Adventures in Wonderland*, by Lewis Carroll 1865: This story of the sweet, naive little blonde who falls into a rabbit hole has been entertaining young people for ages. But the book, which was penned by Charles Lutwidge Dodgson under a pseudonym, has led to darker interpretations. Some say Dodgson was alluding to psychotropic drugs in his work, and a Chinese territory banned the book in 1931 because the animals featured in the text were given the anthropomorphic powers of speech.

● **Hercules**, Greek mythology: Literature's original stud, Hercules was the son of king of gods Zeus and mortal mom Alcmena. This guy was always running around being a hero, and in Roman times was even the basis of a cult.

● **Emma Bovary**, *Madame Bovary*, by Gustave Flaubert, 1856: I love a story about a lonely lady who begins pursuing outlandish fantasies to ward off boredom and discontent. And that's exactly what Emma does, using adulterous relationships to escape her banal life. When published, this book was considered particularly scandalous.

● **Emma**, *Emma*, by Jane Austen, 1815: Any girl who thinks modern manners are ridiculous should read Austen's book set in Georgian England, when every single part of a young woman's day had to cohere to a stiff code of conduct. That's what makes Emma, a spoiled yet well-meaning troublemaker, such an endearing character.

● **Scarlett O'Hara**, *Gone with the Wind*, by Margaret Mitchell, 1936: Chances are, you've met a Scarlett in your life—a self-consumed, vain little lady who cares only about herself. This type of person can be pretty entertaining, especially when placed against the backdrop of the Civil War. What makes Scarlett particularly lovable is the fact that she ultimately realizes that there is much more to life than the perfect petticoat.

● **Holden Caulfield**, *The Catcher in the Rye*, by J.D. Salinger, 1951: Few characters in literature are as relatable as Caulfield, the narrator of Salinger's masterpiece. Even the most overachieving young person can still identify with the feelings of distance, loneliness, and frustration Holden feels after being kicked out of school, as he trolls about Manhattan on his long way home.

● **Scout Finch**, *To Kill a Mock-*

ingbird, by Harper Lee, 1960: Lee only wrote one novel, and this is it. A profoundly touching story revolving around Southern race relations, the story is told retrospectively from the point of view of Scout, the narrator, as she reflects on her childhood.

● **Holly Golightly**, *Breakfast at Tiffany's*, by Truman Capote, 1958: Although Audrey Hepburn played this part expertly in the movie version, in the original work by Capote Golightly is an entirely more complex (and flawed) night creature. It's a short book, and a worthwhile read.

● **Lolita**, *Lolita*, by Vladimir Nabokov, 1955: This book, about a twelve-year-old girl who becomes the object of an older man's affection, is not for the faint of heart. Still, it's one of the greatest works of literature of all time—and has been inspiring teen minx wannabes ever since its release, with less than auspicious results.

● **Clarissa Dalloway**, *Mrs. Dalloway*, by Virginia Woolf, 1925: This story of a young English woman preparing for a house party is an impressive work of fiction—as it weaves in and out of the titular character's mind, we get a full portrayal of a woman on the verge of crisis. This is also one of the original examples of a "stream of consciousness" narrative style.

● **Daisy Buchanan**, *The Great Gatsby*, by F. Scott Fitzgerald, 1925: Equal parts fascinating and frustrating, the beautiful woman across the bay in this masterpiece is both a gorgeous muse and the catalyst for the end of one man's Jazz Age. This book captures a golden period in American history.

● **Lord Sebastian Flyte**, *Brideshead Revisited*, by Evelyn Waugh, 1945: I see modern-day Sebastians all the time: handsome, winsome, aristocratic blonds with the world at their fingertips. Lord Flyte is an Oxford student with a teddy bear and a drinking problem. This book proves that even families that look perfect from the outside are often anything but.

● **Sherman McCoy**, *The Bonfire of the Vanities*, by Tom Wolfe, 1987: This book takes place in New York City in the 1980s, a time when, fueled by a solvent Wall Street, the city was at its most decadent and hedonistic. Sherman, a spoiled WASP whose involvement in a race-fueled incident leads to his bitter defamation in the tabloids, is at the center of this story. Who doesn't love reading about a scandal?

● **Patrick Bateman,** *American Psycho,* by Bret Easton Ellis, 1991: Few characters in fiction have been as completely materialistic or completely mental as the protagonist of this serial-killer classic. He brags about Gucci loafers in one breath, then kills a hooker with a chainsaw in the next. Anyone intrigued by either fashion *or* murder will find this a page-turner.

● **Santiago,** *The Old Man and the Sea,* by Ernest Hemingway 1952: This is a shorter work (which is good for anybody out there with an attention-span problem), but a literary genius like Hemingway doesn't need excess pages to tell a good story. This one features an aging fisherman named Santiago and his mission to catch the biggest fish of his life.
● **Lady Ashley,** or Brett, *The Sun Also Rises,* by Ernest Hemingway, 1926: Another classic from Hemingway, this book revolves around Jake Barnes, a war veteran dealing with both physical and mental

injuries. Brett is his love interest and proves that women have their own problems trying to overcome trauma.

● **Hermione Granger,** *Harry Potter* series, by J.K. Rowling, 1997–2007: I know, I know—I thought these were kids' books too. And I admit that I am not the biggest fan of Harry Potter himself. But the character I do love is Hermione Granger, the independent and fearless girl wizard who saves Harry's ass on more than one occasion.

● **Hana,** *The English Patient,* by Michael Ondaatje, 1992: The female protagonist of this book (and later, of the breathtaking movie by Anthony Minghella) is a young nurse caring for a WWII victim. She must look human pain in the face, listen to one of the most heartbreaking love stories ever told, and try to find her own place in this world—all before her twenty-first birthday.
● **Estella,** *Great Expectations,* by Charles Dickens, 1860: There's a bit of Estella in every girl out there—the part that wants to be beautiful, young,

and able to fall in and out of love at will. But as Estella finds out when her childhood playmate Pip catches up with her later in life, sometimes it's better to let yourself be free than always in control.
● **Celie and Nettie,** *The Color Purple,* by Alice Walker, 1982: This heartbreaking and inspiring book, about two African-American sisters growing up in the South in the 1930s who refuse to let either violence or time get between them, is the perfect book to read if you want a good cry.

● **Hester Prynne,** *The Scarlet Letter,* by Nathaniel Hawthorne, 1850: This is one of those books that you read in school, and you hate it because you were forced to study it. But revisit Hawthorne's great work—it's all about adultery, sin, and guilt. Like a modern tabloid, but you don't have to be embarrassed about being caught reading it.
● **Jane,** *Jane Eyre,* by Charlotte Brontë, 1847: This book isn't short, so don't even think about this as a quick read. But it is an epic, moving story about an English girl who begins life as an orphan and spends the rest of her life trying to find herself.

● **Elizabeth Bennet,** *Pride and Prejudice,* by Jane Austen, 1813: Elizabeth is one of those fictional characters whom nearly every actress wants to play—and why not? Energetic, pretty, and too smart for her own good, she's the kind of gal every girl wishes she could be. Austen's story about Elizabeth's convoluted attempts to find love has been a fabulous read for nearly two centuries.

● **Mary Lennox,** *The Secret Garden,* by Frances Hogdson Burnett, 1910: Mary is a spoiled and sullen little child when her parents die from a cholera outbreak and she is sent to live with a distant relative in a fancy pile of bricks in the English countryside. And she very may well have stayed that way her whole life, had she not stumbled upon a secret garden on the mansion's grounds.

● **Anthony Patch,** *The Beautiful and the Damned,* by F. Scott Fitzgerald, 1922: Anthony is a rich young man of the Roaring '20s, with nary a care in the world. He is perfectly content to live in New York on his family's fortune. But as he finds out, life—and marriage—is more complex than he expects.

PLAYS

Hey, I love a good production of *Chicago* as much as the next person—all that black lace and sheer black paneling and nearly naked dancers (both boys and girls!) writhing around. But to read—ah, yes, remember reading?—a good drama is just as enjoyable as blowing the chunk of change on the Broadway version.

1. *Romeo and Juliet,* by Shakespeare: the quintessential love story.

2. *Hamlet,* by Shakespeare: a good tale of madness, obsession, and classic Freudian father-mother issues.

3. *Cat on a Hot Tin Roof,* by Tennessee Williams: Read the play first, then rent the film with Paul Newman and a gorgeous Elizabeth Taylor.

4. *Pygmalion,* by George Bernard Shaw: the rags-to-riches story that inspired *My Fair Lady.*

5. *Waiting for Godot,* by Samuel Beckett: A play entirely about waiting for something that never occurs? It's good, I promise.

6. *Suddenly Last Summer,* by Tennessee Williams: an insanely good play about insanity.

7. *Who's Afraid of Virginia Woolf?,* by Edward Albee: the insanity continues, this time in an academic marriage.

8. *Closer,* by Patrick Marber: Love is hard, really hard, especially when it involves strip clubs.

9. *A Streetcar Named Desire,* by Tennessee Williams: the play that gave us Marlon Brando (back when he was really, really hot).

10. *The Crucible,* by Arthur Miller: an original cautionary tale about the dangers of mob mentality.

Documentaries to Know

When I was a young person, documentaries had a bad rep. And I think that's because the only ones I was exposed to were ridiculously boring and awful school-mandated stories about government policy or poorly directed history biopics. It wasn't until I was a young adult that I realized that not all documentaries are painful to watch. Some of them are not only interesting—they're inspiring! Some of the jazz on the History Channel is not only informative—it's enjoyable! (And some, in the case of Madonna's *Truth or Dare*, are just straight-up entertaining.) So, if you're afraid of the documentary, don't be. And if you're ready to get your feet wet in that genre, here are a few suggestions to check out.

● *Grey Gardens* (1975): In the fashion world, this is perhaps the most referenced ever. It focuses on a peculiar mother-and-daughter duo who live in their own world in East Hampton. (In 2009, Drew Barrymore starred in the movie version.)

● *Paris Is Burning* (1990): This is the film that gave us terms like *Vogue*-ing and *legendary*, and is actually the poignant tale of drag balls in New York City in the 1980s.

● *Marc Jacobs & Louis Vuitton* (2007): Jacobs started his career by making grunge a fashion movement but landed at the helm of one of Paris's most important fashion houses. This film documents how he creates his magic.

● *Lagerfeld Confidential* 2007): Karl Lagerfeld is an unparalleled fashion icon whose career has been long, impressive, and unique. This film chronicles his life—and fans, like Hollywood actresses and real European royalty—at Chanel.

● *Gimme Shelter* (1970): The same people responsible for *Grey Gardens* gave us this unique look at the Rolling Stones. *Gimme Shelter* has been called the greatest rock-and-roll documentary in existence.

● *Bowling for Columbine* (2002): Michael Moore is not exactly the most fashionable man on the planet, but even those of us obsessed with the shoe of the season have to acknowledge that he has made some brilliant points about the world today. (See also: *Sicko, Fahrenheit 9/11.*)

● *Madonna: Truth or Dare* (1991): Before the kids, before kabbalah and before the charity work, Madonna had an insatiable desire for fame, performance—and herself. This documentary chronicles her Blonde Ambition tour and the hungry woman that once was.

● *Deep Water* (2006): This is the story of a man with a dream, and how determination and hope can sometimes lead the human spirit—literally—into unchartered waters.

POETRY

The sixth century Greek poet Simonides explained his artistic medium thusly: "Painting is silent poetry, and poetry is painting that speaks." I often regret not having given poetry its due (I always half-assed poetry classes), but now when I find a good rhyme, it moves me more than a whole marathon of my beloved reality TV programs. The good thing about poetry is its variety of forms and long history. From peers of Simonides' era, like Homer and Euripides, to romantic-era writers like Wordsworth, to rock stars like Jim Morrison who made their poetry into songs: It's a long, varied, and illustrious history. Take Pete Doherty, the English musician. He made a mess of his life, but he knows how to rhyme. Here is a short list of some of my favorite poets:

W.H. Auden (1907-1973)
Lord Tennyson Alfred (1809-1892)
Elizabeth Bishop (1911-1979)
William Blake (1757-1827)
Robert Browning (1812-1889)
Chaucer (c. 1342/43-1400)
e.e. cummings (1894-1962)
Euripides (480-406 BCE)
Emily Dickinson (1830-1886)
T.S. Eliot (1888-1965)
Robert Frost (1874-1963)
Allen Ginsberg (1926-1997)
John Keats (1795-1821)
Homer (unknown)
Ted Hughes (1930-1998)
Philip Larkin (1922-1985)

Robert Lowell (1917-1977)
John Milton (1608-1674)
Jim Morrison (1943-1971)
Edgar Allen Poe (1809-1849)
Ezra Pound (1885-1972)
Anne Sexton (1928-1967)
Percy Bysshe Shelley (1792-1882)
Shel Silverstein (1930-1999)
Shakespeare (the sonnets) (1564-1616)
Wallace Stevens (1879-1955)
Dylan Thomas (1914-1953)
William Wordsworth (1770-1850)
Walt Whitman (1819-1892)
William Butler Yeats (1865-1939)

● *Buena Vista Social Club* (1999): Wim Wenders documented the lives of some of Cuba's best—but long forgotten—musicians and their own unique brands of sound, love, and life.
● *Murderball* (2005): It may sound like an odd idea—quadriplegic rugby players taking each other on in steel wheelchairs. But the unbridled competitiveness and strength of these players—in the face of disability and adversity—aren't merely a game.

follows the famous Anna Wintour and her partner-in-crime Grace Coddington as they put together the all-important and celebrated September issue.

● *An Inconvenient Truth* (2006): Al Gore may not be the most exciting man to watch on film, but this documentary is an important observation on the future of our world and the consequences of environmental change.

● *Hoop Dreams* (1994): There's a little bit of jock in all of us, even those without a shred of athletic ability. (I was captain of my high school volleyball team, *thankyouverymuch*.) This is the captivating journey of two inner-city basketball stars and the temptations they face as they chase their NBA dreams.

● *Valentino: The Last Emperor* (2008): The Valentino label was built by two men, Mr. V and Giancarlo Giammetti, over nearly five decades. It was a love story, a story of glamour, a story of vision, and—after the two men retired—a story about how the fashion industry had changed forever as a result. This is the funny, poignant, frightening, and amazing story of that five-decade-long journey.

● *Super Size Me* (2004): Morgan Spurlock did something that I've always wanted to do: He ate fast food every single meal every single day for an entire month. In the end, he was unhealthy and near death. Which is why I don't want to do that anymore.

● *The Kid Stays in the Picture* (2002): Hollywood doesn't often make men like Robert Evans: a producer of seminal films, the boyfriend of seminal actresses, and a man with a seminal drug problem. This film chronicles his highs and his lows, and is full of good gossip about a bygone era.

● *Man on Wire* (2008): In 1974 a Frenchman walked on a tightrope wire between New York City's now-destroyed Twin Towers. This documentary is almost as nerve-racking to watch as it would be to perform such an incredibly dangerous stunt.

● *The September Issue* (2009): Having worked at *Vogue* magazine, I can vouch for this documentary's all-access pass into one of fashion's biggest, most important style bibles. It

Epilogue

WELL, THAT'S IT. That's everything a young girl needs to know to become a responsible, successful adult. I hope you've had a giggle and, at the very least, learned a little something about being a lady.

But please, bear in mind my goal isn't to create troupes of boring, Puritan, conservative young women who don't show any skin and don't have any fun. (Shudder at the thought!) If the one thing you took out of this book was that smart girls don't show their boobies on webcams, that's enough for me. If all you learned was that the drunkest girl at the party isn't automatically the most fun and probably not the most interesting, I'm fine with that too. Let's say you still wear crop tops—fine. As long as you know the breadplate is to the left of your dinner plate, I'm happy. Even if you never go to Europe or never throw a dinner party, but you've gained the confidence to swap the string bikini your slutty friend talked you into buying for a sensible one-piece, I feel like I've performed some sort of service.

For me, this book was a reaction to a larger problem: Too often the girls I see put on society's pedestal—worshipped and photographed and given TV shows—are standing up there for the wrong reasons. (They're probably slouching up there with their girlie parts hanging out, unable to differentiate between Austria and Australia, but that's not my point.) Sloppy sluts, sex tapes, bad table manners—it's terrifying. I grew scared that if girls weren't instructed in at least a tiny bit of decorum, the skanks would only continue to grow in number.

What I think we need to focus on are the young people, both famous and not, who respect themselves enough to live their lives in a fun, sensible manner. What we need more people to say is that the good girl always wins. Etiquette, style, manners, self-preservation, self-respect, a sense of humor, being a good girlfriend: These are the important hallmarks of a true lady. And we need more girls who know it.

I'm going to leave you now with some words from Winston Churchill. I know he may seem an odd choice—strange to think of Churchill as having wisdom to impart to young women as they enter adulthood and navigate the challenging waters of temptation (this was the guy who once told a woman who accused him of drinking too much: "But I'll be sober in the morning; you'll still be ugly"). But hey, you just read an entire book by a bearded, twenty-something Midwestern fashion journalist on what it takes to be a lady. These are some words to remember as you look to your future, as you put your life together and make the big decisions:

"These are the years! Don't be content with things as they are. Don't take no for an answer. Never submit to failure. Do not be fobbed off with mere personal success or acceptance. You will make all kinds of mistakes; but as long as you are generous and true, and also fierce, you cannot hurt the world or even seriously distress her. She was made to be wooed and won by youth. She has lived and thrived only by repeated subjugations."

WINSTON CHURCHILL

Notes on the Model

MY FRIEND BYRDIE BELL, who so generously agreed to be the faces of both the Lady and the Tramp in the book, was born Evelyn Byrd Bell in Chicago, Illinois, to an advertising-executive-turned-*New York Times*-best-selling author father and a jewelry designer mother. Stylish, talented, and always up for a good time, she's equal parts old-world class and new-world cool. She is a direct descendant of a long line of Evelyn Byrds, the first of whom was the eldest daughter of Colonel William Byrd, the founder of Richmond, Virginia. (There's a fabulous story about the first Evelyn Byrd being presented at King George I's court and leaving quite an impression: "I have heard much about Virginia, but no one told of its beautiful Byrds," the king reportedly quipped.) Also on her mother's side are bloodlines to the Norway monarchy. Her father Ted Bell is the bestselling author of the book series that follows Alex Hawke through international exploits in works like *Tsar, Spy,* and *Assassin.* (On a lighter note, Byrdie's great-grandfather on her father's side was the inspiration for the character Thurston Howell III on *Gilligan's Island.*) She lives near me in New York City, and is nice enough to let me hang out with her sometimes.

Acknowledgments

IN ALL HONESTY AND ALL HUMILITY (two traits I'm not exactly known for), I must say that without the people mentioned here, this book would not have happened. And not just because I'm helplessly disorganized, grumpy, and easily distracted. If it were not for these guys and gals, whom I'm so lucky to have as friends and professional peers, I would never have thought about doing a collection of humorous essays about etiquette.

The first two I must express my gratitude to are Penguin's affable Ben Schrank and the talented art director Rodrigo Corral, a persuasive duo who convinced me that a modern guide for young women can be smart and sophisticated. These two pointed me toward two other pivotal people: the wondrous (and now a best-selling author in her own right) Laura Schechter, who patiently helped put my ramblings into digestible texts as my editor, and Ben Wiseman, the wise man who illustrated the first edition of *Classy*. That original adaptation was the framework for this new book, which was put together under the serene guidance of Anne Heltzel and Vivian Kirklin.

As the book took shape, more and more wonderful people lent their expertise, which was both solicited and unprompted. These include my parents, my original copy editors, Bill and Carol Blasberg; and the saintly, lovely Lyle Maltz, whose patience with me knows no bounds. (Lyle also generously agreed to be photographed for the "Good Boy, Bad Boy, Gay Boy" spread on pp. 197-199, for which I'm very grateful.) I would be remiss not to thank my brother Chris Blasberg for a lifetime of support and torture, as well as the rest of my extended family (Aunt Tina, Aunt Mary, and so on), and my oldest girlfriends from St. Louis: Maria Zemen and Maja Heyduk.

I am indebted to my friend, the photographer Douglas Friedman, for generously taking so many pictures for this book, including the spreads of

Byrdie looking ladylike and not-so-ladylike. Thanks also to the great Terry Richardson, a photographer who is used to shooting everyone from presidents to porn stars, but who agreed to take some shots of me. The makeup artist Alexa Rodulfo kindly lent her services, for which I'm very grateful, and I have to thank the Misshapes and Jared Abbott for helping me with the book's playlists.

In various phases of editing, many of my friends took the time to give me creative criticisms and advice—which were surprisingly constructive at times, given the types of criticisms we normally discuss! This list includes such smart and beautiful ladies as Lauren Santo Domingo, Claire Bernard, Dasha Zhukova, Anamaria Wilson, and Katie Lee. One of my dearest friends from high school, Diane Brendel, was also a valuable resource for the quotes seen throughout the book.

Throughout my career and putting this book together, many other people in my life lent additional critical skills, including (but not limited to) the following: verbal support, professional encouragement, free meals, free drinks, good advice, great gossip, and/or true friendship. These include those previously mentioned, as well as Fabiola Beracasa, Nate Berkus, Christopher Bollen, Chris Brenner, Jen Brill, Bob Colacello, Edward Enninful, Rosetta Getty, Katie Grand, Marjorie Gubelmann, Daphne Guinness, Amanda Harlech, Lazaro Hernandez, Genevieve Jones, Dan May, Jack McCollough, Alison Mosshart, William Norwich, Stefano Pilati, Caroline Sieber, Tara Subkoff, Andre Leon Talley, Taylor Tomasi Hill, Arden Wohl, and Francesco Vezzoli. Further, I must thank the various editors and employers who have given me a career of opportunities, insight, and training in an industry I've always admired. This list includes Glenda Bailey and Kristina O'Neill from *Harper's Bazaar*, Stephen Gan and Cecilia Dean from *Visionaire*, Amy Astley from *TeenVogue*, Antony Miles and Sophia Neophitou from *10magazine*, Dirk

Standen and Nicole Phelps from Style.com, and Anna Wintour and Laurie Jones from *Vogue*.

Finally, and this is no moot point: I must throw myself onto the altar of the true ladies of this world—and, perhaps even more importantly, the tramps. I've realized that a book like this would not be relevant if it weren't for such a rampant disparity between good and bad behavior in our culture. Think about it: if there weren't so many ill-mannered skanks out there, I wouldn't have this occasion to be a *New York Times* best-selling author. (That's a moniker that will never get old!) Without so many bad-mannered lushes on the street and in the media (whom I am far too discreet to mention by name—but you know who I'm talking about), there would be no book needed to tell the difference between these two female castes.

Without so many of the wonderful women I have crossed paths with in the past decade, who have navigated success and modesty so well in their own lives and careers, I might not have been able to write so expertly on the topics covered in this book. If I hadn't met so many genuine young women, I might not have been inspired to discuss what it takes to be a civilized, successful, intelligent citizen. So a big thank you to the beloved friends and beautiful women who have reminded me what a lady should be like, including Kirsten Dunst, Mary-Kate Olsen, Ashley Olsen, Milla Jovovich, Kate Bosworth, Jacquetta Wheeler, Lou Doillon, Alexa Chung, Jessica Alba, Nicole Richie, Natalia Vodianova, Karlie Kloss, Eugenie Niarchos, Tatiana Santo Domingo, Vanessa and Victoria Traina, Leigh Lezark, Julia Restoin-Roitfeld, Barbara Bush, Lily Donaldson, Joy Bryant, Margherita Missoni, Chloe Sevigny, and Emma Watson.

It's a long list, but there are more classy females out there (even if, at times, it's hard to find them). So, for them, a preemptive extra-special thanks to the many more ladies whom I hope to meet!